Here's what they said about the first edition of

Getting the Most From Your
Yellow Pages Advertising

"Last year, American businesses spent $8 billion dollars on Yellow Pages advertising. For many small businesses, it was their only form of advertising. Yet many small business owners are unsure about how to get the most out of their Yellow Pages advertising. To help them, Barry Maher . . . has written a practical guide to Yellow Pages advertising . . . [providing] insights and advice for small business owners."
—*Los Angeles Times*

"If you now make use of yellow page advertising in telephone directories, you will be especially interested in what [Maher] . . . has to say about choosing the right ad size, creating the ad that will generate the most response, and how to select the right categories to advertise [under]."
—*In Business*

"An informative overview of the entire advertising process, including evaluating and selecting the right Yellow Pages book, choosing the right ad size, determining how many ads to run, creating the ad likely to generate the most calls, and dealing effectively with the phone company and sales reps. He also offers guidance on tracking ads and explains how to . . . analyze the competition."   —*Professional Electronics*

"The bible of Yellow Pages advertising is Barry Maher's book *Getting the Most from Your Yellow Pages Advertising* . . . It's plump with cost cutting tips . . . a super resource."
—*Save Your Business a Bundle: 202 Ways to Cut Costs and Boost Profits Now* by Daniel Kehrer (Simon & Schuster)

"Maher takes the mystery out of Yellow Pages advertising. He tells you how to make it work and what to do when it doesn't. A great new resource for small businessmen."   —*Direct Marketing News*

"The inside scoop on how to make your Yellow Pages advertising dollars pay off . . . Find out what the sales rep won't tell you. Design an ad that really pulls."   —*Business Opportunities Digest*

"The nation's foremost authority—consultant, speaker, expert witness—on Yellow Pages advertising."   —*Dealer Communicator*

"Aimed at small businesses in general and written with sympathy for their concerns, the book takes on the topic of Yellow Pages with zeal and humor—while offering practical help in getting the directories to work for you." —*Instant & Small Commercial Printer*

"Valuable insights." —*Restaurant Management Today*

"THIS GUY IS FOR REAL! Any [who] listen to his ideas WILL GAIN!" —Ben Caswell, Ben's Transmission

"[Maher] has helped thousand of businesses turn their Yellow Pages into gold . . . a complete, step by step program for developing Yellow Pages ads that get the call." —Southwestern Bell Telephone

"Discover effective design, layout and copy writing techniques . . . Learn how to design an ad that will get YOUR business the call, even when surrounded by others ads selling the same product or service."
—*Success Symposium*

"Recommended reading." —Pacific Bell

"I recommend *Getting the Most from Your Yellow Pages Advertising* to all Yellow Pages advertisers. You'll learn how to design an effective ad, keep score on your ad and deal with the sales people when they goof."
— *San Francisco Examiner*

"A comprehensive approach to planning and implementing a successful Yellow Pages advertising program." —*Dentist*

"Guides readers on how to get the best return from their Yellow Pages advertising . . . improve response, enhance profits." —*SNIPS*

"Provides the stimulus to get your prospecting and your advertising in gear." —*The Competitive Advantage*

"Practical advice on the complete process, from deciding whether to advertise at all to turning callers into customers . . . The advice is detailed and backed by marketing data that should help improve the reader's directory-buying decisions." —*Fitness Management*

"Anyone who has dealt with the Yellow Pages people would welcome the book. . . Wise ad people have said placing a substantial schedule in several phone books is only slightly more complicated than dealing with the U.S. Army." —*Des Moines Register*

"Businesses may be spending 25% of their gross [in the Yellow Pages] and be spread too thin, or they may be overspending at 1%. To make key decisions to best business advantage, an independent and authoritative perspective is crucial. *Getting the Most from Your Yellow Pages Advertising,* by Barry Maher, offers [just that]." —*Retailer News*

"Maher is considered by many to be the foremost independent authority on Yellow Pages advertising."
—*Air Conditioning, Heating & Refrigeration News*

"Tremendous insight into Yellow Pages advertising."
—Dr. Gregory S. Keller, Cosmetic Surgery Center

"An invaluable resource on getting the most bang per buck in advertising . . . the book clears the way through the jungle of options and clearly delineates what is as well as what isn't effective. I recommend it wholeheartedly." —Michael Parker, Parker Plumber

"PIP Printing's retail centers rely on yellow pages advertising to reach business printing consumers every day, but without following a carefully planned strategy, our yellow pages messages could be easily overlooked. Maher's book offers . . . straightforward guidelines for insuring maximum effectiveness for yellow pages advertising." —Susan Falk, PIP

"When I want to remember something in a book, I dog-ear the page and highlight the passage with a yellow felt-tip pen. My copy of *Getting the Most from Your Yellow Pages Advertising* has a lot of dog-eared pages with highlighted sentences. I have also found Barry Maher's book to be a very valuable resource as I communicated with members of the American Rental Association on ways they can use the yellow pages most effectively." —Frederick Anderson, American Rental Association

"Cash in on Yellow Pages advertising with a book entitled *Getting the Most from Your Yellow Pages Advertising* by Barry Maher."
—*Pharmacy Newswire, NARD Journal*

Other Telecom Titles from Aegis Publishing Group:

Telecom Business Opportunities
The Entrepreneur's Guide to Money Making in the Telecommunications
Revolution, by Steven Rosenbush
$24.95   1-890154-04-0

Winning Communications Strategies
How Small Businesses Master Cutting-Edge Technology to Stay
Competitive, Provide Better Service and Make More Money,
by Jeffrey Kagan
$14.95   0-9632790-8-4

Telecom Glossary
Understanding Telecommunications Technology, by Marc Robbins
$9.95   1-890154-02-4

Telecom Made Easy
Money-Saving, Profit-Building Solutions for Home Businesses,
Telecommuters and Small Organizations, by June Langhoff
$19.95   0-9632790-7-6

The Telecommuter's Advisor
Working in the Fast Lane, by June Langhoff
$14.95   0-9632790-5-X

900 Know-How
How to Succeed With Your Own 900 Number Business,
by Robert Mastin
$19.95   0-9632790-3-3

The Business Traveler's Survival Guide
How to Get Work Done While on the Road, by June Langhoff
$9.95   1-890154-03-2

Phone Company Services
Working Smarter With the Right Telecom Tools, by June Langhoff
$9.95   1-890154-01-6

Money-Making 900 Numbers
How Entrepreneurs Use the Telephone to Sell Information,
by Carol Morse Ginsburg and Robert Mastin
$19.95   0-9632790-1-7

GETTING THE MOST FROM YOUR YELLOW PAGES ADVERTISING

Barry Maher

Aegis Publishing Group, Ltd.
796 Aquidneck Avenue
Newport, Rhode Island 02842
401-849-4200
www.aegisbooks.com

Library of Congress Catalog Card Number: 97-73918

International Standard Book Number: 1-890154-05-9

Printed in the United States of America. First printing in 1988 by AMACOM. Second edition, completely revised and updated, by Aegis Publishing Group, Ltd. in 1997.

10 9 8 7 6 5 3 2 1

This book is available at a special discount when ordered in bulk quantities. For more information, contact Aegis Publishing Group, Ltd. at 800-828-6961.
.

Library of Congress Cataloging-in-Publication Data
Maher, Barry.
Getting the most from your yellow pages advertising.

1. Advertising.   2. Telephone—Directories—Yellow pages.
3. Advertising layout and typography.   I. Title.

HF6146.T4M35   1997   659.13'2   97-73918
ISBN 1-890154-05-9

ACKNOWLEDGMENTS

I'd like to offer my sincere thanks and appreciation to the hundreds of individuals, businesses, and associations who gave of their time and their expertise to help make this book possible. People such as Bert Michaels of Statistical Research, Inc. (Westfield, NJ), Larry Small of YPPA, Deborah Mahoney of Simmons Market Research Bureau (New York), Doug Berdie of Consumer Review Systems (St. Paul, MN), Sidney Feldman, Ph.D., of Indiana University Northwest, Blanche McGuire of Ketchum Directory Advertising, Fred Smykla and Sherri Starr. Thanks also to all the thoughtful, quotable advertisers such as Terry Johnson of Dial One, and all the publishers who assigned people such as Mary Kay Schuck of Southwestern Bell to answer all those questions. And special thanks to Bob Mastin of Aegis Publishing. And, and, and . . . .

To mention everyone would take another book. And some of them prefer to remain anonymous.

My thanks to all the design experts who contributed to Chapter 10, and particularly to Linda Utsey, who's as generous and patient as she is knowledgeable. Thanks to everyone at BellSouth who helped me to access its *Designline—Effective Yellow Pages Layout and Design* (copyright BellSouth Advertising & Publishing Corporation) and for all their help with the layout sections.

TABLE OF CONTENTS

INTRO

Introduction: Confusion in the Marketplace

Yellow Pages advertising can be the lifeblood of a business or it can be little more than your monthly donation to the directory company. You can spend 25 percent of your gross on it and be spread too thin; you can be overspending at one percent. Even when the funds are properly allocated—good directories, effective headings, appropriate ad sizes—the ads themselves can be so poorly designed as to be virtually worthless.

Whether you're an established business or a first-time advertiser, this book will enable you to create the most effective—and cost-effective—directory advertising program possible. The goal is to make you money, and, if possible, to save you money while doing it.

Before going any further, however, a little historical perspective is in order.

Yellow Pages History—Smedley Strikes Out

On February 21, 1878, a day that will live forever in the hearts of telephone company accountants and CEOs everywhere, the New Haven District Telephone Company issued the world's first classified telephone directory (see Figure I-

Figure I-1 The world's first classified telephone directory.

LIST OF SUBSCRIBERS.

New Haven District Telephone Company.

OFFICE 219 CHAPEL STREET.

February 21, 1878.

Residences.	*Stores, Factories, &c.*
Rev. JOHN E. TODD.	O. A. DORMAN.
J. B. CARRINGTON.	STONE & CHIDSEY.
H. B. BIGELOW.	NEW HAVEN FLOUR CO. State St.
C. W. SCRANTON.	" " " " Cong. ave.
GEORGE W. COY.	" " " " Grand St.
G. L. FERRIS.	" " " Fair Haven.
H. P. FROST.	ENGLISH & MERSICK.
M. F. TYLER.	NEW HAVEN FOLDING CHAIR CO.
I. H. BROMLEY.	H. HOOKER & CO.
GEO. E. THOMPSON.	W. A. ENSIGN & SON.
WALTER LEWIS.	H. B. BIGELOW & CO.
	C. COWLES & CO.
Physicians.	C. S. MERSICK & CO.
Dr. E. L. R. THOMPSON.	SPENCER & MATTHEWS.
Dr. A. E. WINCHELL.	PAUL ROESSLER.
Dr. C. S. THOMSON, Fair Haven.	E. S. WHEELER & CO.
	ROLLING MILL CO.
Dentists.	APOTHECARIES HALL.
Dr. E. S. GAYLORD.	E. A. GESSNER.
Dr. R. F. BURWELL.	AMERICAN TEA CO.
Miscellaneous.	*Meat & Fish Markets.*
REGISTER PUBLISHING CO.	W. H. HITCHINGS, City Market.
POLICE OFFICE.	GEO. E. LUM, " "
POST OFFICE.	A. FOOTE & CO.
MERCANTILE CLUB.	STRONG, HART & CO.
QUINNIPIAC CLUB.	
F. V. McDONALD, Yale News.	*Hack and Boarding Stables.*
SMEDLEY BROS. & CO.	CRUTTENDEN & CARTER.
M. F. TYLER, Law Chambers.	BARKER & RANSOM.

Office open from 6 A. M. to 2 A. M.

After March 1st, this Office will be open all night.

Source: Southern New England Telephone.

1). It came within two years of the invention of the telephone, and within a month of the inception of the first commercial telephone service.

It came without walking fingers, without multicolored
ads or stadium maps, without coupons or audiotext or complicated discount programs. It wasn't even yellow. Just a single card, and only seven classifications. There were three
physicians, two dentists, two hack & boarding stables, seven
stores, factories, etc., and eight listings under *Miscellaneous,*
including the police station, the post office, a lawyer, and
something called *Smedley Bros. & Co.*

I have this image of the Smedley brothers, Seth and
Salvatore. Seth has spent three weeks talking Salvatore into
shelling out the money for this telephone machine. Now the
two of them, along with little brother Sam, Sam's second
wife, Sarah, and the rest of the company, stand around day
after day waiting for the darn thing—the expensive darn
thing—to ring. To ring and generate all that business that
Seth and that cocksure telephone salesman—the one with all
the testimonial letters and fancy projections—were so sure
of.

Perhaps someone will need an emergency "miscellaneous" in the middle of the night, or will somehow be able to
figure out some other reason for calling.

Smedley Bros. & Co. notwithstanding, the telephone
directory was off and running. Before long, directories had
been established in New York, Boston, and Chicago (See
Figure I-2). By 1892, the Los Angeles phone book had nine-
ty-two listings, forty-two more than New Haven's first directory, but, of course, Los Angeles had twelve thousand people.
Businesses included a real estate agent, a cemetery, and the
University of Southern California. People didn't use the
directory to look up phone numbers. There weren't any. They
just picked up the phone and asked the operator for their
party by name. They used the directory to see who had a
phone.

Before the turn of the century, publishers were printing

Figure I-2 A page of "F" Entries from the Chicago Telephone Directory of 1886.

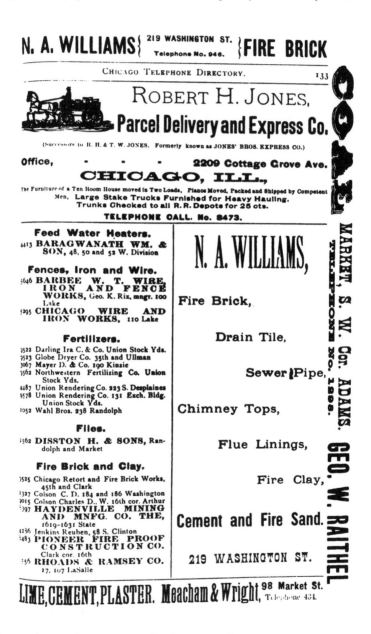

the classified section of the book on yellow paper. Classifications had become somewhat more exact; *Miscellaneous* was no longer a major heading. Stores that sold both paint and lumber were allowed to list their names in both places.

For a small fee of course.

A breakthrough came when some genius stumbled upon the idea of letting businesses say a few words about themselves under their listings. Eventually, the display ad was discovered, followed almost immediately by the even-bigger display ad (see Figure I-3). Unfortunately, this came too late to save Smedley Bros. & Co. By then even Seth was convinced that the Yellow Pages was a waste of money. The Smedley brothers had gone back to advertising on matchbook covers, bowling shirts and pens. In 1898, the company went out of business before anyone had ever found out what kind of business they were in.

Your First Yellow Pages

Let's suppose you've just opened or just bought a small business. It's a furniture shop. Monday morning, 8:43 a.m. (seventeen minutes early), you open the doors for the first time. At 8:49, you discover your expensive new computerized cash register voids out any sale over $7. And at 8:54, in walks your very first Yellow Pages salesman. (If your business is in Los Angeles, it won't take nearly that long.)

He's wearing a well-cut gray suit, carries a leather attache case, and his socks match. He tells you he's going to make you rich and famous.

From the attache—maybe it's only leatherette—come statistics. Some are just numbers, seemingly plucked from the air without attribution, perhaps even contradictory.

"Do you know that 81 percent of the population uses Yellow Pages," he says. "That 91 percent are influenced by the larger ads, 83 percent by color . . . that 87 percent of all perception is visual . . . that 77 percent of those who do business with you once are likely to return . . . that 89 percent of

Figure I-3 A display ad from the Chicago Telephone Directory of 1886, prototype for today's Yellow Pages.

CHICAGO TELEPHONE DIRECTORY.

129

EDW. E. HARBERT & CO.,

Manufacturers of and Dealers in

Electric Supplies

Electric Bells, Elevator Calls,
Speaking Tubes, Electric
Gas Lighting Apparatus, Burglar
Alarms, House and Hotel
Annunciators put
up to order.

All kinds of Batteries and Electric Apparatus
Renewed and Repaired at Short Notice.

SATISFACTION GUARANTEED.

No. 159 La Salle Street. Telephone No. 209

Magneto Call Bell.

Source: *The Donnelley Directory Record*, Reuben H. Donnelley Corporation.

Figure I-4 A display ad from the Chicago Telephone Directory of 1886, prototype for today's Yellow Pages.

the people in the area use our book."

"I'll need a little time," you say.

"I wish I could give it to you," he says. "I really do. And it's not that I'm trying to pressure you. I don't work like that. But, as usual, we're running late. The directory is closing. Once it's closed, I couldn't get my own mother in."

"Well, can't you . . ." you try.

"Heck, I'm so swamped with advertisers, it's only a fluke I made it in here in the first place. If I hadn't seen your "Grand Opening" sign as I was driving by, and my last appointment hadn't finished up early . . . ."

Just then, in comes your first customer. At the same time a shipment of patio tables arrives that should have come the week before. The phone rings. After a few minutes, the directory salesman decides he has to go. You make arrangements to meet on Friday. He'll squeeze you in right before the deadline.

That night you ask your brother-in-law about Yellow Pages. He owns a printing franchise, and he shows you a piece he got from franchise headquarters:

> The Yellow Pages telephone directories are the final link in the advertising cycle that results in delivering the customer directly to your front door. All of the other media dollars create a recognition factor which pays off for you when the customer opens his Yellow Pages directory and sees our name and logo.

Your other brother-in-law works for a large national roto-tiller company. He sends you some information the advertising department got from the Yellow Pages Publishers Association (YPPA). YPPA is an industry group, an association of directory publishers and national Yellow Pages advertising agencies. Hardly an unbiased bunch, but the studies they commission are done by respected independent research companies like Simmons Market Research Bureau (New York), and Statistical Research, Inc. (Westfield, NJ).

According to Simmons, well over 80 percent of the

adults in this country use the Yellow Pages. The ongoing study by Statistical Research involves over 10,000 random telephone interviews every year. It says Americans refer to the Yellow Pages 52 million times a day, more than 19 billion times a year.

Maybe the Smedley Bros.
Should Have Been More Patient

YPPA says businesses spend more than 10 billion dollars a year on Yellow Pages advertising. More businesses advertise in the Yellow Pages than in any other medium.

Nineteen billion references a year. Nine billion dollars. The numbers are astronomical. The testimonials can be astounding. Perhaps you spend an evening at the library.

In her book, *Setting Up Shop: The Do's and Don'ts of Starting a Small Business* (McGraw-Hill), R. B. Smith calls Yellow Pages, "the ultimate advertising vehicle . . . . For many, if not most, small businesses, the Yellow Pages will be the primary source of advertising and, therefore, customers."

In *Honest Business* (Random House), Michael Philips states that "Sometimes, [Yellow Pages] are such an important source of clientele that it is not worth starting your business until you can be listed in the phone directory."

In *New York* magazine, the president of American Direct Mail estimates that Yellow Pages advertising brings in 75 percent of his new business. A plumber mentioned in a *Los Angeles Times* article attributes 95 percent of his new business to it.

In "America's Search for Quality," a study conducted for the Whirlpool Corporation by Research & Forecasts, Inc., more consumers named Yellow Pages as an important source of product information than any other advertising medium.

About now your checkbook is warmed up and ready to go. Your main worry is that the salesman will be so busy Friday, he won't have time to get you in the book.

Confusion in the Marketplace

Friday, you discover it's not going to be that easy. No matter how nice a guy your sales rep might be, how well-manicured his fingernails, how sincere his manner, and how honest his face, the fact remains that aside from 15 minutes Monday morning, you've never seen him before in your life. Chances are good you'll never see him again. And you have decisions to make, expensive ones.

The $200 ad he mentioned Monday turns out to be $200 a month, not $200 a year. Besides, you've never designed an ad. The salesman reminds you he does it all day long, everyday, but he seems in such a rush. And do you really want to pay this kind of money for an ad that looks just like everyone else's?

Then he tells you the ad you were considering is much too small. What's more, it's the wrong kind of ad: you can't use the border you wanted, and no bold type, no artwork.

"And it's going to be buried at the very end of the heading," he says.

You take the phone directory he's carrying and turn to the classification. When you decided a Yellow Pages ad was a good investment, you'd been thinking in just those terms, *a* as in *one* Yellow Pages ad. Under *Furniture*.

Only the book has no heading for *Furniture*. It has:

Furniture Dealers—New
Furniture Dealers—Used
Furniture Designers
Furniture—Custom Made
Furniture—Renting & Leasing
Furniture Repairing & Refinishing
Furniture—Outdoor—Dealers
Furniture—Outdoor—Renting
Furniture—Outdoor—Recovery & Repairing
Furniture Stripping
Furniture—Unfinished

And this doesn't take into account several furniture frame, furniture wholesale, and furniture manufacturing headings. There is also:

Antiques—Dealers

Baby Carriages & Strollers

Barbecue Equipment

Bedding

Beds—Disappearing

Beds—Retail

Bedspreads—Retail

Benches

Carpets & Rugs, Dealers—New

Carpets & Rugs—Pads, Linings & Accessories

Chairs—Renting

Clocks—Dealers

Curtains—Retail

Cushions

Draperies—Retail

Electric Appliances—Small (Several Headings)

Fireplace Equipment (Several Headings)

Garden & Lawn Equipment & Supplies

Garden Ornaments

Hammocks

House Furnishings

Hotel & Motel Equipment & Supplies

Interior Decorators & Designers

Interior Decorators' Supplies

Kitchen Cabinets & Equipment—Household

Lamp Shades—Retail

Lamps—Retail

Linoleum Dealers

Mattresses—Dealers

Mirrors
Office Furniture & Equipment (Several Headings)
Patio Equipment & Supplies
Pictures—Retail
Quilts—Retail
Ranges & Stoves—Dealers & Service
Rattan, Reeds & Willow
Second Hand Dealers
Stools
Refrigerators & Freezers—Dealers & Service
Slip Covers
Springs—Coil, Flat, Etc.—Distributors & Manufacturers
Stereophonic & High Fidelity Equipment—Dealers &
    Service
Stoves—Wood, Coal, Etc.
Tables
Television & Radio—Dealers & Service
Upholsterers
Venetian Blinds—Dealers
Wardrobes

And there are probably several other possibilities, depending on your products and services.

"*Obviously,*" the rep says, "your ad under *Furniture Dealers—New* isn't going to bring in people who are looking under *Beds* or *Tables* or *Office Furniture & Equipment*, is it?"

Obviously, this stuff can cost you a fortune. You haven't really figured out an advertising budget yet, and you have no idea how much you should be spending. You look for the competition, to see what they're doing. After all, Yellow Pages may work for plumbers and chiropractors but how do you know it works for furniture shops?

Your main competition, Phil's Phurniture Phantasies,

isn't there. He's not even listed. You look at the directory's cover. Enlightenment.

"You're not with the phone company," you say. "You're not with *any* phone company."

"Of course not," the rep looks at you as if your ears are leaking brain fluid. "I told you—Confabulated Publishing. Better than the phone company. Twice the area at half the price! And we're spending $3 million to make ours *the* phone book in this area. With bigger ads—37 percent more bang for your buck—full process color, white page banners, coupons, bus schedules . . . ."

And maybe at this point, another salesman strolls in. From a neighborhood book, or a countywide book, or a phone company book, or an Internet Yellow Pages, or the Chamber of Commerce directory, or the Greater Midwestern Independent Telephone Directory, Tide Schedule and Feed Catalogue.

How much should you spend? How should you spend it? And where?

Remember the good old days, when you could just list your firm under *Miscellaneous* and leave it at that?

The Bottom Line

Whether you are a brand new business or you've been around for 20 years, the questions remain. The following pages offer the best available answers to all the questions advertisers, ask and to those they never ask but should. And when there are no simple answers? At least, you'll know that, and you'll know your options. Very likely, you'll end up with more hard knowledge about Yellow Pages advertising than a number of the people who'll be coming in to sell it to you.

This book is the product of extensive research, along with hundreds of interviews and contributions from advertisers, advertising researchers, Yellow Pages publishers and associations, advertising agencies, graphic art specialists, trade groups from various industries, and many others. The statistics cited as evidence are the most reliable I have been able to uncover. If anything, I have been overly skeptical, which is usually safer. I have tried to be objective; I've been a small business owner myself.

And since 1986, I've been a consultant to Yellow Pages advertisers of all sizes. *Time* magazine, called me "Easily the most widely respected consultant, speaker and writer on the subject." Who am I to argue with *Time* magazine?

I should tell you, as a matter of honesty, that I also work with Yellow Pages publishers and with various advertising media that compete with Yellow Pages. And before 1986, I was a Yellow Pages salesman myself—with one of the largest directory companies in the world, GTE Directories. As a matter of ego, I'll add that I was their number one rep worldwide, which means, I hope, that the programs I designed worked. It also means that even back then I spent large hunks of my life talking to a huge cross-section of advertisers about their advertising—about what worked and what didn't.

As I said before, my goal is to make you money, and if possible, to save you money while doing it. After reading this book, you may decide to spend less in the Yellow Pages, you may decide to spend more. But—with competition increasing among phone companies and directory companies, and with advertising rates increasing in spite of the competition—at least you won't be bluffed or stampeded into unnecessary, ineffective, or counterproductive advertising. And you'll get far more value out of each dollar you do spend.

CHAPTER 1

"Is This Stuff Really For Me?" Why Advertise at All—and Why Yellow Pages?

Why Advertise at All?

I am always amazed, in this over-advertised society, where more and more ads compete for our attention every day, how many small businessmen consider advertising a luxury. Like caviar, advertising is something they think they can afford only in small nibbles, if at all.

New companies go into hock for leasehold improvements, spare no expense for painting and decorating, spend fortunes on equipment, hire and train any number of employees, but scrimp on the one thing that brings people in the door. Then they wonder where all their customers are. In the sad tradition of the Smedley brothers, businesses *routinely* go out of business before anyone's ever heard of them.

It is self-evident perhaps, but please carve this into the top of the mahogany desk that sits in your backroom hideaway:

Office Furniture Does Not Bring in Customers.

Neither does your stationery. Your help doesn't bring in many, not at first. Even your exorbitant rent contributes little initially, unless you're dependent on passersby. And guess what? All that ultramodern, high-tech equipment that will do the job better than anybody else in town? Pawn it. Take it to the swap meet. It's not worth anything unless you have customers to use it on.

In most businesses—probably in yours—advertising is a necessity. Not necessarily Yellow Pages advertising, but advertising. It's a necessity like your lights and your heat. You wouldn't think of running your business without light or heat.

Advertising brings in money. I don't know how many times I've had a small businessman tell me, "Sure, the competition can afford to advertise like that. He's making a fortune."

It doesn't work like that. Not usually. Advertising is not a trip to the Caribbean. You don't say, "Gee, I've made a lot of money this month. I think I'll take out a full page ad in the *Daily Globe* to celebrate."

Businesses don't get big and then start to advertise. They advertise and then get big.

This is not to say that you should go out and buy all the advertising you can get your hands on. Or that you should waste a penny of your advertising dollar if you can avoid it. You advertise to make money, to keep your employees busy, to pay for all those other expenses, and to eat. If an ad doesn't make you money you cancel it.

Ad salesmen will try to sell you advertising as prestige. They appeal to your pride, the thrill of seeing your name splashed across the page, looking prosperous and important, "as big and successful as anyone." They'll shame you into it. "This guy works out of a lean-to and look at the size of his ad!" Or "Every other pharmacist in town is going to be in our flyer."

Prestige and the look of success can be vital to a business. Nobody's going to buy a $100,000 telecommunications system from a guy who looks like he should be marketing tin cans tied together with string. But if you're buying advertising primarily for pride, as many people do, and that pride isn't being translated into profit, wouldn't you really rather have a Mercedes?

And don't confuse advertising with charity or civic mindedness. It is good business to be a part of your community. Charity is even more important than good business. Give and give again. But remember, putting ads on page 36 of a 48-page advertising supplement in the back of the high school yearbook is not advertising, it's charity. The money that goes into this sort of thing shouldn't come from your advertising budget.

You advertise to make money: to get more business and to hold onto the business you've got.

As the World Turns: Customer Turnover

The marketplace is never static. No matter who you are, no matter what your business, you're always going to lose some customers with the passage of time. I had a boss who used to tell us that businesses have a complete customer turnover every three years; I've also heard seven years. Actually, this is one of those business statistics that varies hugely from concern to concern, from situation to situation. The point is, you will always have customer turnover.

Pacific Bell has a series of brochures, each with a reproduction of a single page supposedly selected at random from the white pages of a particular phone book. All the listings that have been changed in the last year are marked in colored ink. On the pages I've seen, anywhere from 28 percent to 64 percent of the listings have been changed—either added, removed or altered. I don't know how many pages Pacific Bell may select at random to get the ones they use. I do know that in one year, in one California city of about 112,000 households—325,000 population—records show 60,490 new phones were connected and 54,274 disconnected. Your customers do leave the area, and new people arrive all the time.

Customers move, customers die. They're also lured

away. The old cliche has some truth: Your best customer is your competition's best prospect. Sometimes customers just don't need what you have to offer anymore. Some you'll even drive away deliberately—if their credit is bad or they're too much of a problem. And no matter how good you are, once in a while, somebody's going to get upset and head for your competition.

You're gonna loose'em so you gotta replace'em. Granted, you'll get a certain amount of new business if you just sit on your fat laurels and do nothing: referrals, people who have seen your store, former customers returning. Perhaps you talk to a few people once a month at your Rotary meeting. If that's going to be enough to keep the bills paid, the kids in college and you, your spouse, and your creditors perfectly satisfied, fine. You've got a rare situation.

Otherwise, you need to advertise.

But why Yellow Pages?

A Major Disadvantage?

Does it make sense to advertise in the Yellow Pages? According to G.M. Siegel's *How to Advertise and Promote Your Small Business* (John Wiley & Sons), "almost always and for almost every business."

The only major disadvantage listed in a comparison of advertising media by the Bank of America's *Small Business Reporter* is that Yellow Pages use is limited to active shoppers—who are exactly the people you're most interested in reaching.

The Statistical Research, Inc. study mentioned in the Introduction estimates that 52 percent of those who refer to the Yellow Pages make a purchase within 48 hours. And 79 percent of those who don't buy are very or somewhat likely to buy in the near future.

The numbers are self-evident. Nobody reads the phone directory just to see how it's going to turn out. Nobody except a Yellow Pages salesman, or a Yellow Pages consultant, opens the book simply for the fun of looking at the ads.

The only reason people will ever look at your Yellow Pages ad is because they are seeking what you're selling. And that's the basic difference between directory advertising and other advertising media.

Directional and Non-Directional Advertising

Newspapers, magazines, radio, television, billboards, direct mail, sports schedules, visors, whatever, even your sign out front—that's you, the businessman, in search of the customer. "Come to us for great selection, good prices, the finest food, the most reliable service." "Call us when your Aunt Millie switches on her hair dryer and blows every circuit in the house."

When you place your ad in the newspaper, on the TV, splashed across that expensive billboard on Highway 61, your first goal is to capture those people who have an immediate need: for a new car, a pool cover, a wedding cake, a plumber.

Sometimes you're trying to create an immediate need where none existed previously. This can be done with temporary price reductions or special offers to motivate the customer to act: "Just the thing for your French poodle—a sequined dog collar that glows in the dark and plays the Marseillaise. And today only, a free bag of dog food with every purchase."

Often, as an advertiser, you're simply hoping to gain name recognition and to plant an image, so when people eventually do have the need they'll think of you.

If your ad is good enough and big enough, it manages to steal the attention of a few people from Dear Abby and Doonesbury and the latest government scandals. Obviously, those who already need what you're selling are more likely to look. But how many of them drop the paper or switch off the TV, and either snatch up the phone or rush down to your business? Probably just the guy with the backed up plumbing that's forming a puddle at his feet. The rest finish the paper, watch the second half of that Green Acres rerun, or keep on driving past that expensive billboard.

Then later that evening they go shopping—for the car, the pool cover, the wedding cake. Or maybe they wait a week, or a month, until the Yugo dies or a storm tears the old pool cover to shreds. Maybe they still remember your ad. They ought to, you've been running the darn thing every other day for the last seven years.

Name recognition advertising does work. It works especially well for larger companies and successful national franchises. There's a strong correlation between recognition and the size of your advertising budget. If you're with Midas, and, instead of dying, the Yugo just loses its muffler on the freeway, the owner may well think of you.

So maybe they remember you and you've got a sale. Unless, of course, they want to shop another place or two as well, or they've forgotten your address, or your phone number, or—if you don't do quite as much advertising as Midas Muffler—your name. Or perhaps they want more information, such as how late you're open if you handle insurance claims, or how quickly you can get them back on the road.

Maybe they remember. But you should never forget that your advertising is not nearly as memorable to others as it is to you. If Profit and Greed Mutual cancels your earthquake insurance, would you recall the name of the agency that advertised its "San Andreas Special" in the *Pennysaver* the week before.

And when *your* sinks start backing up, how long are you going to spend searching for the plumbing ad in yesterday's newspaper? Or sitting in front of the TV waiting for the commercial you saw last week to reappear?

That's when the Yellow Pages comes into play. People in the business call it directional advertising, which simply means it's where customers go when they're in search of the businessman. When they're looking to buy. When they finally notice the house needs painting, the stereo needs replacing, when little Jimmy wraps the family Buick around the cannon in front of the VFW. When they don't know or don't remember a specific business they want to deal with, or they need more information, or they just want to see what competitive concerns have to offer.

That's why Midas Mufflers spends over $11 million a year in phone directories and calls them, "our most important service advertising medium."

"Television ads get the attention," the president of Midas once said, "but our Yellow Pages ads get the sales."

Your local Yellow Pages is not only a listing of virtually every pertinent business in the area, along with addresses and phone numbers, but it's also a guide to that tells the customer many of the things he needs to know about those firms. And about your firm: what services you offer, what brands you carry, how long you've been in business, if you have a credit plan. Often it's the first image your potential customer gets of you.

Where else do you appear side by side with all your local competition? And the Yellow Pages are in every home, every business, available to almost everyone. At 3 a.m. Christmas morning, when the dog topples the Christmas tree through the picture window and a distraught parent desperately needs a glass man for the first time in 11 years, he or she is going to reach for the Yellow Pages and start reading the ads.

The Importance of Directional Advertising

According to Samuel W. Shoen of U-Haul International, "Everything else we do in marketing communications is in preparation for closing the sale in the . . . Yellow Pages. That's why we're number one . . . the biggest advertiser in the directory business." And what he meant by the biggest was 20,000 display ads in 5,000 phone books under 35 different headings.

Directory advertising complements all your other non-directional advertising. Your newspaper ads may have generated excitement for your pool business, but if the customer doesn't act immediately he might well end up in the Yellow Pages trying to remember who you are. If you're not there or you're difficult to find you've just generated a sale for your competition—probably the competition that sounds most like you, or whose ad looks most like your newspaper ad.

The same is true for your referrals, which are, after all, your best advertising. You did a great job taking the pictures at Mr. and Mrs. Simian's anniversary party. But six months later, when Mrs. Simian recommends you to one of the ladies at the club, she probably won't recall your exact name and address. It's not likely to be, "Oh, you must go to Harry Hollenzollern. He's at 273 State St. His number is 555-1345." It's more likely she'll say, "You know, dear, the one with the studio down by the pier. I think it was Henry or Hubie something or other."

Major manufacturers like GM and Zenith spend millions selling people on their products. When those people start looking for where to buy those national brands locally, you want to be where they can find you.

Phone directory advertising can even make your sales force more effective, as in: "What was the name of that company who called on me last month about this? Where did I put that brochure?" And for the right businesses, the Yellow Pages can generate lead after lead.

When Everybody Knows You

What about the businessperson who says, "I don't need Yellow Pages. I've been in town 20 years. Everybody already knows me."

Let's assume that, because of the giant glass bubble over the town, nobody new ever enters. So people know you. But do they always think of you? Maybe so, if you're their regular beauty parlor and they've been going to you for seventeen of those twenty years. Maybe not, if you're the contractor they haven't called since they built the bombshelter under the flowerbed back in 1959. The less frequently your customers need you the less likely they are to think of calling you when the need arises.

If you think everybody knows you, ask yourself if everybody calls you. Why not? Are others getting calls out of the Yellow Pages—calls you could get if you reminded people about your business, if you let them know that you carry parts for every vehicle ever made, or that besides being more experienced than anybody in town, you offer a low-cost maintenance plan for fleet service.

Suppose someone simply wants your phone number. Directory assistance isn't free anymore. In a small academic study published in the *American Journal of Small Business*, marketing professors, R. W. Jackson and A. Parasuraman reported that, even when the name of the business was known, two-thirds of their respondents went to the yellow rather than the white pages when looking for a phone number or an address. And remember, once your customers get into the Yellow Pages, they're surrounded by ads trying to lure them away from you. Of course, if everybody knows you, maybe everybody—at least all your present customers—already has your number, perhaps in their Rolodex or their card file or written on the wall above the phone.

In a classic study, a company called Neff Plumbing of Youngstown, Ohio was given three new telephone numbers. Each number was placed in a different size Yellow Pages ad and nowhere else, and a meter was placed on the phones. The phone which appeared in a simple in-column bold listing received 241 calls. The number which appeared in a 1 1/2-inch in-column ad received 443 calls. The phone linked to the large display ad received 1382 calls. Not surprisingly the biggest ads got the most calls. What is surprising is that over half the calls to these new numbers were from old customers. Even they were getting Neff's number from the Yellow Pages.

The Neff study is so old it's practically folklore. And Neff Plumbing and Heating itself has gone the way of the Smedley Brothers. The results, however, have been verified over and over and over.

President Dewey, GTE and
Ryder Trucks: Who Should Advertise?

A GTE sales aid says that 42 percent of those who refer to GTE's Oxnard, Santa Paula, and Thousand Oaks, California directories refer to one of the top twenty-five classifications (top, that is, in number of references). A similar visual claims that 43 percent of the Santa Maria, California referrals came from the top *fourteen* headings! Obviously, your salesman might forget to show you these visuals if your main heading wasn't one of those mentioned.

Once upon a time, I had more faith in the polls that predicted victory for President Dewey back in 1948 than I had in these two sales aids. They seemed to be more a test of which headings are easiest for certain respondents to remember. I was wrong. According to Statistical Research, Inc., nationally the top twenty-five headings get 44 percent of the references. The top fifty get 56 percent.

Of course, over one quarter of all references—more than 5 billion by current figures—were made for headings not even in the top 150. Still, such studies do point to the obvious truth that phone directory advertising works better for some businesses than for others.

Ryder Truck Rental, for instance, attributes 80 percent of its "occasional, short-term rentals" to directory ads. Homelite did a study that found that over half of potential chain saw buyers consult Yellow Pages. But that study isn't going to be of much use to someone opening a boutique selling high-fashion hockey shorts.

Chances are you bought this book because you had a fair idea that phone directory advertising of some kind could work for your particular business. Chances are you were right, but let's take a look.

Getting Gas or Seeking Information

I buy gasoline two or three times a week. For the most part, I go to the same few places. When I do go someplace new, I just grab whatever's handy or cheapest or a brand I'm familiar with. I don't have to think about it. It's a minor purchase. One I'm used to making. One I'm comfortable with. I may be prejudiced in favor of a particular brand of gasoline because of national advertising or favorable experience, but I feel I already know all I need to know to make a purchase.

I know where to buy gas, I know where to buy groceries, I know which convenience store to use if I want a pack of twinkies at 2 a.m. I don't think about these things. I don't go to the phone directory.

But suppose my car needs a tune-up. I've tried several mechanics since I've been in Santa Barbara, but I've really never been all that thrilled with the results. I've got no fixed buying habits that tell me how to deal with the situation. I'm looking for someplace new. I'll give it more thought than if I were just buying gas, and I'll be seeking more information.

Directory advertising works when customers are seeking information—even if it's just your established customers seeking your address or phone number. It works particularly well on:

1. Those without established buying patterns such as recent arrivals to the area, business people from out-of-town, visitors and tourists. Newcomers need new sources for most everything, and two of the first things they get when they move in are a phone and a phone book. Others might have been in town for years but are new to your market. The family with its first baby has a whole new set of needs, so does someone who has just taken up skiing, or significantly increased his or her income. Still others may have always dealt with one firm, until that firm raised its prices enough for them to decide they'd better shop around.

2. Shoppers who for one reason or another—price, quality, selection, novelty—want to compare several different businesses. Do people shop before they select your type of product or service? Or, as with restaurants, do they frequent many different establishments? In general, the more shopping customers do the more likely they are to

have been inspired by the millions of dollars the directory publishers have spent over the years to get people to let their "fingers do the walking." And when times are tough, they do even more shopping around and need more information before they buy. Sometimes shoppers are simply looking for a place to buy a specific brand name or get a brand-name product repaired.

3. Infrequent buyers who may have been in town for fifteen years and never had a need for a chimney sweep until now. As I stated before, the less frequently people need a type of business the less likely they are to know who to call when the need arises, and the more likely they are to be seeking this kind of buying information. That's one reason why service businesses and emergency service businesses advertise so heavily in directories. Few of us need a bail bondsman during the course of the year. But when we do need one, simply because we've needed one so infrequently, we go to the Yellow Pages.

Obviously, businesses whose customers usually phone first should give serious thought to advertising in the phone book. These include service businesses that go out to the customer, businesses that make appointments or reservations, and those that give phone estimates or price quotes. If consumers are going to be calling by necessity or for convenience, give them a reason to call you instead of the guy down the street.

Finding a Brain Surgeon

The more important the purchase, the less likely the consumer is to rely strictly on what he can discover in an ad. Take the most extreme case. "Who would get a doctor out of the Yellow Pages?" business people always ask me. "No one," I answer. "But in the absence of a referral, what better place to begin searching? To find out who in the area does tummy tucks or bunion operations. To look for specialties, services, qualifications. To get a first impression."

Actually, I *have* found doctors strictly through the phone book, though it seemed too pat (or too stupid) to admit it while selling the ads. And I imagine thousands, if not millions, of others have too. This is not to say that you don't check them out every other way you possibly can. Thankfully, my insurance always paid for a second opinion.

As a matter of fact, ***Physicians & Surgeons*** is consistently one of the top two or three most heavily referenced headings in the Yellow Pages.

The professions discovered the Yellow Pages back in the early 1980s. Despite the changes they've all faced since then, and despite the proliferation of advertising outlets—and the proliferation of practice-building theories—more professionals still advertise in the Yellow Pages than anywhere else. An American Bar Association survey found Yellow Pages to be the best medium by far for lawyers—who apparently averaged an $8 return for each advertising dollar they spent there. (Obviously legislative restrictions on personal injury awards could lower that rate of return.)

A few years back, one county medical association said that doctors who advertised in the phone directory would be "summarily called before the executive committee . . . to explain their actions." The organization's president insisted that taking out a simple bold type listing constituted unprofessional conduct. At least he did until he was informed that the Federal Trade Commission had ruled that medical advertising was a definite benefit to consumers and could not be prohibited.

"It is my hope that tradition will prevail over law," he replied. It didn't. Soon, studies were reporting that over 25 percent of those without a regular physician said they'd used the Yellow Pages to find a doctor. And more than a few MDs were saying that directory advertising was, "the single most significant thing a doctor can do to build up a practice."

The managed care explosion has changed that somewhat. But even now, the majority of potential patients don't belong to a managed care system. And for those who do? As one doctor told me, "When an HMO restricts its members to five or six or ten doctors, providing nothing more than names and addresses, what better place than the Yellow Pages to look for additional information?"

The *Physicians & Surgeons* heading is second only to *Attorneys* in terms of dollars spent by advertisers. *Insurance* is third and *Dentists* fourth.

But How About High Fashion Hockey Shorts? Studies of Other Products and Services

Table 1-1 shows Statistical Research, Inc.'s, "National Yellow Pages Usage Study Report on Most Frequently Referenced Headings." This ranking is solely by estimated number of references. These are raw references with no regard as to whether a purchase was actually made or whether the person using the book was shopping for a new business to deal with or simply looking up a phone number. A high ranking for your heading doesn't necessarily mean you should start pouring the bucks into directory advertising.

On the other hand, there are about 1,500 to 2,000 headings in the average city directory; even if yours isn't listed here at all, that doesn't mean the Yellow Pages can't work for you and work very well. It may work even better for you than for many businesses whose headings are listed far above yours. After all, a swimming pool contractor doesn't need to get nearly as many customers from a directory as a restaurant to make a lot more money.

What's more, different types of businesses do better in different areas and different books. There are even headings—like *Water Well Drilling & Service*—that might not be in many directories, which can generate call after call in others.[1]

In a separate study, Statistical Research, Inc. inter-

---

[1]Throughout the book, I'll be talking about customer calls and contacts generated by the Yellow Pages. We all know that in dealing with many businesses, customers often, or even always, call in person—not over the phone. Sometimes they even send faxes, letters or e-mail. But you don't

viewed over 14,000 adults who had actually purchased one or more of 24 different types of products or services in the pre-

Table 1-1 The National Yellow Pages Usage Study Listing of Most Frequently Referenced Headings.

Heading Classifications	Number of Annual References (in millions)
1. Restaurants	1,265.4
2. Physicians and Surgeons—Medical M.D.	1,242.7
3. Automobile Parts—New & Used	907.1
4. Automobile Repairing & Service	689.2
5. Pizza	495.9
6. Automobile Dealers—New & Used	415.9
7. Attorneys/Lawyers	349.1
8. Beauty Salons	337.2
9. Insurance	305.2
10. Department Stores	297.6
11. Hospitals	256.1
12. Plumbing Contractors	249.4
13. Dentists	238.6
14. Airline Companies	233.1
15. Hardware—Retail	221.0
16. Banks	216.7
17. Florists—Retail	208.9
18. Lumber—Retail	192.9
19. Veterinarians	169.6
20. Tire Dealers	157.5
21. Automobile Renting & Leasing	142.1
22. Theaters	132.8
23. Real Estate	128.0
24. Furniture—Retail & Non-Specific	120.2
25. Hotels	119.6
26. Pharmacies & Drugstores	115.1
27. Glass—Auto, Plate, Window, etc.	113.1

want to keep reading, "a call, a visit, a fax, etc." and I don't want to keep writing it. So usually it'll be just "call" or "contact." Of course, in some industries a customer contact is little more than a lead; in others it's practically a sure sale.

28.	Appliances—Household—Dealers	112.3
28.	Grocers—Retail	112.3
30.	Schools—Academic—Colleges & Universities	101.0
31.	Printers	96.2
32.	Carpet & Rug Cleaners	95.4
33.	Travel Agents & Bureaus	95.2
34.	Churches	94.9
35.	Electrical Contractors	92.8
36.	Appliances—Household—Major—Service & Repair	92.4
37.	Building Materials	91.3
38.	Sporting Goods—Retail	88.0
39.	Computers—Dealers	86.9
40.	Motels	80.5
41.	Contractors—General	77.0
42.	Service Stations—Gas & Oil	76.3
43.	Rental Service Stores & Yards	71.8
44.	Government Offices—U.S.	70.1
45.	Television & Radio—Service & Repair	69.8
46.	Electronic Equipment & Supplies—Dealers	68.6
47.	Plumbing Fixtures & Supplies	68.3
48.	Automobile Body Repairing & Painting	66.6
49.	Book Dealers—Retail	66.3
50.	Automobile Wrecking	65.7
51.	Movers	65.1
52.	Photographers—Portrait	64.0
53.	Government Offices—State	63.8
54.	Office Supplies	59.5
55.	Schools Academic—Secondary & Elementary	59.0
56.	Taxicabs	58.6
57.	Carpet & Rug Dealers	57.5
57.	Pet Shops	57.5
59.	Cleaners—Dry	57.3
60.	Government Offices—City, Village & Township	55.8
61.	Pest Control Services/Exterminators	55.6
62.	Television—Cable, CATV & Satellite	53.9
63.	Roofing Contractors	53.0
64.	Paint—Retail	51.2
65.	Videotapes & Discs—Renting & Leasing	50.8
66.	Apartments	48.9
67.	Golf Courses—Public	45.9

Source: Statistical Research, Inc., Weitfield, NJ.
Reprinted with permission of the Yellow Pages Publishers Association (YPPA).

ceding 30 days. (see Table 1-2). On average 28.8 percent of all purchasers of these particular products and services referred to the Yellow Pages before making their purchase.

For these particular products and services, on the average:

28.8 percent of all purchasers referred to the Yellow Pages before making their purchase.

And among those purchasers using Yellow Pages:

74.7 percent looked at one or more Yellow Pages ads.

89.8 percent contacted one or more of the businesses seen in the Yellow Pages.

48.2 percent identified Yellow Pages ads as influencing where they made the purchase.

65.3 percent made the purchase at a business seen in the Yellow Pages.

33.6 percent were first time customers at the business.

31.9 percent of everything spent on these products and services was spent by purchasers who used the Yellow Pages before making the purchase.

At best, surveys like these offer approximations and averages. Eventually—before you invest any money—we're going to have to determine just how well your particular business is likely do with a given size ad under a given heading in a given directory.

Table 1-2 The Role of the Yellow Pages in the Purchase Decision.

Product/Service	Percentage of Purchasers Who Use Yellow Pages	Among Purchasers Who Use Yellow Pages, Percentage . . .				
		Who Look at Ads	Who Contact Store Seen in the Yellow Pages	Who Say Yellow Pages Ads Influenced What They Bought	Who Buy From Firm Seen in Yellow Pages	of Spending Involving Yellow Pages Users
Air Travel (contacted airline directly)	47.5%	51.9%	95.8%	38.5%	67.4%	42.7%
Attorneys	32.1	66.6	92.4	44.9	57.4	30.6
Auto parts	29.5	80.2	95.1	56.6	68.6	24.9
Auto repair	31.8	75.6	93.0	51.3	68.9	44.4
Auto/truck rental or lease	51.6	80.8	98.0	60.7	54.1	50.4
Bank services	24.2	72.1	93.2	31.8	63.7	n/a
Beauty salons	24.4	63.1	94.1	19.3	86.7	27.2
Carry-out food (except pizza)	30.6	65.2	86.1	27.1	80.7	36.3
Electronic products: includes TV's, VCR's, stereos, home computers, similar products	21.0	82.4	87.4	58.1	59.0	28.1
Floor coverings	24.0	82.9	83.7	69.6	24.0	31.1
Florists	31.0	71.0	87.9	37.4	31.0	34.3
Furniture	19.3	74.1	77.7	58.0	19.3	24.5

Home contractors: includes plumbers, painters, carpenters, electricians, exterminators, and similar contractors	44.2	82.8	90.3	55.2	59.7	37.0
Insurance	31.3	83.6	95.7	62.9	54.6	34.5
Lawn & garden supplies: includes power equipment, hand tools, seed, plants, fertilizers, insecticides, similar products	13.0	79.8	85.2	56.2	69.2	23.8
Loans	22.5	66.7	92.7	32.9	56.4	19.0
Major appliances	25.1	83.7	91.4	67.3	61.8	29.0
New, used cars & trucks	19.7	84.1	81.9	51.8	49.3	23.3
Pizza carry-out	38.1	62.1	92.4	31.5	92.5	41.2
Real estate	29.2	78.0	87.3	55.5*	53.6	n/a
Restaurants	9.5	70.5	79.8	34.7	71.5	14.0
Sporting goods	17.2	72.4	88.5	50.6	60.2	20.7
Tires	31.7	80.0	92.4	50.5	67.9	32.7
TV/radio repair	45.2	82.9	94.1	54.9	76.3	53.0

Source: Research study copyrighted by the Yellow Pages Publishers Association, conducted by Statistical Research, Inc. Westfield, N.J.
* Percentage who say Yellow Pages Ads influenced where they bought or listed.

Businesses Selling to Businesses

Many business people have said to me "I can see how Yellow Pages advertising works when you want to reach the average consumer, but we sell strictly to other businesses." Do businesses use Yellow Pages to make purchases like consumers do? Of course. Don't you?

Think about it. Research from Chilton Research Service (Radnor, PA) and others indicates that from 30 percent to 40 percent of Yellow Pages references are made for commercial purchases. And commercial purchases are larger. Businesses probably use the Yellow Pages more than any other kind of buying aid—even slightly more than the Thomas Register. In a few areas, publishers even separate their normal directory into a business-to-business book and a consumer book. That's so purchasing agents won't have to wade through ads for hairdressers and toy stores, and so publishers can sell twice as many ads to firms that need to reach both the commercial and the consumer market.

Commercial customers do use phone directories to find the same types of products and services consumers use Yellow Pages for. If, for instance, they need a plumber, a painter, a caterer or a printer. Or they need janitorial supplies, office equipment, furniture or temporary help. And if a bid is required, the Yellow Pages may be the best place to find all those who are qualified to submit one.

But what if you're selling widgets, industrial machinery, raw materials or outside production services like welding or tool making? Here I'd be a lot more cautious. A lot more. According to *Business Marketing* magazine, almost half of these kinds of suppliers don't advertise in phone directories. Of course, that also means that over half do. And I've known many who have achieved excellent results.

As to whether customers for any particular type of supplier look in the Yellow Pages, you're going to have to evaluate that on a case-by-case basis, using the methods and criteria furnished in this book. Often it depends on your area. How many of your potential customers are even within the coverage of your local phone book? If you're a welder maybe they all are, and *Welding* is a usually a good heading. If you're selling tool presses you might have only a couple potential customers locally, if that. Then too, the more heavily industrialized the area and the better the representation of industry within the phone directory, the more likely industrial customers are to have fallen into the habit of consulting it.

Another thing to remember: When they have the name of a supplier in mind, commercial shoppers seem much more likely than ordinary consumers to simply turn to the white pages. Studies report only about one-fourth of business people who are looking for a specific firm use the Yellow Pages, though with consumers in general the figures range from about one-half to two-thirds.

If a Yellow Pages salesman comes to sell you a big full-color ad under *Circuits Printed & Etched* and you tell him you don't have any local customers, he may tell you that you should buy an ad anyway, because many of your customers maintain libraries of directories from all over and when they're looking for you they'll go to your own directory to find you. This may sound like a stupid reason to buy. If so, good. It is. Tell the salesman you'll be glad to buy an ad when he guarantees to deliver a book to each of your out-of-town customers.

If your potential customers are spread across the state or the nation, ask yourself: How do they normally buy? Are there buying guides or specialty directories they habitually consult? How likely are your customers to look in their local phone book for what you have to offer? If they do look, will they find similar suppliers in their own backyard and will that keep them from calling you even if you're in the book too?

Covering a far-flung market is going to cost you some money, because unless you're doing extensive national advertising in other media, just listing your name and number isn't apt to send enraptured customers dashing to their phones. Advertisers may have trouble believing that, but unfortunately it's true. Federal Express gets by on 4,500 bold listings.

You aren't Federal Express.

So if you're new to directory advertising, sample the wine before buying the vineyard. All you need is a sip. If you have no local market, select *one* town or city with as many possible customers and as little competition as possible. More than likely, it'll be the place that's sending you the most orders right now.

But take out an ad, not a listing. A listing in a far-off directory is merely an aid for those seeking you by name—making it easier for them to find your number. Only unless you're a national concern, how many of them are going to be looking in their Memphis directory for the number of a St. Louis business?

If and when you're ready to jump in more heavily, one contact through a national Yellow Pages agency—a Certified Marketing Representative (CMR)—can put you in any or all of over 6,000 directories. (See "Becoming a National Account" at the end of Chapter 8 for minimum requirements.)

What's Next?

We've talked about the kind of customers who use Yellow Pages, be they consumer or commercial, and some of the kinds of businesses the Yellow Pages work for. Now open your local phone directory to the main heading for your business. What do you see? Make sure you're looking in the dominant directory in your area, the one with the most ads, most likely the one put out by the dominant phone company. Who advertises there and to what extent?

How many of them are doing it because they're losing money? Some might be; you'd be surprised. It's amazing how many business people have no idea of the effectiveness of their advertising. Later, we'll find out if they know what they're doing. For the moment, all you need to get is a general feel for the importance of phone directory advertising to your particular type of business in your particular market.

At least now you know what your competition thinks of it. Quiz time:

1. Can you envision your prospective customers using the Yellow Pages for any of the reasons we discussed?

2. Is your business in the most frequently referenced headings?

3. Is there significant advertising—anything more than bold print listings—under your heading in the dominant local phone book?

If any one of these three factors is the case, you should give serious consideration to Yellow Pages advertising. We're not talking full page, full color ads yet, just serious consideration.

CHAPTER 2

Yellow Pages Everywhere— Choosing Among Directories

Okay, so you think Yellow Pages might be for you. But which Yellow Pages? Back at the furniture store, you've seen the sales rep from Confabulated Publishing: "Twice the area at half the price." And from the neighborhood book: "Just your particular market, where everyone around here shops anyway. Why pay for wasted circulation?" Why indeed?

Then there's the directory from Tel & Tel Unlimited, the phone company that used to have the monopoly for Metropolis, the big city right next door. It's expanding the coverage of its Metropolis directory to include your area too. "Eight hundred thousand people are already using our book."

The Spanish-language Paginas Amarillas tells you about massive Hispanic buying power. And don't forget the Asian Yellow Pages. The Women's Pages are serious and businesslike. The Gay Yellow Pages explains that the average gay male earns over $51,000, the average gay female more than $42,000. And then there's the Internet Yellow Pages, "the wave of the future."

By the time the guy from your telephone company

phone book arrives—the phone company that used to have the monopoly in your area—you know that the Hispanics, the Asians, the women, the computer users, and the gays are already covered. So are the people who shop in the neighborhood, those who shop across "twice the area" and those who shop in Metropolis.

Apparently, the only one who's going to be using your phone company's book is you, and you're not in the market for furniture.

Types of Phone Directories

To make this chaos a little easier to contemplate, it might be useful to classify the different types of Yellow Pages directories.

The Core/Dominant Book

In the beginning, there was the *Core* or *System* book, often considered "The Official Phone Book," put out by the local telephone monopoly. The territory the book covered was often arbitrary, determined more by telephone company service boundaries—the area in which you could make a local call—than by actual calling and shopping patterns. The *Core* book always contained white pages with residential and business listings, though sometimes white and yellow pages were broken up into separate volumes. Occasionally, the Yellow Pages were further divided into a consumer and a business-to-business book.

With telephone company deregulation, with no single local phone company providing monopoly service in an area, there is no longer any "official phone company book." Still, you can expect to find a dominant local phone company— and expect it to be the former local monopoly—and it will publish the dominant local phone directory with complete listings for your entire area. To keep things simple, we'll continue to refer to this dominant local book as the *Core* directory.

Once the dominant phone company disappears, the dominant directory as we know it today is likely to go with it.

The Neighborhood Book

The "just your particular market, why pay for wasted circulation?" directory. A *Neighborhood* book serves a smaller, more localized part of the area already covered by the larger *Core* book. It might be published by the dominant local phone company itself as an additional book, but more often it's done by an independent publisher or by another phone company. (Yellow Pages publishing can be extremely lucrative, with after-tax profit margins often in excess of 20 percent.) For our purposes, independent publishers and phone companies publishing in areas where they aren't the dominant local phone company will be lumped together, and their directories described as "independent" or "competitive" books.

Neighborhood books may or may not have a true white pages section with business and residential listings.

The Overlay Book

The Confabulated Publishing rep with his, "twice the area at half the price," was talking about an *Overlay*. *Overlay* books cover territory from all or part of two or more directories in one volume. Independent publishers frequently overlay established directories because that "larger area, lower prices" story is an extremely effective sales hook. Telephone company publishers will often extend the coverage of one of their *Core* books to overlay all or part of a directory of a nearby competitor. Overlays may or may not have white pages with business and residential listings.

Other directories beside *Core*, *Neighborhood* and *Overlay* fall into the category of *Specialty* books.

The Specialty Book

A specialty book can be a true Yellow Pages—meaning a general-interest directory—but for a specific segment of the population (e.g., Asians, Hispanics, women). It can also be a specialized directory with classifications of use to a particular occupation (e.g., travel agents or architects) or to a group with a particular interest (e.g., boat owners or restaurant-goers).

Little-Noted Benefits

If having more Yellow Pages salesmen hanging around the store than customers has you plunging into despair, take heart. What some have seen as "the cancerous growth of directories," others have welcomed. *Consumer Reports* called the proliferation of competing directories "a little-noted benefit to both consumers and businesses." Competition holds the line on prices. And you were so negative about paying for seven different books when one used to work so well.

But remember what you used to pay for that one directory? Competitive directories only got off the ground because advertisers were fed up with those prices. And fed up with year after year of rate increase piled upon rate increase. In the heyday of Yellow Pages monopolies, it was often 8 to 10 to 20 percent a year.

In Yellow Pages school, I was taught that ad rates were based on the book's circulation and the cost of putting the book together. Not until I had gained the exalted privilege of an occasional lunch with the company's top echelon was I made privy to the actual formula: "Whatever the market will bear."

I once talked with some Yellow Pages old-timers about the way they used to work one particularly high-priced directory: a team of sales reps would arrive, "put on their white shoes at the city limits, rape, pillage and plunder, then vanish until next year." One critic called the Yellow Pages, the closest thing to a legalized protection racket. The attitude was often, "you know you have to have it and this is what you're going to pay." Ad sizes got bigger and bigger, and everything got more and more expensive.

With competition from both additional directories and other advertising media taking aim at those Yellow Pages dollars, all that has changed. Rates might still be based on what the market will bear, but the market won't bear what it used to. Most of the white-shoed hit-and-run experts have vanished for good, especially at the leading publishers; and elsewhere they've at least put their white shoes back in the closet. The industry as a whole is far more service oriented, and far more concerned with turning out the best possible product. They have to be or they're going to be left behind. Research and marketing information are improving constantly. Enlightened directory publishers have realized that if they don't take care of their advertisers they soon won't have advertisers to take care of.

To me, the most amazing indication of this transformation came with the publication of the first edition this book. As critical as I sometimes am of directory companies, most of the major publishers hailed the book. Many of them bought copies for their advertisers and/or their sales force, and a few of them even contracted with me to conduct workshops for their advertisers. Hardly the reception I would have expected.

How To Chose a Book

Usage is everything. When you're deciding on a directory, evaluate it as the end user would see it. The first time an independent book comes into an area, it usually fills up with ads because advertisers are just buying low price. It's great to get the same size ad at half the cost, but if nobody uses the book that bargain may be the most expensive ad you ever buy.

The dominant local phone company will tell you that people have been using its *Core* book for the last fifty, eighty, one hundred years, so people are going to continue to use that book. They've called themselves "The *Real* Yellow Pages," "The *Official* Yellow Pages," and "The One and Only." In the days of the local phone monopolies, *Forbes* once quoted a competing independent publisher as saying, "merchants think the phone company book comes from Mt. Sinai." It didn't. And it certainly doesn't now. And just because people used it in the past doesn't necessarily mean they're going to use it in the future.

Ketchum Directory Advertising is a major advertising agency that buys ads on a national basis for large corporations. Over the years they've monitored the competition between independents and dominant local phone company *Core* books.

"We've found," says Blanche McGuire, senior vice president, director of marketing strategy, "that people generally don't care what directory they're reading as long as it has what they want. In one study, about half the consumers kept more than one book in the house—to cover all the shopping areas."

"The independents," McGuire says, "are a force to be reckoned with." But having said that, she continues: "In virtually every market the [dominant local phone company] *Core* book is still by far and away the primary reference."

Generalizing about directories nationwide, McGuire said: "There is never a single instance in which we at Ketchum wouldn't recommend people go into the *Core* book. Others may be half price, but in terms of usage [the dominant local phone company] *Core* book would still be the best buy. In some areas we might recommend an independent or a non*Core* phone company book too, but virtually always as a secondary book. And never to the exclusion of the local *Core* directory."

As I said before, without a local telephone monopoly, there is no longer any such thing as the official telephone company directory. Still, in most markets, we can expect the *Core* directory published by the former local telephone monopoly to remain the dominant directory—the directory with the greatest consumer usage—for some years to come. The lead they've established is too great to be overcome quickly.

Still, competitive books will make gains—especially those with the backing of the major players in the industry. And eventually some will become the dominant books in their markets. In some areas at least, Yellow Pages coverage might someday be more like that of radio, where you have several stations that reach different segments of the market, where no one station, no matter how dominant, reaches everyone, and where sometimes you might want to go with more than one.

Know Who You're Dealing With

Obviously, if no one bought advertising in them, there would be no second and third and fourth telephone directories for advertisers to complain about. But since you don't control every other advertiser in town, your job is not to help the books live or die but simply to determine which, if any, of them are cost-effective ways for you to reach a worthwhile segment of your potential customers.

In some markets this is easy. Much like what Nielson and Arbitron do for TV and radio, the National Yellow Pages Monitor (NYPM) provides syndicated surveys with objective, third-party data on Yellow Pages directory possession and usage—which directories people have and which directories they use. National advertisers use this information with confidence. Local advertisers, however, are far more likely to be shown studies done by the directory companies themselves.

Even if your rep does have NYPM figures, use them with care, and determine just exactly what the study is measuring. Perhaps your rep pulls out one that "proves" only 14 percent of those surveyed use the little *Neighborhood* book you were considering. Not particularly impressive—unless you realize that this particular NYPM survey is for the entire metropolitan area. The *Neighborhood* book reaches only a fraction of that territory. Within its own distribution area—the only area you're concerned about reaching—its numbers may be much more impressive.

National Yellow Pages Monitor studies are not available in every market. And with every publisher out there making all manner of claims, you have to be able to evaluate the different books by yourself.

The first thing you want to know when you're checking any directory is the most basic: Just who are you are dealing with here? In the worst cases, independent reps deliberately give the impression they're with the dominant local phone company.

One scenario goes like this: The rep dashes in, waving your business's current ad pasted on a copy sheet. Clearly visible on one corner of the copy sheet is the famous walking fingers logo.

"Yellow Pages," he announces. "Do you want to run your ad in our book just like it is or would you like to make some changes?"

One suspicious advertiser questioned the rep repeatedly. "You're from the real Yellow Pages?" she asked.

"Of course."

"The phone book?"

"The phone book. The real phone book. Now what I'd suggest you do this year is . . . ."

They went over the program: increasing one ad, balancing that with a cut in another which, uncharacteristically, the rep didn't seem to mind. Then he wrote up the contract.

"My God!" exclaimed the advertiser. "My rate's been cut in half!"

"Well, you see, this year we're charging a lot less."

An obvious impostor.

According to Southwestern Bell, when it set up a separate subsidiary, Southwestern Bell Publishing, to handle its books, some competing reps told advertisers that Southwestern Bell no longer had a Yellow Pages directory.

"We're publishing the phone book this year," is a claim to be accepted no sooner than, "We're printing the money now." "We" may be publishing a phone book too, but Yellow Pages publishing produces far too much revenue for any dominant local phone company to simply let somebody else take over the business for a year or so. Phone companies sometimes do contract with independent publishers to produce directories for them, but the directory is still the phone company directory, reps will always identify it as such, and the utility name will be on the cover.

If you have any doubt about who you're dealing with, call the dominant local phone company business office. The walking fingers logo and the "let your fingers do the walking" slogan are public domain in the United States. Anybody can use them.

Beware also of strange invoices or unfamiliar "renewal" notices that come through the mail (see Figure 2-1). Make sure they're actually from the publisher you think they're from. Instead of paying your bill or renewing the ads you have, you could be buying a listing in some kind of national Yellow Pages. I may be one of the few people who's ever seen the inside of such a directory. It was a bizarre combination of the traditional and the innovative. Traditional, in that it re-introduced the worthless **Miscellaneous** category. Innovative, in that it had addresses like, "213 S. Main, no state given," and phone numbers like "317-000-000," to prevent those annoying nuisance calls.[1]

Still, John Gauling, the former CEO of Pacific Bell's directory subsidiary, wasn't referring to companies who misrepresent who they are when he told the *Wall Street Journal*: "This has become a down-and-dirty little competitive business. People will do whatever it takes to convince businesses that they have broad market coverage."

Considering Market Coverage

Aside from price, if you're considering an independent or a non*Core* book instead of your dominant local telephone company, it's probably because of the book's particular coverage. Your bakery only attracts customers from the 49,000 people within a one mile radius, but to be in your *Core* Springfield directory you have to pay for the entire 357,987

---

[1] There are, of course, legitimate national directories such as AT&T's consumer and business-to-business directories for toll free numbers, and, of course, the various Internet Yellow Pages.

Figure 2-1 A Misleading direct mail solicitation.

DIRECT MAIL
ADVERTISING DEPARTMENT
YELLOW PAGES

NOTICE

Yellow Pages

FEBRUARY 2, 1987

TELEPHONE DIRECTORY

THE YELLOW PAGES

DISTRIBUTED AND MADE AVAILABLE TO BUSINESSES AND PROFESSIONALS NATIONWIDE.
THIS IS NOT AN INVOICE. THIS IS A SOLICITATION. YOU ARE UNDER NO OBLIGATION TO BUY.

With your approval, you will be listed in the next Edition appearing as follows:

Smedley Bros. & Co.
21111 Dead End Ct. 555-555 $ 90.00 per year.

Classification   *Department Stores*

001718

Please indicate below any changes or corrections on your order that you may require

Name _____
Address _____
City _____ State _____
Zip _____ Telephone _____

☐ Listing is correct as shown above. Please print as is.
☐ Changes required.
☐ My check is enclosed

Please make your check payable to Telmaster   A return envelope is enclosed for your convenience.
Not affiliated with A.T.&T. Yellow pages.

PLEASE RETURN THIS ORDER FORM WITH YOUR CHECK

Source: The Yellow Pages Publishers Association.

bodies it reaches. How far is somebody going to drive for a doughnut? Or perhaps you move houses all over greater Goose Tuft, an area covered by parts of four different *Core* directories published by three different dominant local phone companies.

This is where *Neighborhood* and *Overlay* books can have their greatest advantage. This is especially true if the *Core* book remains locked into utility company service boundaries set decades ago—boundaries that aren't necessarily those of the market area in which people tend to shop and merchants want to advertise.

And just as *Neighborhood* and *Overlay* books target specific areas, *Specialty* books target specific demographic groups.

The demographics of those who use local *Core* books are largely determined by the coverage area's population. Yellow Pages users in general tend to be somewhat younger and more upscale than the statistical average, but that's largely because these are the people who *in general* make the most purchases. Obviously, user profiles vary widely from classification to classification within a directory—those looking under **Shoes—Orthopedic** will be very different from those checking **Child Care Centers**. If, however, virtually all the clientele for your customized shuffleboard shufflers are in the 15.6 percent of the population over 65, then you'll probably be tempted by the rep who tells you that, with his Leisure Land Directory, every bit of circulation you're paying for is within the market you need to target.

It is a thing of wonder and beauty to find a directory with perfect coverage (for your business anyway), whether that's a geographic area or a demographic group. Just keep in mind *usage*. Do the people who are supposed to use this particular directory really have any use for it? Have the publishers done their homework, have they uncovered a niche in the marketplace, a consumer demand that justifies the product? In buzzword-ology, is this directory "market-driven," or have they merely invented another excuse to sell advertising?

Figure 2-2 YPPA Chart on Yellow Pages Demographics.

Demographics

1	2	3 WEEKLY USAGE (REACH)	4 AVERAGE FREQUENCY TOTAL POP	5 PERCENT OF USES TOTAL POP	6 PERCENT OF POPULATION	7 USAGE INDEX
TOTAL	ADULTS 18+	58.3	1.9	100	100	100
SEX	MALES	57.5	1.9	48.0	48.2	100
	FEMALES	58.8	1.9	52.0	51.8	100
AGE	18-24	63.4	2.3	16.1	13.4	120
	25-34	64.6	2.3	26.1	21.3	123
	35-49	64.8	2.0	33.0	31.3	105
	50-64	57.6	1.7	15.8	17.9	88
	65+	39.7	1.1	9.0	16.1	56
EDUCATION	HIGH SCHOOL	34.7	1.0	6.7	12.7	53
	H.S. GRAD	55.9	1.6	33.1	37.3	89
	SOME COLLEGE	66.4	2.2	27.9	23.1	121
	COLLEGE GRAD+	67.8	2.2	32.3	26.9	120
HOUSEHOLD INCOME	UNDER $10,000	43.0	1.3	5.7	8.8	65
	$10-$25,000	53.1	1.8	19.0	21.9	87
	$25-$40.000	63.6	2.1	23.6	23.1	102
	$40-$60,000	69.3	2.3	26.4	23.4	113
	$60,000 OR MORE	68.5	2.2	25.3	22.8	111
CENSUS REGION	NORTHEAST	52.7	1.5	17.1	20.6	83
	MIDWEST	60.4	1.9	23.9	24.0	100
	SOUTH	57.1	1.9	34.5	34.5	100
	WEST	64.4	2.2	24.5	20.9	117
COUNTY SIZE	AA/A	55.1	1.5	34.1	40.6	84
	B	63.8	2.1	33.9	29.7	114
	C	64.0	2.3	18.7	14.6	128
	D	51.8	1.6	13.3	15.1	88
		The average weekly usage or "reach" by the demographic subgroups.	The average number of uses per week for each demographic subgroup.	The distribution of uses in a typical week within each subgroup.	The distribution of the adult population within each subgroup.	The result of dividing column 5 by column 6. As an index, it is used to compare strength of Yellow Pages usage by demographic subgroup.

HOW TO READ THIS CHART

Of adults who live in "B" counties, 63.8% use the Yellow Pages at least once in an average week (col.3). The average number of uses per week is 2.1 (col. 4). This group's share of Yellow Pages uses is 33.9% (col.5); however, within the total population distribution, "B" counties represent 29.7% (col.6). The resulting index of 114 means that adults who live in "B" counties account for 14% more of the references to Yellow Pages than the average adult (col.5 ÷ col. 6).

The information contained in this brochure was compiled by Statistical Research, Inc. (SRI), an independent research firm headquartered in Westfield, New Jersey. SRI has been commissioned by the Yellow Pages Publishers Association (YPPA) to conduct an ongoing national study to measure consumer Yellow Pages usage.

The study design measures overall usage, frequency of usage, type of usage and end results of usage.The research methodology utilizes a random digit dial telephone number sampling technique with one randomly selected adult interviewed in each household. Interviews are conducted throughout the United States on a daily basis over 12 four-week measurement periods annually. In 1996, an average of over 500 interviews was conducted per month among persons 18 or older.

This report highlights the study results from 1995 and 1996 combined, based on an arithmetic average of the results each year. This combined sample size of 11,941 interviews, (5,796 in 1995 and 6,145 in 1996) increases the statistical accuracy of estimates over that for each year separately.

COUNTY SIZE DEFINITIONS

  AA/A All counties in the 21 largest metropolitan areas.

  B All counties not included in AA/A that are in metropolitan areas with more than 85,000 households.

  C All counties not included in the two preceding groups that either have more than 20,000 households or are in a metro politan area with more than 20,000 households.

  D All remaining counties.

Source: Yellow Pages Publishers Association. Copyright 1997. Used by permission.

Is Smaller Big Enough? Neighborhood Books

Riverdale is a part of Metropolis. Archie and Jughead used to live there. So did Beaver and Wally. The area is much more urban now. Yet, recent studies of shopping patterns show that Riverdalians still do most of their business—and make most of their phone calls—within three to five miles of home. Whether that's because of the extensive retail development, habit, traffic, a sense of community, or a fear of the outside world is hard to say.

Riverdale is perfect for a *Neighborhood* book. No more wading through the two-volume Metropolis directory—page after page of faraway firms with strange sounding names—just to find a local fix-it shop. What's more, the population of Riverdale is now quite elderly. Little old ladies like Mrs. Cleaver find the smaller books easier to handle, and little old ladies don't travel far anyway.

Publishers of *Neighborhood* books contend, and probably correctly, that the larger the *Core* directory the greater the chances of acceptance for a convenient localized book. As an advertiser in a *Neighborhood* book you get greater visibility plus a larger ad at a lower cost, and you have fewer other businesses competing for attention. You can advertise services like "Free Delivery" and "Free Pick Up" that wouldn't be profitable over a larger area. And even a business too small to afford anything significant in its *Core* book can get cost-efficient results out of the right *Neighborhood* book.

Even the best *Neighborhood* books, the ones that work, are still not substitutes for *Core* directories. Their publishers don't claim they are. Usage figures are almost always far lower. Such directories tend to work better for smaller-ticket items, for things people won't drive very far to buy, and for minor services performed cheaper or more conveniently by somebody local. If Mr. Cleaver is looking for a baker or he wants a pizza delivered, he's not going to be doing a lot of shopping around. He wants someone good; he won't deal with just anybody, but mostly, he wants someone close.

If, however, he's buying a car or a yacht, or having the

house recarpeted, he wants more of a selection and he's probably going to a bigger book.

Most products and services fall somewhere between cars and croissants, of course. And that's where it becomes most important that the territory the *Neighborhood* book covers is a viable marketplace: one that people do shop within; one with a big enough selection of businesses and different types of businesses that people won't always feel the need to turn to their *Core* book. So they get more and more into the habit of using the *Neighborhood* directory.

Overlays

Overlays are big enough. Theoretically anyway. In central Illinois, an area of 116,000 people is divided into 10 different *Core* directories published by seven different dominant local phone companies. The *Overlay* publisher simply put the marketplace back together and satisfied a need.

On the other hand, in Santa Barbara, California, where I live, a competitive publisher tried to put in a directory covering Santa Barbara, Santa Ynez (40 miles away), Solvang (45 miles away), Lompoc (50 miles), and Santa Maria (75 miles). These towns are in the same county, but *nobody* in Santa Barbara shops in Santa Maria or Lompoc. Therefore nobody in Santa Barbara used the county-wide *Overlay*.

Some Santa Marians and Lompocians (Lompockers?) do shop for certain items in the relatively big city of Santa Barbara, so many Santa Barbara businesses advertise in the Lompoc and Santa Maria *Core* directories. The question for the competitive directory was, how frequently will those shoppers be dissatisfied with what they find in their local *Core* book and reach for the *Overlay*? And when they do, will they be any more satisfied with what they find? In this case, the answer was *no*. Because Santa Barbara merchants didn't advertise in the *Overlay*. Nobody they knew ever used it. After a few years the book disappeared.

The problem with *Overlays* is that they're often too big, giving directory users coverage they neither need nor want.

Specialty Books

You judge a *Specialty* book for a certain group just like you would a *Neighborhood* or an *Overlay*. Is this a group you want to target? Does the group have a need or a desire for the directory? Do the businesses the book contains—or will contain—make up a coherent marketplace? One in which the members of the group tend to shop? How often will they have to go outside the scope of the directory to find what they want?

In some areas, Spanish, Chinese or other foreign language directories have an almost captive audience. They give the non-English speaking access to directory information they may not be able to get elsewhere and let them know where they can do business in a language comfortable to them. Of course, just because the directory is in a potential customer's language doesn't mean it will get used. Usage of Hispanic directories, for example—though it's probably growing—is often lower than expected. Hispanics simply tend to get more of their buying information from TV, radio and word of mouth.

In areas where even households can be divided by languages, there are also bi-lingual books. For a single price, your ad runs in both the English and the foreign language sections. Besides verifying usage, take extra care to verify the translation.

Obviously, groups that speak a different language tend to shop where that language is spoken. But is an African-American, an Indian, a woman or a gay likely to use a Yellow Pages directory simply because it's targeted for him or her as a member of that particular group? Let's look at some numbers. A few years back, a Southwestern Bell usage study for its Silver Pages directories proudly proclaimed that 79 percent of all senior citizens in Silver Pages areas had received the book. Ninety-five percent of those still had it. Forty-seven percent of *those* said they had used it at least once. That means, by

Southwestern Bell's own figures, 35 percent of the seniors in Silver Pages cities had used the directory at least once, to look up some business in some category.

Thus, if you'd bought an ad you were in a book people were using. That's good. But these figures aren't even in the same ballpark as the numbers normally associated with a *Core* directory, which, without competition, will be used by close to 90 percent of the people in the area—and the *average* user will open the book 35 to 40 times a year.

Besides the classified directory, the Silver Pages offered a magazine section and a listing of local government and social services for the elderly. But the principal inducement to get the old folks to use the book and patronize its advertisers was the senior's discount program offered by the advertisers. Only before the first Silver Pages book hit the streets, publishers of regular phone directories began tagging businesses that offered senior discounts with special logos—at no charge to advertisers. So seniors didn't have to use a separate directory with a limited number of businesses or carry a special I.D. card, and advertisers didn't have to pay to offer seniors that incentive. In spite of a huge investment by a major publisher, a vast amount of hype and Bob Hope's best efforts as spokesman, the Silver Pages soon disappeared.

If you advertise in many *Specialty* books you aren't necessarily offering a discount. Are you betting that these people would be dying to shop with you . . . if only they knew you were black or a woman? Or Lithuanian? If you are a member of the group you're trying to reach, is that how you shop? You know better than I. If you're not a member, be very skeptical that hordes of Lithuanian women will arrive at your doorstep because of an ad you put in "their" directory.

Offering discounts as incentives is good, but unless you offer those discounts within a complete directory, what you'll have is little more than a coupon book or a cumbersome flier. With any *Specialty* book, pay particular attention to how many people you'll be reaching within your market and how the book is going to get to them. I mean, how does a publisher distribute a directory to Lithuanian women? If the women have to sign up for it or go pick it up or even call an "800" number, how many are going to bother?

All that said, the *Community Yellow Pages*, the gay Yellow Pages for Los Angeles, contains over 400 pages and recently published its 16th edition.

Directories for Specific Occupations or Interests

Limited directories geared to specific occupations— builders, aerospace engineers, interior decorators—or aimed at groups with a specific interest such as computer owners or resort-goers are a different story and for the most part one outside the scope of a book on Yellow Pages, general-interest, directories.

Just a quick word. If your business deals with groups with such specialized needs, you may know that the right directory—either in use or proposed—could be a real help, especially if it offers information they need beyond what's available in a regular phone book. You still make the salesman prove usage. Then make sure the directory's going where the publisher claims, that it's being promoted enough to get people to open the thing, and that when it *is* opened the user can find what he needs inside—so he won't be turning to his local phone book.

Once More . . .

I repeat one final time. For any directory, no matter what the coverage, no matter what the price: A book which nobody uses doesn't cover anything.

Obviously, the amount of advertising in a directory is an important indication of how seriously the book is being taken, but never buy simply because you see your competition's full-page, process color, glow-in-the-dark ad there. You might just be repeating his mistake. I've seen books in which up to 80 percent of the advertisers cancel from one year to the next.

What About the Publisher?

For any directory or directories you're still considering, be they from the dominant local phone company or Confabulated Publishing, you should ask yourself the following questions:

—Is the publisher reputable and will they be available if you have a problem?

—How committed are they to making the directory work or even to putting out another edition next year? So they take pains to get your ad right. And so the placement advantages you might gain from seniority will be worth something.

—What kind of advertising are they doing to get people to use the directory?

Even major publishers often aren't willing to spend the money necessary to really make a book succeed with the public. Ask specifically about where their advertising is being placed. Dollar figures can be deceiving: the company may be including the cost of sales and production.

Are Their Listings Accurate, Complete and Up to Date?

If the end-users of the book, the people you're trying to reach, can't find the local movie house that has been downtown for 50 years or the pharmacy across the street—if the numbers they do find have been changed or disconnected—then the book will find a quick home with yesterday's melon rinds and last Tuesday's coffee grounds. Accuracy and completeness are where the independent books sometimes break down.

Do the publishers buy the latest and most accurate listings from the phone company just before they go to press? Do they compile their own (and if so how)? Or perhaps they simply purchase the old listings from the last telephone company book, a book that may have been published a number of months before?

Completeness in the Yellow Pages goes beyond a simple listing of all the businesses. People go to the Yellow Pages seeking information—not just names and addresses. Though a lot of ads in a directory doesn't mean you should automatically buy, a poor supply of ads means a poor supply of information. Consumers can get that from TV.

When Does the Darn Thing Come Out?

When will the directory be distributed? When I was with GTE, we once started signing advertisers in June for a directory that published the following May.

The independents like to canvas before businesses have committed their ad dollars to the dominant local phone company's *Core* book. They tend to get their directories out first too. Originally, the idea was that people would say, "Oh, the new phone book," then toss last year's *Core* book into the trash. Of course, this only worked until the new *Core* book arrived. Then the competitive book—if it had nothing more going for it than confusion—would itself get tossed or just stuck at the bottom of the pile under the phone.

In any case, directory users have become more sophisticated, likely to judge the directory or directories they wish to keep more by merits than by timing. Still, if you're a new business, a good competitive book that comes out early enough can, at the very least, help tide you over until the *Core* book hits the streets.

White Pages—The Other Half of the Book

Does the directory you're considering have *real* white pages? Some independent books have none at all. Some pretend to, but what they actually have is a section on white paper which is nothing more than an alphabetical listing of the businesses that have decided to advertise in the thing. Most independent books do have complete white pages, and that's important to you as an advertiser.

How many of your friends and acquaintances are listed in the Yellow Pages? If Mrs. Cleaver has to grab the local *Core* book every time she wants to use the white pages, how likely is she to toss that one aside and reach for a second book when she wants to find a florist or a tile setter? Which one will end up on the bottom of the pile?

If, on the other hand, the white pages and the Yellow Pages of your local *Core* book are already separate, a competitive book without white pages loses nothing.

Circulation and Distribution

An independent book rode into a western town a little while back. It offered a 69 percent savings on ad costs and combined the coverage of three different local *Core* directories from two different dominant local phone companies. The total circulation was 137,078. Combined circulation of the *Core* directories for the identical area was 274,297. So unless the phone companies were printing an extra 137,219 books just to be on the safe side, somebody somewhere was getting shortchanged.

Such discrepancies are commonplace (though they're sometimes difficult to detect since coverage areas don't always match up so neatly). Ask the rep from your independent publisher just who gets a book and who doesn't. Do businesses get one for every phone, one for the entire business, or as many as the distributor can dump on them?

Phone booth distribution usually accounts for some circulation discrepancy. How important are phone booth directories to your business? If you own a cab company, a motel, or a towing operation they could be crucial. Independent publishers may or may not provide books for pay phones in bars or restaurants, but the books won't be tied down and tend to disappear. And independent publishers can't put them in phone company phone booths. Of course, phone companies are getting lax here too.

I mentioned earlier that newcomers without established buying patterns are a great potential source of new business. What book do they get when their phone is installed? If they move into the area six weeks or six months after an independent publisher's distribution will they receive a directory? If so, how will the independent publisher discover these people? New homeowners and new businesses are relatively easy to locate, but how about renters? Some independents buy the lists of new installs from the local phone companies and do an excellent job of getting their book out.

Will directories be in each room of every hotel and motel in the area and will they be replaced when they disappear?

Can the general public conveniently get replacements for lost books?

Of course, circulation figures—whether for the dominant local phone company's *Core* book or a competitor—can easily be inflated. Often what they really represent is the number of books to be printed. Since books are held for secondary distribution—to newcomers and as replacement copies—nobody knows in advance how many will actually be circulated. But passing out phone books is expensive. How does this year's proposed circulation compare with what was actually circulated last year? If too many books are being held in reserve, you might wonder if the only purpose they'll ever serve is to provide impressive numbers.

Circulation can also be inflated by multiplying the number of books distributed by the average number of people in each household and business that gets a book. The publisher drops off one directory, but it "circulates" among five people. A phone book may indeed be used by the entire household, and it's helpful to know the population of the market covered, but how many books is the publisher distributing to cover that market? After all, if they drop off a book at a GM plant does it "circulate" to 9,876 employees? Just imagine, if they donated one to the library the whole darn town could use it!

You would also do well to ask how the book is distributed and how the company verifies that distribution. I've seen stacks of books dumped in the lobbies of apartment houses and office buildings and heard of dumpsters overflowing with directories because nobody checked up on the part-time workers hired to pass the books out.

A few years back, in Kern County, California, prosecutors in the consumer fraud office alleged that the publisher who did the directory for the Better Business Bureau had delivered books to less than half the addresses promised. The BBB sued its own contractor on behalf of its advertisers.

Special Features

As one publisher used to say, telephone books are "Yellow Pages and much, much more." Any number of studies have found that people like the "much more"—the extra features like zip codes, government listings, first aid advice, seating charts for auditoriums and stadiums, Internet guides, community fact-finders, audiotext (recorded consumer tips, horoscopes, weather, stock prices, etc.), pictures of missing children, crime prevention information, hurricane tracking maps, and so on. Is anyone going to tell a survey that they don't like free mileage charts or bus schedules? Still, anything that gets people to hang onto the book and open it is of benefit to the advertisers inside.

According to a Ketchum Directory Advertising study, the most important special feature in determining usage is a good headings index. That should be clear to anyone who has ever tried to find anything under any of the Yellow Pages non-existent categories. According to Statistical Research, Inc., zip code information is the most heavily used special feature, followed by street maps, public transportation maps (especially heavily used in metropolitan areas), and guides to local attractions.

Grided locator maps, with correspondingly coded display ads, are the best way I've seen to pinpoint a business' location within a city.

Older people especially like large type and wide columns for easier reading. But publishers sometimes use both of these—and thicker paper—to make a sparse directory appear thick and worthy of the area it's supposed to cover.

Other Considerations—Money

Does the publisher you're considering require advance payment? All or in part? That may be because they are using your money to print the book. If it is required, are they giving a significant discount for paying up front? When are the other payments due? Your dominant local phone company usually will give you credit, tacking your monthly Yellow Pages charge right onto your phone bill. And the first bill doesn't come until the directory is published and on the street. But dominant local phone companies also charge a lot more.

What is the procedure for cost adjustments if somebody screws up your ad?

If you go out of business or become disabled, will you be liable for the cost of the whole year's advertising? If you disconnect your business phone, will your advertising billing stop immediately? (If you've paid in advance find out if and how you can get a rebate.) What happens if you sell the business? If you're advertising with your telephone company, the new owner signs for the advertising when you transfer the phone. If for some reason he doesn't want it, he simply gets a new number. In either case, your billing should stop. Make sure it does.

If the ads are cut rate, at whose expense are they cutting costs? Rates for the local *Core* book being what they are, there is usually plenty of room to cut costs and still turn out a world-class directory, probably one with a gold-plated cover and a diamond-studded spine. There's even more short-term money in turning out a piece of garbage. No gold, no diamonds, maybe even no cover. Many independent publishers do manage to do just as good a job in terms of the look of the directory as the phone company publishers and sometimes

Summarizing Questions

1. Who are the publishers?

2. Is there a demand for this directory among those consumers you want to reach?

3. How committed are the publishers to the directory's success?

4. Are their listings current, complete and accurate? How extensive is current advertising in the book ?

5. When does the directory publish?

6. Does it have white pages?

7. Who gets a directory and who doesn't—and how does the publisher verify promised circulation?

8. What useful features does the directory offer?

9. How will you be billed and how are adjustments given?

10. Will the book and/or your ad look cut-rate?

better.

Especially with smaller independents, the training the sales reps receive can be slipshod. They may know little about designing ads. They can have accuracy problems. And he or she may have no idea if, for example, your ad infringes on a trademark, leaves out a legally required address or license number, or makes a claim that could get you into legal difficulty.

A rep from a major publisher can be just as ignorant, but major publishers have extensive post-sales departments—not as extensive as they once were perhaps, but thorough nonetheless. Post-sales not only checks ads for spelling and little things like phone number accuracy, but in most cases they also try to make sure everything is done by the book, so that Mercedes Benz doesn't come after you—and the publisher—because you used its logo without permission.

A very small publisher may not have an art department, but you may not need one. Likewise, if you're confident about the ads you have or of your ability to design new ones yourself, a lack of post-sales scrutiny might not be a problem. Just be even more careful on the copy than you would normally be.

So What Do You Think?

Now that you can see all that can be wrong with a directory, consider this: Why not be in all of them? Virtually all directories offer businesses one free listing. If they don't they aren't going to be complete directories, are they? Free is a good price. I'd take that. Other competitive books might convince you as far as the price of a tiny cut-rate ad. One or two might be possible secondary books for your advertising—one might even stand a chance of eventually becoming the dominant local book.

If you're thinking about investing significant money in any competitive directory, it should be evaluated in exactly the same way we'll be evaluating your dominant local phone company's *Core* book.

Taking Control of the Situation— How to Get Started

In the chapters that follow, we'll be planning your Yellow Pages program—discussing what types of ads are available, the advantages and disadvantages of each, discovering just how well Yellow Pages can work for your business, and determining which ads, if any, you want in which books. I'll show you how to stretch your ad dollars and how to get the greatest possible return on those dollars, with the smallest possible risk. Before we can do any of that, however, you need to gather a little information.

Taking Control

A directory will close to advertisers—stop taking ads—three to five months before it's actually published and hits the streets. Often it closes to current advertisers a week or so before it closes to new advertisers, but once it is truly closed, it is closed. In the first few days after the close, an act of God *might* get a minor change or two made in your ad. Don't count on it.

Never wait until the last minute to begin working on

your Yellow Pages advertising. You don't want to be stampeded into hasty decisions by looming closing dates. And though it may close last, always try to deal with the dominant local phone company's *Core* book first. Get the other reps to leave their literature. Ask them the questions we covered in Chapter 2. Let them, if they choose, give you their whole pitch. Just explain up front that you aren't signing with anyone until you finish with the *Core* directory. (Unless, of course, it's too late for you to get into the *Core* directory and you want the competitive book to tide you over until you can.) I've seen too many advertisers who felt they had to underfund what should have been their primary directory because of what they had already spent on other books.

To get started, you can either wait for the rep from the dominant local phone company to come to you, or you can take charge of the situation. I strongly recommend the latter.

Making a List and Checking it Twice

The very first thing to do is to begin a list: "What to put in the Yellow Pages ad(s)."

Later, we're going to cover ad content thoroughly, as part of an extensive section on ad design, so you don't have to rack your brain. Just jot down random ideas as they occur to you and grade them as to their importance. If you're already a Yellow Pages advertiser, start the list with all the different copy points in your current ad. The phrases that work best when you're selling one-on-one to customers will also work best in your directory ad, so get them in there. Tape the list to your desk or some countertop where it's handy, but not where it will get covered up by accumulating debris. Now and again look it over. Try to think of better, more precise and more concise ways to express your ideas. Then, scratch out the old and scribble in the improvement.

Know the Closing Date

You need to find out when your local *Core* directory closes. Do not call the phone company business office. They don't know anything about Yellow Pages, and they'll just put you on hold anyway. Get the number of the *Yellow Pages* office from directory assistance or look it up in your *Core* directory under *Advertising—Directory & Guide*. If the number isn't local, it should be toll-free. If it's not toll-free, call collect.

Try to get the close date from a customer service person or a receptionist or secretary. Yellow Pages reps are probably no less—or more—honest than any other group. But since every advertiser wants to be handled at 4:45 p.m. on the day the book closes, on this one point reps are sometimes tempted to fudge. In any case, you do not want to be handled anywhere near the closing date. Remember the fall of Saigon? The average Yellow Pages close is only slightly more disorganized than that. Up to 80 percent of directory errors that are attributable to the sales force occur in the last 20 percent of the sales canvas. And even if mistakes aren't made, your rep won't have the time to give you his best possible effort. Earlier in the canvas he may have nothing but time.

You'll also need to find out when the reps are going to be working your area. In smaller towns they may only be physically present for as little as two or three days. You might even discover your advertising has to be handled from start to finish over the phone. Phone accounts tend to be smaller and more straightforward and under headings with "less potential," which means less likely to buy that big old full-color ad. Handling advertisers by phone keeps costs down—and profits up—and, theoretically anyway, makes the advertising cheaper for everybody. That's fine as long as everything is crystal clear between you and the phone rep. If problems develop, drive in and do it in person or have the company send a rep out to see you.

Upgrades and New Installs— The Phone Company Gets Theirs

If you're advertising in a local phone company phone book for the first time, there's one thing you might not have, even though you may have been in business for years, and very successfully at that. It's one thing without which you often can't get into the phone company Yellow Pages: a business phone.

Many telephone company publishers will require you to get one, even though you've been doing business on your residential line since 1984, and your 6,017 customers all know your number by heart. The phone company is finally gonna get the extra bucks. The good news is that, if you want, you can keep the same number. You just get to pay more money for it.

Because of the growth of the SOHO (small office/home office) phenomenon, some telco publishers have tentatively begun to sell advertising on residential lines. It's cheaper for you than upgrading to a business phone, but in most cases it means being listed in the Yellow Pages exactly as your residential phone is listed—e.g., under *Smith, John* rather than *JS Worldwide Enterprises*. You should be able to put the name of your business inside any ad you buy, but customers looking for your business name alphabetically are not going to find it (nor for that matter will anyone calling directory assistance).

If you do decide to upgrade your residential service, your Yellow Pages rep might be able to handle it when he comes out to visit. Otherwise you might have to call or—God help you—visit the phone company business office. If you tell whoever handles your request that you don't want the upgrade to take effect until the directory comes out, the extra charges won't begin until then.

Similarly, if you don't have a business phone yet, you should be able to have the telephone company advance you a phone number for the directory. You can buy all the ads you need and, in theory anyway, the phone doesn't have to be installed until the book hits the streets. Just be certain the telco business office knows the number is for the Yellow Pages, and that the number they give you is actually the number that'll finally be installed. Often they won't guarantee the number, and you'll need to have the phone activated before the date the directory closes in order to make certain the number you put in the book is accurate.

If your business won't be open until sometime *after* the book publishes, consider having the business phone installed in your home or office or even on the construction sight, then transferred later. Save yourself the agony of trying to survive those first few months without being in the phone book. You could even put voice mail on the line with a little pitch and the date of your opening. Maybe might even a coded phrase, "mention you called early," good for a subsequent discount.

Most independent publishers don't care if your phone is a business phone or not. If you don't have one, they, and everyone else, will have more trouble finding you.

Cold Calls and Why Not

You've got your business, you've got your phone, you know when the local *Core* book closes, you may or may not already have ads in the directory from previous years. Next comes the preparation.

Old-school directory publishers—the ones with those white-shoed, hit-and-run experts still selling for them—are going to hate one piece of advice more than anything else in this book. And it's the piece of advice that will save you the most money:

> **Never make an appointment to see your Yellow Pages rep until you're fully prepared. Never. And never let a rep just walk in on you out of the blue and handle your account.**

Remember your Yellow Pages rep is a commission salesman. If he (or she) is a good one he'll want to make sure you have the best possible ads, and that each and every one really does draw for you. Nonetheless, he is on commission. The more you buy, the more he makes.

Typically, appointment or no appointment, when the rep arrives, the advertiser is bogged down in an average work day.

He's not even quite sure what he's got in the directory. The sales rep is. He's checked it over and he knows 1,016 reasons why that business needs more and bigger ads. Heck, the laziest rep in the country can dredge up 804 reasons just winging it, with no preparation at all. You'll wonder how you ever managed to stay in business with nothing but a skimpy little half-page ad. And under a major heading like *Macaroni Machinery*, too.

So even if you're sure you just want to renew what you have, do your homework before you make the appointment. The better your preparation the less likely you are to be talked into something you may regret afterwards. Besides, no program is so good it can't be improved.

More Free Input

Nevertheless, when you call to find out about the close of the *Core* book—before you're ready to set the appointment—talk to your rep too. If he's not there, have him call you back. Put him to work. Ask him to design you a new ad or, even better, have his spec artist design a new ad. It may have already been done using the copy, and sometimes the artwork, from the ad you had last year. If it hasn't, or if you've never had an ad, you might give him some input about copy and any particular style of ad you might be looking for. A good rep will take this opportunity to find out about your business, so he can help you tailor your copy and your Yellow Pages program to fit your specific needs. He may even want to set up a preliminary appointment. That's great. Just as long as he understands that you won't be finalizing anything at this point. You simply want to see the best spec ad possible.

From the publishers point of view, the spec ad is designed to tempt you into spending more money. But it doesn't commit you to anything. And it can be one more good source of ideas. Some spec ads are of surprisingly high quality. Others aren't.

Classified Information—Unclassifying It

While you have your rep on the phone ask him a few questions:

"What, Mr. Yellow Pages Rep, is the circulation for the Riverdale book this year?"

It may take him a moment, but he'll get the figure for you.

"One hundred thousand even, Mr. Businessman."

Now you have the close date and the circulation. Intoxicated by such candor, reckless with success, you press on:

"What's the rate increase?"

"What?"

"The rate increase?"

"Oh. Not much."

"How much?"

"Hard to say. Depends on what you have. It varies. It's not much though. And circulation's way up. Way up. With all the new people moving into Riverdale and all that new construction. Anyway, we'll go over all that when I get out there."

It's like a politician's press conference. If you're lucky, you'll end up with an answer like, "About 4 or 5 percent. A lot of ads not that much. A few a bit more."

What you really want, what you need, and what you have a right to—as a customer, a citizen of the United States of America and a patriot—are the specific prices of the ads. Specific prices. Insist. Be nice about it—salesmen are people too, at least many of them are. But definitely insist. Tell the rep that otherwise he'll have to come out to you at least two more times. Once to give the prices, a second time to handle the program.[1] This advice is what old-school publishers will hate second most about this book. But you can't do any real-

---

[1] If the publisher happens to have a Neighborhood book for your area as well as the Core book (ask if you don't know), then you should always schedule two visits. Tell the rep to bring the Neighborhood directories from the last two years. As we'll see later, without a preliminary appointment you won't be able to evaluate a Neighborhood book properly.

A Little Information

From customer service:

- the close date of the directory
- when your area is to be worked
  - in person or by phone?

From your rep:

- if a spec ad will be available
- circulation figures
- if there's a telco *Neighborhood* book for your area
- rates and discount programs
  - for you current sizes
  - for those of your main competition
  - for any display ad sizes not in the heading
  - for any and all other sizes in which you might be interested

istic planning if you don't know the prices of the ads—*including any applicable discount programs.*

If it's easier for him or her, have your rep send you a tear sheet from the directory or a sales visual with the different prices of the different size ads clearly marked. I'd like to see the publishers provide a sheet with size and prices to all their advertisers, and they could mail whatever propaganda they'd like along with it. If your rep would rather give the prices over the phone, you can both open your current directory to your main heading, and you can pencil the prices in as he gives them to you.

Remember, even though the book is printed and distributed just once, these prices are *monthly*. Your commitment, however, is for a full year.

Be sure to get the rates for the ad sizes of all your main competition and any sizes of display ads that might not appear under the heading. If you're an advertiser, get the price of your current ads and all the other sizes you're curious about, but finish off by asking about at least one or two that are smaller than your present ad. With most publishers, when you cut your advertising, your rep loses money, so that'll get his attention and make sure he does his best preparing your account.

If you're not yet an advertiser, finish up by asking the prices of the largest ads. That'll get his attention, too. In the course of your preparation, if you need any more prices, feel free to call back.

CHAPTER 4

From Squint Print to Full Page—Different Types of Yellow Pages Ads

All Yellow Pages directories are categorized by the number of columns of alphabetical listings on an average page. Two-column books are usually small, a little taller than a hard-cover novel. Three-, four- and five- column books are all phone book size, but with a different number of columns per page and different size print in the columns. Obviously, two- and three- column books tend to serve smaller areas. Five-column books are found most frequently in California, under Pacific Bell and GTE. In the rest of the country, four-column directories predominate even in the largest cities.

Regardless of the number of columns in the directory, the Yellow Pages ads inside run the gamut from simple listings, small space and trademark ads to display ads, which vary from a quarter of a column to a full page.

"What Do I Get for Free?"—Squint Print and You

In a state of nature, before the Fall, when man was pure, businesses were simply listed alphabetically in columns under their particular headings: name, address, phone number. Every one had the same size typeface. A stranger couldn't tell one from another, but maybe there were no strangers in those days.

Nowadays every business is still listed in-column alphabetically. (That's why it's called a directory: Your pterodactyl needs taxidermy, you page to *Pterodactyls—Stuffed & Breaded*, and the book "directs" you where to go.) With your

Regular listings in a five-column book:

Danny's Dead Dinosaurs
   1212 La Brea 555-1066
Frank's Freeze-dried Fossils
   3 N. Pelucidar Ln 555-1492
Stiffs R Us
   Westside Mall 555-1776
Ted's
   555-1789

In a four-column book:

Danny's Dead Dinosaurs
   1212 La Brea 555-1066
Frank's Freeze-dried Fossils
   3 N. Pelucidar Ln 555-1492
Stiffs R Us
   Westside Mall 555-1776
Ted's
   555-1789

In a three-column book:

Danny's Dead Dinosaurs
   1212 La Brea 555-1066
Frank's Freeze-dried Fossils
   3 N. Pelucidar Ln. 555-1492
Stiffs R Us
   Westside Mall. 555-1776
Ted's
   555-1789

In a two-column book:

Danny's Dead Dinosaurs
   1212 La Brea 555-1066
Frank's Freeze-dried Fossils
   3 N. Pelucidar Ln. 555-1492
Stiffs R Us
   Westside Mall 555-1776
Ted's
   555-1789

business phone, you get one "free" in-column listing in your telephone company book under the heading of your choice. Most independent directories and telephone company *Neighborhood* books provide the free listing as well. Some businessmen believe they should be listed free under every applicable heading. The directory companies do not share this belief.

Your free listing—which at least in your telco book you pay for by having the phone—is your basic name, address, and phone number. It's in "squint print"—small enough to encourage advertisers to want a larger size.

Anything more than this freebie, placed in the alphabetical in-column listings under any heading, constitutes paid in-column advertising.

In-Column Advertising: Listings

The simplest and least expensive in-column ad in any book is the regular listing (RL). It's just like the one you get free. Yellow Pages salesman have been known to froth at the mouth when businessmen refer to these as "advertising." It's worth watching. Some books offer semi-bold listings (SL)—which are little more than regular listings in all capital letters—either in addition to, or instead of, selling regular listings.

The next size is the bold listing (BLN): your name and phone number bold, the address in small print. The advantage to the bold listing is that it can be seen. If no one else is bold and you don't want to be aggressive, you can get away with just the squint print. Otherwise, if a heading is of any importance to you and if you have customers looking for you by name, your in-column listing should be at least a BLN. Squint print surrounded by bold ends up lost, looking like part of someone else's ad.

You may want to use extra lines for your e-mail or website address, and alternate call numbers to list your fax number.

Under your bold listing—or even your regular listing—you can add extra lines of copy (ELs).

Danny's Dead Dinosaurs
1212 La Brea **555-1066**
Frank's Freeze-dried Fossils
3 N. Pelucidar Ln **555-1492**
Stiffs R Us
Westside Mall **555-1776**
Ted's
. . . . **555-1789**

RICK'S RESTAURANT
127 W. Maurice. **555-1812**

Doesn't tell the customer much.

RICK'S RESTAURANT
Cajun food, 24 hours
127 W. Maurice **555-1812**

gives them a reason to come in.

You can also add alternative call numbers (AC) with appropriate captions:

RICK'S RESTAURANT
Cajun food, 24 hours
127 W. Maurice. **555-1812**
after midnight 555-1815

Doctors who don't advertise love to buy extra line after extra line, detailing all their specialties, qualifications and associations. A bold listing with 10 or 12 extra lines makes for a good-sized non-ad that not only provides valuable information, but grabs a lot of space. Some publishers, however, limit the number of extra lines you can buy. In any case, once you get more than one or two, it's usually cheaper and certainly more effective to go to a small space ad.

The Space Ad

A space ad is just that: space in-column under the name of your business. It's also called the business card ad and the in-column informational. Your name is bold, and—as in all the listings mentioned above—it will appear exactly as you

Examples of half-space ads.

listings mentioned above—it will appear exactly as you recorded it with the phone company. At least, in telco books it will. A thin line border surrounds the ad. Address and phone number usually have to run across the bottom in small type (if you have a published address). In between, you put copy. Type sizes and styles are very limited.

Space ads are 1 column wide. They usually start at 1/2 inch high (1 HS for one half-space) and proceed at 1/2 inch intervals.

1 inch (2HS)
1 1/2 inch (3HS)
2 inches (4HS)
2 1/2 inches (5HS)
3 inches (6HS)

Not all publishers offer all sizes. Some have an additional (even cheaper) 3/8 inch size. Others have replaced the 1/2 inch with a more expensive 3/4 inch ad. Some offer sizes above 3 inches. And some, while they usually keep the same codes, have decreased—or occasionally even increased—the size of the half space unit, thus increasing or decreasing the length of the ads.

Generally, you can't use much artwork in a space ad. That means no special borders, no photos, not even Visa and Mastercard logos. Most publishers do allow you to stick a single cut—a piece of artwork—such as a logo in the medium and upper sizes. It's a big increase in visibility for a variable extra charge—at GTE that meant another 20 percent. Nowadays some publishers allow two small pieces of artwork.

More In-Column: Trademark Ads

The trademark ad (TM) is actually two pieces. First, comes the ad itself: the business name, in bold across the top, the logo below on the right, and on the left a few lines of copy. Underneath logo and copy comes what is called a "where to buy line." It's called that because it's the introduction to the listing below, and that's about all you can say, something like *Where to Buy, For Information Call* or *For Service Phone.*

If you don't want such meaningless phrases in your ad, the space can be left blank. The second part of the ad contains your basic listing—name, address, and phone number—either in bold, semi-bold or squint print. Since your name already appears in bold across the top, the cheaper lettering is usually sufficient across the bottom—unless the number is too small to read. If you choose, your listing can run below an italicized caption indicating location or the type of outlet listed, such as *Main Office,* or *Warehouse and Showroom.*

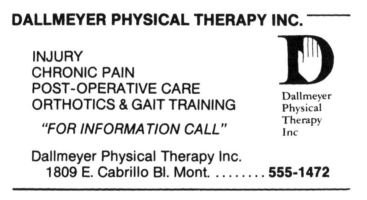

DALLMEYER PHYSICAL THERAPY INC. ⎯⎯

INJURY
CHRONIC PAIN
POST-OPERATIVE CARE
ORTHOTICS & GAIT TRAINING

"FOR INFORMATION CALL"

Dallmeyer
Physical
Therapy
Inc

Dallmeyer Physical Therapy Inc.
1809 E. Cabrillo Bl. Mont. **555-1472**

Source: David A. Dallmeyer Physical Therapy, Inc. Santa Barbara, California. Graphic design by RAVE & Associates, Santa Barbara, California.

Such is a local trademark ad. You're charged for both the ad and the listing underneath it. You have your business name in there twice, which may not hurt but takes up space. There's no art but the logo, and the layout is fixed. Your big design options are whether or not to leave out the "where to buy" line and whether or not to add a caption.

I don't want to hinder your creativity but as far as the "where to buy" goes, *For Free Estimates Call* or *Call Toll Free* is usually about the best you can do. Unless what you come up with something of real value, remember, white space—in this case yellow space—sells a lot better than empty phrases.

But, whereas the "where to buy" line takes up space inside the ad, adding a caption increases the size of the listing. If your location is an advantage, this is the place for *In Riverdale* or *On the South Coast*.

If you can get a space ad with a cut for about the same price or less—sometimes it's much less—forget the local trademark.

The reason the ad is so limited is that it's not designed for local businesses so much as it is for national companies and brand names like Goodyear Tires, Ford, Carrier Air Conditioning, or Kodak.

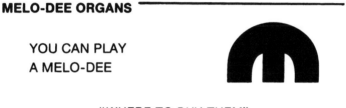

MELO-DEE ORGANS

YOU CAN PLAY
A MELO-DEE

"WHERE TO BUY THEM"

RIVERDALE

Night Music
   345 River Rd. .555-1645

With a national trademark, the brand name appears across the top, above its logo and copy. The *Where to Buy Them* and even *For Information Call* make a bit more sense, because underneath are alphabetized listings of local business that carry the brand. The caption above the listings might be something like *Authorized Dealers,* or *Sales and Service.* Several captions might divide the listings by location (*In Millersville, In Riverdale*), or by function (*Wholesale Distributor, Sales Offices, Warrantee Service*).

The trademark ad is normally 1 inch high. Not counting the listings underneath. If it's 2 inches high it's a custom trademark (CTM) and the logo may be top center, top left, or top right.

One particular advantage to the trademark ad is that the name on the top of the ad doesn't have to agree with the name listed below, which can come in handy if you have your own brand or a trade name different from your business name that you want to promote.

The Trade Name Listing

The trade name listing is just like the trademark ad, but without the ad. The brand name appears in bold type, alphabetically in-column, followed by the caption: *Authorized Distributor, Service and Repair*, whatever. Underneath is your name, usually all capitals in regular type, your address in regular print, and your phone number.

The trade name price is roughly comparable to that of a simple bold listing. Extra lines of copy and alternate call numbers are available in both the trade name and in the listings beneath trademark ads.

COOL-AIRE AIR CONDITIONERS

AUTHORIZED SALES & SERVICE

JIM'S CLIMATE CONTROL
1798 Wallace Rvdl............................**555-4447**

COOL-AIRE AIR CONDITIONERS

AUTHORIZED SALES & SERVICE

JIM'S CLIMATE CONTROL
new, used, rebuilt
1798 Wallace Rvdl................555-4447

Display Advertising

If you want to know what a display ad is, open your directory. The first thing you notice is probably a display ad. Display ads are those ads not placed in among the alphabetical in-column listings. However, unless they're full page ads, there should be in-column listings on the page with them, so they're part of the heading. They can have fancy borders, artwork, and variety of type styles and sizes. And as an advertiser you have greater freedom on how you lay the thing out. See Figure 4-1 for an example of a display ad.

Figure 4-1 A display ad.

Source: Reprinted with permission from BellSouth Advertising & Publishing Corporation.

Display ads come in all sizes, from 1/4 of a single column to a full page. So far the 2-page ad is still a rarity. Ads are priced in almost direct ratio to their size. An ad twice as big will be about twice as much: sometimes more, rarely less unless a discount program is in effect.

The ads hyping Yellow Pages, the phone company, and/or

various charities that you see throughout the book are just filler to make the paging work out correctly. Occasionally, you might find a "product sell" display ad, extolling the merits of a particular product under the appropriate heading, but without a phone number or even the name of a local dealer.[1]

Different publishers offer different size display ads. The following pages show the most common and some of the main aberrations. Don't worry about the designations; in spite of attempts at standardization they can still vary from publisher to publisher. I have included some of the most generally-accepted traditional ad codes.

---

[1] In a few directories, you might even see product-only ads under classifications where they aren't strictly appropriate: ads for toothpaste under DENTISTS, for car insurance under AUTOMOBILE DEALERS—NEW CARS. This is an experimental practice that most publishers don't allow.

Figure 4-2 Examples of standard display ads, two-column books.

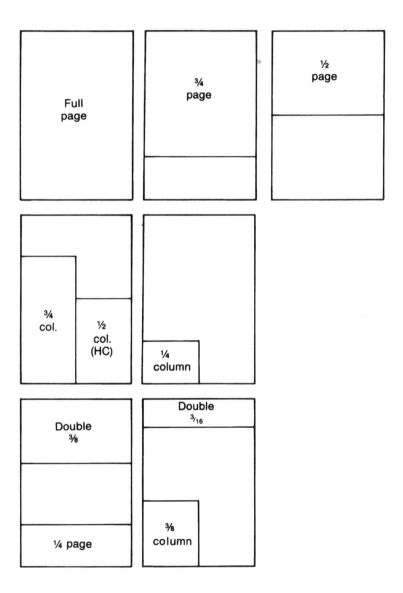

Figure 4-3 Examples of standard display ads, three-column books.

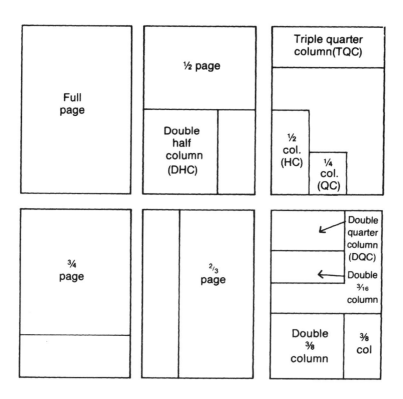

Figure 4-4 Examples of standard display ads, four-column books.

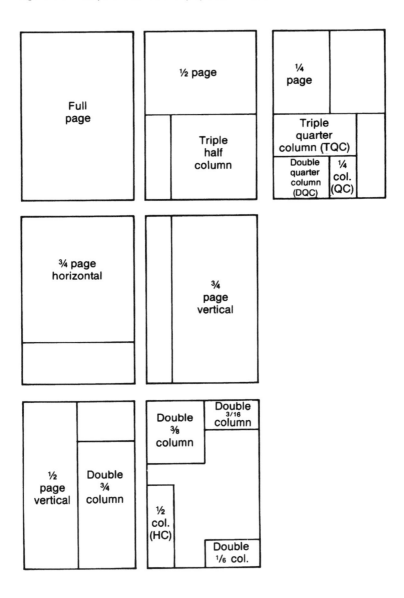

Figure 4-5 Examples of standard display ads, five-column books.

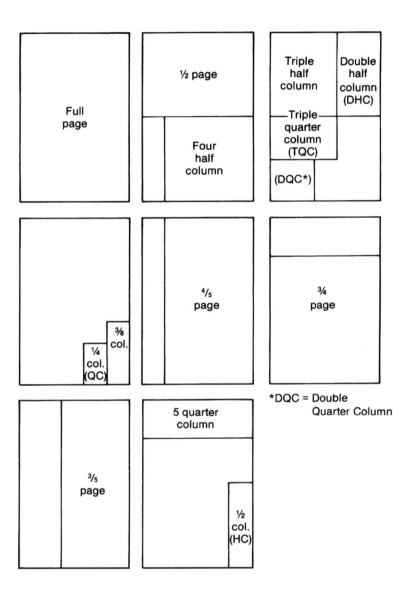

CHAPTER 5

The Main Considerations— In-Column and Display; Size, Placement, Color

Knowing what you can buy is only the beginning of your quest for truth, beauty and knowledge of Yellow Pages ads. Inquiring minds also want to know:

- Do display ads pull better than in-column ads?
- Are bigger ads really better?
- How are display ads placed in the heading, and how important is that placement?

All these and many other questions will be answered here in Chapter 5. We'll also talk about the effects of adding color to your ad. And since what you can afford may have some small bearing upon the decisions you'll be making in the following chapters—knowing what works best doesn't help if you can't afford it—we'll have a few brief, preliminary words on your advertising budget in general and on Yellow Pages spending in particular.

In-Column Verses Display

When you advertise in-column you are trying to do one or all of three things:

1. Make certain you can be found by people checking the alphabetical listings for you specifically, and provide these customers with information they need so they don't decide to call someone else (either instead of or in addition to you).

2. Distract those who are looking for another business and tempt them into your camp.

3. Grab the attention of those customers who are most up for grabs—the ones who don't have the name of a specific firm in mind.

Obviously, in-column advertising will do better than a display ad in terms of number one: hanging on to those customers who are searching for you alphabetically in-column. Some people might be looking specifically for you among the display ads, but a good-sized in-column ad, perhaps with a logo, can get their attention too—if they're looking hard enough. According to Statistical Research, Inc., 63.2 percent of those who go into the Yellow Pages already have a firm in mind. This varies considerably from heading to heading, but you have a better idea than Statistical Research ever could of how many of them will be looking for you.

Of course, even with a display ad you will still have a listing in-column. You can't get a display ad without having one. It's called an anchor: name, address, phone number followed by "see our ad page 322." The display ad will give them more information than they would have gotten from the in-column ad. And, unless it's a very small display, it should make you look like a bigger, more successful business. The disadvantage is that they may not turn to page 322. But even so, your address and phone number is still right there in front of them, provided, of course, they don't get distracted by someone else's ad.

Which brings us to reason number two for advertising in-column; to steal a few of those people who are looking for another firm. The vast majority will call the firm they had in mind, but a few won't. You might be able to get some of the others to call you as well, and end up with their business.

Now granted, most people seeking a specific business are looking in-column. Some of them are going to have to run right over your in-column ad to get to the firm they're seeking. But do you really think a little in-column ad without borders, bold type, or much in the way of artwork has as much chance of catching the eye as a full-blown display ad? All else being equal, it doesn't.

Now for reason number three—grabbing those customers who have no specific firm in mind. Under a heading with any significant display advertising, people without a firm in mind are not looking in-column. Not most of them. And with all the limitations of advertising in-column, it's very difficult to steal their attention from the displays where they are looking. Publishers cite figures like three out of four or four out of five of those who look at any ads look at display ads, not in-column. If anything, the discrepancy is even greater when you consider only those most in need of the information in the ads, those most up for grabs—those without specific firms in mind.

I have never seen a "which ad would you call first," study where an in-column ad pulled anything like a good-sized display. If you're under a developed heading and you really want a decent share of the up-for-grabs customers, an in-column ad is not what you want.

Display Ads—Is Bigger Better?

Bigger is more expensive. We all know that. But is it better? At one point, Terry Johnson was spending $193,000 in 27 directories to advertise his A.A. Johnson Plumbing, Heating and Air Conditioning. Twenty percent of his gross.

"With a big ad," Terry says, "you're substantial, reliable, important. Here today, here tomorrow. With a small ad, you're nothing, nobody."

Jack Reding of Reding Painting of Santa Barbara has one ad in one book—the biggest ad offered. "It gives me credibility," he says. "People call the large ads for estimates, but more importantly, large companies call the large ads because they figure you can handle the large jobs."

You will hear—and business people like to believe—that consumers turn to the smallest ads, figuring those firms don't have to charge as much to pay for their advertising, or figuring some companies buy larger ads to compensate for poorer quality. A few consumers might reason that way. One or two might even choose your ad, or even your squint print listing. I wouldn't want to count on these people to make my living.

"As a general rule," says the Small Business Administration, "the larger the ad the larger the response." I could quote variations on the above from any number of marketing and advertising books, and any number of studies. Size is undoubtedly one of the main reasons why display ads work better than in-column. When your ad is bigger people think you're bigger. And more successful. They think there's probably a reason for that success. They think you do more volume, and that you're probably cheaper. They think smaller is less volume, possibly more expensive, maybe less professional, maybe just starting out. The guy with the big ad may work out of his garage, but the guy with the small ad looks like he does.

At the very least larger ads are more visible. The first ad the consumer sees is not necessarily the first ad he calls. Maybe the business isn't close enough, or isn't open when he needs it. Maybe it doesn't have just what he's looking for, or maybe it looks too expensive or too cheap, or doesn't meet with whatever other criteria he has. So he'll move on to the next ad that catches his eye. If that doesn't satisfy him, he'll move on again. But the more visible your ad, the sooner you'll be seen, the better your chances are of getting a call. One of the first ads seen will probably be the first ad called. How many other calls are made also depends on the consumer.

And bigger ads allow you to convey more information, more ammunition for convincing him to give you that call.

Some publishing companies have visual aids: "This size ad is twice as big as our smallest ad, but with effective copy and a good illustration, it will draw five times the results." "This ad is four times the size and 15 times as effective." The numbers are impressive, but ignore them.

In 1963, Sidney P. Feldman and Jean C. Halterman published a copyrighted study called, "Consumer Use of the Yellow Pages in Kansas," and got the figures on which some of these visuals are based. Doctor Feldman stresses the "in Kansas," and the "1963"—both of which the visuals omit—and that he was studying two specific headings under very specific circumstances. Any number of studies have been done since then, but that's still all that can ever really be studied—specific headings under very specific circumstances.

Effectiveness of various ad sizes is going to vary according to the heading, the amount and type of advertising there, the quality of copy, artwork and layout in the ads, and their placement. No one can tell you that if you double the size of your house cleaning ad you're going to get five times the response. The numbers won't translate from one situation to another. Still, that doesn't invalidate the conclusion that, everything else being equal, a bigger ad gets a bigger response.

Again, every single study of print advertising I've ever encountered—academic and non-academic—suggests a strong link between size and effectiveness. Anybody surprised by that revelation obviously hasn't lived in this country long. Or did you really think all those advertisers were spending all that money just to subsidize printers and publishers?

Yellow Pages advertisers with big ads complain about their cost. So do smaller advertisers, so do advertisers in any medium. But the guys with the larger ads are usually the ones who are the most satisfied with the results. Of course, if they weren't happy with the stuff they wouldn't have the larger ads, would they?

When I was selling, the quarter-column display, the smallest display ad we offered, was the most difficult to get an advertiser to renew. The smaller the ad, the more likely the advertiser is to complain about the response. And the more likely he is to claim, "All I get are price shoppers—people who don't care about quality or selection or service or anything else except getting the absolute lowest price."

Some people—for whatever reason—do turn to the smallest ads first. If they were concerned with quality, selection and service would they really start there? Others only get far enough into the category to call the small ads because they are shopping price and they're calling everyone in the book. Customers who call one firm or two or three often stop long before reaching the tiny ads.

The independent Jackson and Parasuraman study I mentioned in Chapter 1, "Yellow Pages as an Advertising Tool for Small Businesses," concludes advertisers should "be prepared to buy an ad large enough to be effective." In the Statistical Research, Inc. study, 69 percent of the ads looked at were the largest size ads on the page.

In its advertising handbook, the National Office Products Association advises its members that "unless you are by far the largest dealer in town and you want everyone to know it, do not buy an ad larger than your [competition]." Otherwise, the N.O.P.A. says, you'll start a size contest benefiting primarily the directory publisher. So much for capitalism and competitiveness. Still, assuming you can get similar placement in the heading, and assuming you can keep the competition from going any larger, this isn't bad advice, provided you follow the second part of it and "develop a better ad [than your competition]—one that will get you noticed and set you apart . . . ."

Remember all we've said about size. But also remember that even the most die-hard Yellow Pages rep would have to admit: The largest ad is not always the best ad.

Display Placement—Size and Seniority

Bigger ads get better placement. Display ads are placed by size, largest ads go first, closest to the front of the heading.[1] Ads that are the same size are sometimes placed alphabetically, but for the most part they're placed by seniority: Those who have had the size the longest get priority. And if you cut your ad in size from a half page to a quarter page, you not only go behind all the half-page ads, you go behind all the existing quarter pages too.

One typical publisher places like-size display ads in this order:

1. Existing ads by seniority.

2. Ads increased from smaller sizes.

3. In-column ads increased to display.

4. Ads transferred from another heading.

5. Ads cut back from a larger size.

6. New ads in order of purchase.

Obviously, if ads are being placed in such strict order, the positions into which they're going to be put on the page must be ranked in order too. Generally, on any given page, upper takes precedence over lower, outside—away from the fold—takes precedence over inside. On a two page spread, the upper left is usually first position, followed by upper right, lower left, lower right, and then the corresponding inside positions.

Under the size and seniority system, the only way to get closer to the front of the heading is to go up in size. And that's the only way that businesses can leap in front of you. Your rep can guarantee you that. But no one can guarantee you position on the page. No one. Headings can and do start anywhere. And where they start changes every year, depend-

[1] A very few directories still place their display ads alphabetically without regard to size, a few others strictly by seniority without regard to size. This is not the wave of the future.

ing upon what happens in all the headings that come before yours. If you think your rep is giving you a guarantee on position, get suspicious.

Color and white knockout ads cost more money but give you no better placement than a black ad of the same size.

Importance of Placement

Advertisers covet placement like social climbers covet status. Businesses with positions at the front of a well-developed heading let them go about as often as governments lower taxes. For years, Yellow Pages reps pitched bigger ads and better placement. With size and placement so closely linked, when you did move up, it was very difficult to tell to which was responsible for any additional customers.

Selling placement worked for the directory companies, and worked well. Until one day, some corporate genius glanced up from his profit projections and noticed they were approaching a point where they would have no real placement left to sell. Once you have seventeen attorneys with full page ads, how can you sell full page number eighteen by stressing the importance of being close to the front of the heading? Suddenly, a number of publishers realized that size was what was important. Not placement. What did placement have to do with anything? Where do these crazy ideas come from, anyway?

I remember the day a regional vice president wheeled out the new theory to a roomful of flabbergasted reps. We believed in placement and so did our advertisers, but like an ancient religion it had outlived its usefulness. It had become a god we were no longer to invoke. Not even to make a sale.

The new dogma said directory users sought out the large ads, not necessarily the front of the heading. They were just as likely to turn to full-page ad number eight as full-page number one. Well, okay, almost as likely (a small concession to so much accumulated experience). What's more, we were told, no one really knew if people thumbed through the book from back to front or from front to back. Maybe having the last big ad was as good as or better than having the first. Of course, the first big ad—or was it the last big ad—was not really any better than any other that size anyway.

Oh.

Granted, people do seek out the large ads and others are grabbed by the extra visibility. As for the front to back or back to front "controversy," pick up a directory. Flip through it. If you use your right hand you flip the book front to back. If you're left-handed you probably go back to front. That's why our books open the way they do in the first place. If most of us were left-handed they'd open from the other end. If you're looking for left-handed customers maybe you should try for the last large ad instead of the first. But wait, placement doesn't really make a difference, does it?

Well, actually it does. When asked what attracts them to an ad, people are more likely to say size, layout or artwork than they are position. But as a general rule ads toward the front of the heading do better than ads that come later. Ads on the upper part of the page do better than ads below. Those on outside do better—often much better—than ads next to the fold.

In summary, get the best placement you can. Don't worry about discovering and memorizing paging priorities though. Within any given size, there's not much you can do about where your ad may fall on a given page. But, as we'll see later, you can and should evaluate potential placement within the heading—how close you'll probably be to the front—before you ever decide which size your ad should be.

Just never forget that great placement won't make up for a rotten ad. And a really good ad will go a long way in making up for bad placement, especially in smaller classifications where all the ads may be on the same two or three pages.

Color

Nowadays, color options are almost always available in display ads. That might include process color (an approximation of "full color" for color photos and illustrations), spot color (separated swatches of red, blue, green and/or black within the ad) and white knockout (white rather than yellow background). For in-column and larger space and trademark ads, most publishers will let you use at least one spot color.

The price for a single additional color can be a small premium or it can be as much as 50 or even 60 percent more. And don't be surprised if a process color ad runs 75 percent more than a similarly-sized black and yellow ad.

You can't just buy one or two lines of color. A well-known red logo becomes more identifiable when it's red in the directory too, but you can't just pay for the logo. If anything in the ad is color you pay the full single color price. In which case, get your money's worth and use enough color to grab the attention you're paying for.

That said, when colors are used together it should be with care, restraint and creativity—which is why single color ads are frequently more effective than the amateurish four color ads found in so many directories. More colors may make your sales rep more money, but a poor multicolor ad can end up looking like a 3-D comic. People will see it but they aren't going to try to read it.

With spot color, some publishers offer rich, vibrant hues. Others offer colors that are dull and flat, or washed out. White knockout background makes any spot color brighter and more vibrant. On the other hand, without color the impact of a white background is greatly reduced.

Process color allows you to reproduce color photos and graphics—to add drama and "give your ad the look of real life." The quality of color is vital—even more so than with spot color. A dull greenish tinge to your logo is not going to hurt your ad nearly as much as a dull greenish skin tone in your photograph. Different color processes reproduce different colors in different ways, but no matter what the technique, process color is not really full color. The image in your ad will seldom look exactly like that great photo you supplied.

It's impossible to deny that color is more visible than mere black and yellow. You don't have to believe all the directory companies' studies, just page through any phone book and see how it seizes your attention. It can look like the devil, but used correctly, it can be attractive and effective. Like music, color can effect us on a visceral level and convey a wide range of moods and emotions.

The publishers also claim color adds prestige to the ads—to the extent that people realize that it's more expensive. I suppose that's true too.

And more expensive is the key. Process color, spot color and white knockout can all add visibility, effectiveness and prestige, to your ad. For a price. We'll be speaking more about color in the chapters to come.

How High to Pile It

So far most of what we've covered shows how spending more money can improve your ad's pull. Let's face it, it can. If you stand on a big enough pile of dollars you can be seen for miles around. The real trick though, comes in stacking the pile straight enough to get maximum height for your buck—and only as high as necessary to be seen by those who might actually bring their bucks to you, or call you to come out and pick them up.

Speaking of Spending—
Your Advertising Budget

But before we go into stacking the money straight—before we go into how big and how many, which in turn determines how much—a word or two about your total advertising budget.

Do you have one?

Setting an advertising budget is the easiest thing in the world. (Actually, it's the second easiest—not setting a budget is the easiest.) As Shirley F. Milton says in *Advertising for the Modern Retailer*, all you have to do is develop "a sophisticated projection of sales volume, take a given percentage of that figure, and finally adjust it (to meet your) objectives." In other words, guess how much you're going to sell next year, figure out how much of that (what "given percentage") you should be spending on advertising (which was, I think, the question in the first place), then adjust (change) that figure so you can accomplish what you need.[2]

Anyway, you have your advertising budget (or perhaps you don't have one) and you want to know how much of that to spend on Yellow Pages. Again the answer is easy. You spend however much it takes to meet whatever goals you have. One theory of advertising says you should spend until the last dollar you spend no longer generates more than one dollar in profit. If your goal is to make as much money as possible this is not a bad theory. Advertising brings in money. If it doesn't you cancel it.

Advertising as a Percentage of Sales

If you don't have an advertising budget—or even if you do—you might want find out what percent of sales similar businesses in your line spend on all their advertising. You can get these figures from trade associations or magazines or from the *Robert Morris and Associates National Averages Annual Statement* in your local library.[3] Don't do anything with these figures. They're just to give you a rough idea. Very rough. Even within an industry, they're going to vary wildly.

The Small Business Administration says:

"Knowing what the ratio [of advertising expenses to sales] for your industry is will help to assure you that you will be spending as much or more than your competitors; but remember, these industry averages are not gospel. Your particular situation may dictate that you want to advertise more than or less than your competition. Averages may not be good enough for you. You may want to out-advertise your competitors and be willing to cut into short-term profits to do so.

[2] For a quick explanation of budgeting for all your advertising, see Appendix A.

[3] For other sources, see Appendix A.

Growth takes investment . . . *if you want to expand your market share, you'll probably need to use a larger percentage of sales than the industry average.*" (Italics mine.)

Other reasons to increase advertising expenditures include stiff competition, bad location, low prices (which require volume sales), a large market area, infrequently-used or seasonal goods and services (people forget). You might have a one-time reason: perhaps you've moved, changed your image, or doubled your size.

Little or no direct competition, a high-traffic location, concentrated market area, being really well-known, and having the kind of product or service that generates fixed buying habits, are all things that tend to bring your ad costs down. That's why you're paying the exorbitant rent to be in that mall, isn't it?

The average company probably spends about 3 to 5 percent of sales for all its advertising. Service businesses spend more, retailers less. Hardware stores average 2.01 percent. The National Office Products Association reports that 1.23 percent of sales is the norm for its industry. Expert recommendations on what firms should spend run the gamut. Some would be happy with 3 percent or even, for businesses like retailers, less. Some say 4 to 6 percent, some 5 percent or 10 percent, even 12 percent.

Find out the average for your industry.

Yellow Pages Spending

How do you decide what to spend in the Yellow Pages? And where to spend it? Next year it will be easy. Next year you'll know what worked and what didn't, what to expand, what to cut, what to leave the same.

Next year will be easy. As for this year, continue reading.

CHAPTER 6

Are Yellow Pages Really For You? Evaluating Your Main Heading

If you're a current Yellow Pages advertiser in a local *Core* directory, you may think you already know how well—or how poorly—your main heading works. Pretend you know nothing, because, at best, even if you've been keeping careful records, you know more about the effectiveness of your ad than the effectiveness of the heading. And the investigations we'll be doing in this chapter are just as vital for you as they are for the guy who's opening his doors for the first time.

There are a number of ways to evaluate a heading. Use as many or as few as you need to feel comfortable with the decisions you have to make. The techniques we'll be discussing are valid for any directory—dominant local phone company or independent. Obviously, you'll be doing your main heading in your local *Core* book first, and other headings and other books only later (see Chapter 9), as—and if—necessary.

Stooping to Common Sense

When all else fails you can even try common sense. If you were one of your customers, looking for your product or service, would you look in the Yellow Pages? Under what heading? Ask a few friends and acquaintances. Talk to your customers. Just remember if you're not in the directory now, your customers won't be directory users. Directory users couldn't find you. And if you are in the book, this is just another test of your current ad—an ad which may be great, but may also be not-great. Possibly very not-great. This is no reflection on you. You should see some of the junk even the pros turn out, and ads that might be wonderful in a newspaper or a magazine can fail miserably in the Yellow Pages.

Still, if you increased or cut your ad under your main heading last year how did that effect your business?

Read your trade magazines and trade organization newsletters for their opinions and stories of how others in the trade have done. If you don't already belong you can find industry groups listed in Gale's *Encyclopedia of Associations* in your library. Their input may be less valuable than you'd expect. Many trade organizations have no hard Yellow Pages information; others simply regurgitate material supplied by directory associations. And some of the "how to" pieces in trade magazines are actually written by those in the employ of Yellow Pages publishers. Not that they don't contain useful information. So do the brochures you get at car dealerships, but you don't see those brochures appearing as articles in *Consumer Reports.*

Inside Yellow Pages

As I said, there are many ways to evaluate a heading. But only the directory itself will tell you how your competition has evaluated that particular heading, in that book.

Get the directory, the one you're considering buying into, which means for right now at least your Core book. Open it to the main heading for your business. If you have trouble locating that heading use the index, and make a mental note; your customers may have trouble too. If you can't find your main heading even with the index, you might consider putting your advertising somewhere people are going to see it.

Let's say your heading is something straightforward, and you turn right to *Odor Neutralizers*.

Look carefully. Pay particular attention to your closest competition of course, and to those firms whose position in the marketplace is similar to that which you can envision for your own firm in the coming year.

Now you know what all of the competition is doing as of this year. You know who has in-column and who has display ads, and what sizes. If the display ads aren't alphabetized, their positions will give you a good indication of how long each advertiser has had that size. You have the rates so you have an idea of about how much everybody will be spending if they keep the same size ads in next year's book.

You should have your list of potential copy points beside you. Mark down anything anyone else is saying that might be useful for your ad. Are they offering some product or service you should be offering, or that you do offer and should be mentioning? Look at their colors, their borders, their artwork. Where are illustrations more effective than words? Check out the national advertisers. They've all spent several truckloads of money creating an image. Look to see how their ad carries out that image. The Yellow Pages is one place where you can look as big as anyone. But you'll also want to look as professional. Whose ads are more visible? More appealing? Who would you call and why?

Who's There? Who's Not?

Is anybody missing from the heading? If it's the main heading for your industry and some longtime businesses aren't even listed, you're dealing with an incomplete directory. Other times the competition is there but seems underrepresented.

If it's just one guy, maybe he's getting old or easing off on his business. Or maybe he's one of those people who, when things get a little tight, decide to "save money" by cutting his advertising. So much the better for you.

Remember though, that just as Yellow Pages ads from

national firms and franchises—and even very successful local companies—may be larger than you can afford, they can also be smaller than you need: because more people will be looking specifically for them when they turn to the heading; because a small logo ad for an Allstate Insurance or a Federal Express will trigger recognition generated by all their other advertising; and because far more of their business may come from other sources.

The market niche of a national firm is often very different from your own. A McDonald's can get by with a small ad or even just a listing, but I wouldn't pull the ad for my dinner house because of that. A franchise manager in the Fantastic Sam's discount family haircutting chain tells me they'd rather put their Yellow Pages money into coupons—by direct mail, in flyers and newspapers—and into regional and national TV. But Fantastic Sam's isn't Beverly's Beauty Shop. They're trying to be the McDonald's of hair. They want going to Fantastic Sam's to be a no-brainer—like eating at McDonald's or shopping at 7-Eleven. It's geared to be quick, inexpensive, with no calling for appointments; a place people go without much thought, possibly habitually, certainly without seeking a lot of buying information. (Yet, some Fantastic Sam's franchises do advertise in the Yellow Pages. And I've seen their closest national competitors with ads in directories 30 or 40 miles from their location.)

In any case, if some of your competition is missing or seemingly under-represented in the heading, you've got additional reason to keep checking the heading and the directory.

How many firms from out of the area are advertising in your book? From how far away are they? Note techniques they're using to get people to patronize them instead of local concerns. Are they fulfilling needs the local competition has overlooked?

Learning From History

If you can dig up an old directory or two, check who's gone up in size, who's gone down, who's dropped out altogether, and who's stayed the same. Keep in mind which businesses have grown and which have deteriorated. We're not talking strict cause and effect here. You can't just assume Rampaging Roses became such a tremendous odor neutralizing success simply because it bought the largest ad in the book. Or that Smell Busters went belly up simply because it wasted its money on the same ad. Try to see a pattern. Did the successful, growing concerns usually increase their ad sizes? Did they all decrease, and are they still growing? What did the firms in the position you're in now do in that old directory? How successful have they been? Have their ads gone up or down in size? Again, general patterns are important, not cause and effect. And remember, some businesses rely heavily on Yellow Pages to get started, then cut back when their established clientele has grown to the point where they don't want or don't need as much new business.

From now on keep your old directories. You'll have a record of everything your competition does. You'll always know just what they think of the Yellow Pages.

Of course, your competition doesn't necessarily know what the heck they're doing.

More Checks

In the best of all possible worlds—which as I explained before (see Chapter 3) we don't live in—you could simply ring up the competition and ask them about their advertising. They'd all give you straightforward answers, which—even in the best possible world *I* can imagine—would usually amount to some vague ideas, prejudices, and hunches about how the Yellow Pages did or didn't work for their business.

But a few of them know exactly how well it works for them. (Thirty-one percent according to the Yellow Pages Publisher Association.) Some know practically to the dollar. With their advice, plus the general feeling you gained from all the others, plus the information in this book, you'd have an excellent basis for making your Yellow Pages decisions.

Only your competition isn't going to tell you the truth.

One way around this is the traditional method: You can lie. You can call the local competition and tell them you're opening a odor neutralizer in another part of the country. A small fib. Just be sure they're not seeing through it. Explain you're considering directory advertising with your Core book there, and you'd like their opinion. Call a good selection of all the different size ads, and some with additional colors. If they're busy when you call, set up a better time. You'll find businessmen love to talk about their businesses and their advertising.

You're looking for the actual number of customers different ads generate. For some businesses you might want to ask about the total number of calls too, especially if you tend to sell to a significantly higher—or lower—percentage of callers than others within your industry. And find out what kind of customers advertisers are getting: Who are they and what do they buy? For example, home buyers—who want to know about specific houses—don't look in the Yellow Pages under *Real Estate* nearly as often as sellers, who are searching for a company to list with. *Real Estate* ads should be targeted accordingly.

Are different size ads and/or different copy slants getting different types of customers or selling different products? Ask about other headings, turning to them so you can see what each business has there. In most cases, it should only take a moment to cover all their secondary headings. How big an area do they draw customers from? Besides this one directory, what other advertising do they do and how does it work for them? And while the guy's on the phone, ask if in the last few years he's cut back or enlarged his ads, tried color, added or deleted headings. What happened when he made changes? What does he intend to do next year and why? Note for yourself which ads generate the most satisfaction.

If you don't want to lie or don't think you can get away with it or just need further confirmation, find another heading in the directory that is as similar to yours as possible, at least in respect to how its customers shop. *Painting*

Contractors and *Roofing Contractors* would be very similar, for example. They'd have the same customer base, and painting and roofing customers probably make their buying decisions in much the same way. Barbers and beauty shops, on the other hand, may both cut hair, but each serves a very different clientele, whose buying decisions are made in very different ways. Anyway, find a similar heading with about the same amount of advertising and in the same directory, then make your calls.

When you're evaluating a heading in a *Core* book you can also go to the library. Find a *Core* directory for a similar size city nearby,[1] but not so near that businesses there will consider you competition—a directory with about the same amount of advertising under your main heading. Photocopy the heading, go home and start calling.

When you're evaluating a non*Core* book—whether published by a competitive publisher or your dominant local phone company—you may have to wait until your rep arrives to run your checks. He'll show you last year's book. Non*Core* books can be very volatile, so here you definitely want to see the directory from the year before too, if at all possible. Open them both to the heading and compare. Who went up? Who went down? How many advertisers dropped out completely.

If you're still interested after that comparison, start making your calls. With a new, first-year directory, always phone on at least one similar book the publisher has done someplace else. And make sure the one the rep shows you is similar—the same type of directory—not a *Core* book the publisher did for a dominant local phone company. Don't forget to ask advertisers how long the book has been in their area, and how effective it was when it was first introduced. If the rep doesn't have a book to show you, wait to buy until he does.

The idea behind this research is not to blindly follow your competition, and it's certainly not to base your advertis-

---

[1] It's still difficult to find anything but *Core* directories in libraries.

ing on what strange firms do in some other city. The idea is merely to develop a generalized understanding of the heading and how it might work for you, to make you comfortable with the decisions you have to make. Next year, you'll know exactly what works and what doesn't.

CHAPTER 7

Saving Money— Strategies and Options For Selecting Your Ad

What Are You Trying to Achieve?

By now you should have a good generalized idea of how well your main heading works in your *Core* book, and what the different kinds of ads can do there. Next you have to decide the impact you want to have under that heading: how great a share of the potential business you want to try for.

Do you want to dominate? Sometimes you can. Sometimes you're up against ten or twelve full-page ads, in which case, lower your expectations.

Do you want to do somewhat better than your competition?

Do you want to do about the same?

Do you simply want to get the best possible response for a very limited amount of money?

Do you just want to be there for your present customers?

Maybe what you really want is to put your adver-
· tising money into matchbook covers and embossed
pens.

Let's examine some of the different strategies and
options for helping you achieve whatever your goal may be.

Who's the Competition?

First: only those businesses that draw your type of customers from your market area are your competition. Under
many headings, every business draws from the same customer
pool. But if the potential patients for your clinic will pass over
the first three ads under *Hospitals* because they're too far
away and the next two because they only handle drug
abuse—which you don't—why should you worry about being
bigger or closer to the front of the category than they are?
Know your market. Know your competition.

What the Competition Is Doing:
Domination by Squint Print or Lost in Space

That said, obviously, whatever you do under any heading
has to be tempered by what the competition is doing.
Perhaps you want to dominate. When your rep comes, you go
through his compilation of all the possible Yellow Pages headings related to your toy business and you find *Doll Houses &*
Accessories. It isn't even in this year's book, but over the
years, a number of customers have told you they'd looked
everywhere trying to find handmade doll houses like those
you carry.

You buy the smallest paid listing available, the one the
sales rep refers to as "squint print." That puts the heading in
the book. Nobody else is listed. Every time someone goes
into the Yellow Pages looking for *Doll Houses & Accessories*
you get the call. In your directory, that means that for $4.95 a
month you dominate the heading. Your listing is as good as a
full-page ad.

If the biggest thing under a heading is a regular listing, you can dominate with a bold one. If the bold is the biggest now, the smallest in-column space ad will dominate; providing, as always, that nobody else moves up in size.

The smallest in-column space ad is a good value not only for size but for providing information: for your customers' convenience or for your own. After you buy your regular listing under *Doll Houses & Accessories*, you might want to add an extra line, like "Custom house & furniture only," to eliminate nuisance calls from people who want the kind of cheap tin doll houses you're too snooty to stock. It may not be necessary, but it's not a bad idea, especially when listing under the more generalized headings. If, for example, you simply put your name under *Craft Instruction* and you don't explain you teach only bubble gum sculpting, you're going to get calls for everything from model airplanes to wigwam construction.

Or maybe you have an alternate call number to add:

> In case of emergency call...........................**555-1865**
>
> If no answer, dial......................................**555-1898**
>
> After 10 p.m..**555-1914**

For the same price as the smallest paid listing and an extra line of copy (and frequently a bit less), you can often get a real in-column ad with room for several lines of copy.

Staying In-Column

We've already established that display ads get more attention than in-column ads. If the heading you're considering has nothing but assorted little in-column efforts, a small display ad will make you cock of the walk, right?

Actually, you might be walking by yourself. Smaller display ads appear on the same page as the in-column listings, but solitary 1/4 column and 3/8 column display ads often get shunted off into a corner, far away under a small heading or—under a bigger one—buried on a page full of listings, isolated and easily overlooked.

Don't wander out into the expensive wilderness beyond in-column unless your ad is either large enough or simple and bold enough to be noticed. Otherwise, you can get a bigger in-column ad than anyone else, you can stick a piece of artwork into your present ad, or you can add color.

Some publishers offer a 25 percent or 30 percent discount for putting a display under a heading without any. But that discount is for one year only. Much more inducement comes from the *Yellow Pages Report* from Consumer Review Systems, Inc. of St. Paul, Minnesota. This study indicates that, in general, the first ad seen is the first ad called about half the time. But when there was only one display ad on the page, the first ad seen is called first three times out of four.

But you have to be seen.

Isn't Even Bigger Even Better?

Size is important. This is much of the reason that once a heading develops display advertising, in-column ads can no longer compete. The more display within the classification, the less likely your in-column ad is to attract new customers.

Once you move into display ads, a well-designed eye-catching ad can make up for a lot of size. Nonetheless, you can't get approximately the same response as—much less do better than—your competition without approximately the same size ad. You aren't going to *dominate* them unless your ad is at least as big and probably bigger. Still, I wouldn't buy a display ad more than one size larger than the rest of the competition. Not the first year anyway.

"But, Mr. Businessman," your old-school Yellow Pages rep might say, "even bigger is even more dominant."

Maybe, maybe not. Even bigger is, however, definitely even more expensive. Your second or third year—when you know the heading is making you money—will be time enough to try being "even more dominant." Yellow Pages reps dread handling an account whose ad is several sizes ahead of the competition, because even they can't think of a good reason the advertiser shouldn't cut back. One size larger is usually enough, then dominate with a better looking, better designed ad.

"But gee-willikers, Mr. Businessman. If you go up to the largest ad we offer—just two sizes higher—you might end up with first position in the category. (If the guys in front of you don't go up.) And next year, nobody'll be able to leap ahead of you."

Worry about that next year. In fact, even if you want to dominate, as long as you have the biggest—and the best designed—ad, my advice would be to keep improving the ad itself and wait until the competition was the same size before you considered moving up again. Somebody—maybe even a couple of somebodies—might suddenly get aggressive and jump larger than you for a year. You'll still have the next size down. And the best ad.

"And I can always go larger myself the year after that," is your line. Deliver it confidently.

"But, Mr Businessman," the rep cries. You catch the faintest whiff of hysteria. "If he gets the top size first he'll have the number-one position."

"Oh, pshaw," you reply. Your rep won't know what it means either. "Pshaw." Practice in front of the mirror.

Since nobody can predict where an ad will fall on the page, second and third position are frequently every bit as good as number one. Sometimes better. Ask anyone who ever had his first-position ad orphaned on a right hand page by itself, with the rest of the display ads for the heading on the next page in.

Size and Placement

In spite of these imaginary conversations, you're not ready to see any Yellow Pages salesman yet. I'm not writing the rest of this book only to have you consult it *after* you've signed a directory contract. This, of course, will not prevent me from invoking the ghost of salesmen past to illustrate certain points. It also gives you a chance to listen to someone else besides me.

Say your salesman shows you a sample directory page under **Linoleum Dealers** with a half-page display ad and some smaller ads on it.

"Who would you call?" he asks. "Ninety-one percent of the people we asked said they'd call the half-page ad first."

No doubt. But, first of all, what percent of those people we really looking to buy linoleum? Zero percent. They were in some mall someplace on their way to buy a pair of tennis shoes. They didn't have a firm in mind. They couldn't have cared less what the ads on that page said. They weren't looking for buying information. They weren't going to be attracted to the Congoleum featured in one ad, the sanding and refinishing service in another, the huge showroom mentioned in a third. Copy didn't matter, so what they saw was size, layout, and artwork. That's first of all.

What's second and even more important is that this sample **Linoleum Dealers** page is not from the heading you're buying into. And the situations aren't comparable. Maybe your heading has five pages of those big ads. If you get one too, and they all renew, every one of them would be in front of yours.

Always consider placement when you're deciding on ad size, even if you can't or don't want to dominate the heading. Even if you just want to do a little better than the competition or do about the same. No matter what, you want to get the best possible response for the money you're spending.

No one knows what the other advertisers will do this year. Still, determine where the ad you're considering would be in the current directory. That'll give you some idea of how close you'll be to the front of the heading, of where you'll be in relation to the competition.

"A" Is For Advancement—
When the Alphabet is Your Friend

When display ads are placed by size and alphabet—largest ads first and then alphabetically within any given size—everybody wants a name beginning with "A". And why not? New businesses that haven't chosen a name should obviously take placement into consideration when going into such books. Established businesses that already have a name sometimes change it or adopt a second name, setting up an alternate listing and putting their display ads under that name.[1] Some publishers may require a copy of a D.B.A. statement, certifying the company is now *doing business as* Ace's Taxi Company of Riverdale, A. Smith's Plumbing, A Metropolis Dumpsters or whatever. (Contrary to popular belief, "A" by itself comes before "AA" or "AAA" or "AAAA" or even "AAAAA".) Others insist on a more legitimate sounding name than A Premium Investigators or AAACME Dry Wall.

At least one directory company has a policy requiring a written statement justifying use of such an alphabetically advantageous name—for reasons besides jumping ahead of the competition in the phone book. Nonetheless, many businesses slip through.

"We use the name Abe's Honest Auto Repair for the historical identification and the flowing, memorable sound."

"AACME Dry Wall is named in honor of my maternal great-great grandmother, Zelda Aacmegianski, who came to this country seeking freedom, opportunity, and to avoid being burned as a witch."

Companies that take a second name can usually add their original name in the ad. They should get a bold listing or an in-column ad for their current name, depending upon how many customers are going to be looking for it. Then they can add the reference, "see our display ad under AACME Dry Wall."

If you take a second name. I have no recommendation on this one. You have to decide what to do on your own. Will you be gaining an unfair advantage? Yes. None of us would like our competition doing it. Yet, it's hard to watch

---

[1] In directories published by a local phone company, the phone company itself— as opposed to its directory company—tacks on a small additional charge for alternate listings.

your ad slip back in the heading while newer firms—paying no more money—move in front of you simply because they're Budget or Federal Cabinets and you're Pat's Kitchens.

That's the problem with letting alphabet determine something potentially so important. People's livings are at stake here. You can complain about the system to your publisher and/or your telco, but be careful. They might start charging for placement.

If your publisher uses the size and seniority system of display ad placement—largest ads first, and within a size those who've had that size longest taking precedence—you get better placement only by going larger.

Breaking Out of the Pack, Moving Up From the Gutter

Sometimes moving up a size or two won't make much difference in where your display ad falls within the heading. Sometimes it does. Frequently, you can get stuck behind a block—several pages perhaps—of similar-sized ads, with little to chose between them. Advertisers within a heading have a tendency to buy the same sizes. It's reassurance that they're not spending too much or too little. For a few dollars more for the next size up, you can move up and out of the pack, often much closer to the front of the heading. And one size up can often appear a heck of a lot bigger, and a heck of a lot more successful, especially when everyone else looks about the same.

Additional size can also keep your ad from being guttered, trapped in the inside of the page near the fold. When this happens your response can drop considerably. Be aware that certain size ads can never be guttered—full-page ads, half-page ads when the page is split horizontally, and ads at least three columns wide.

Generally, the smaller your display ad the more likely it is to be tucked into the fold. But the half-page ad with the page split vertically is large and expensive and gets guttered far too often. So does the double three-quarter-column ad, which is basically the same ad, but three quarters of the height. I wouldn't buy either one. The double-half-column ad, usually called the quarter page (because that's what it is in four-column books) isn't as great a problem but still, under a well developed heading, it frequently ends up in the fold.

If guttering seems to be a problem under your heading—if the inside column has display ads instead of in-column listings or filler ads for the phone company or the Yellow Pages—consider avoiding the endangered size. You don't have to memorize anything; any ad at least three columns wide is gutter-proof in four- and five-column books. Usually, the smallest and least expensive gutter-proof ad is the dollar bill size ad—the triple-quarter-column—which is three columns wide by a quarter column high and is cheaper than the quarter page. In two- and three-column books, anything two columns wide is safe.

When the Biggest Gets Even Bigger

Once you get the largest size ad—usually the full page—you're locked in position relative to the ads in front and in back of you, unless somebody cuts back or goes out of business. Or unless the publisher comes out with a still larger and still more expensive ad. (And yes, there is such a thing as a two-page spread, a double-full page.) If you buy the new size, you move ahead of all those now in front of you who don't. Turn it down and every business behind you who takes it slides up in front of you.

The publishers don't call this blackmail. The new larger size is a service to their advertisers: It gives you more room, more chance to get your message across.

Some advertisers feel serviced. Others feel raped. Still, to be fair, who among us wouldn't sell a bigger more expensive product if we had customers willing to buy it?

Just remember, when a larger size comes, advertisers in front of you also feel compelled to move up to keep you from going in front of them. You know your competition. Or you should. You know what the new size is selling for. You're better able to gauge who'll go up and who won't—how much you can gain for the extra cost and how much you might lose by staying pat—than is the salesman. This is one time when advertisers within a heading start making pacts not to buy the bigger ad. I've even heard of them all going down in size. With everybody cutting the same year, each kept the same relative position. Such arrangements keep down everyone's costs, but they also keep everyone permanently in their place.

And anyone who breaks the pact leaps ahead of everyone else—permanently. That's why such arrangements rarely work. If you're happy with your present position and you're sure you can trust your competition, do it. If not, don't.

Going Smaller

Alfred C. McCrea in *The Advertising Cost Control Handbook* (Van Nostrand Reinhold) says that advertising cost control doesn't necessarily mean smaller ads: "It might be excellent business to take large ads . . . to produce expected sales. This is also cost control . . . money is being spent wisely to meet competition."

When it comes to advertising spending, more businesses save their way into bankruptcy than spend their way into it.

Which is not to say that you can't spend your way into bankruptcy.

Sometimes you simply can't afford the ad you'd like, especially if you're trying the medium, the directory, or the heading for the first time and you're unsure of the results. Ask yourself how going one size smaller would hurt you. For example, in terms of placement, your first year in a size and seniority book, you'll probably be at the end of any size you chose. If there aren't many—or aren't any—ads of the next size down, even the last of them should have about the same placement as ads at the tail of the bigger size.

Always consider ad sizes not currently represented under the heading. If you find one larger than what you're considering, you could get better placement without spending much more. If you find a slightly smaller one, you could save money without losing significant placement. And a unique size helps your ad stand out from the herd.

There are some ad sizes that are perceived by the directory user as "just about the same size" as the larger, more expensive ads. They aren't as visible, they won't give you the placement or the extra layout space, but neither will the customer say, "Well, this guy looks a lot smaller than that other guy. I wonder if he's operating out of his garage?"

For example, if you have to save money and if the placement is about the same, is the full-page ad really that much more impressive than the three-quarter page? A three-quarter page that falls five pages behind a full-page ad certainly is going to be less impressive, or at least less successful. But if there's only one of each, I'd much rather have the three-quarter size and fill it with a good ad than have the full size and a mediocre ad.

In five-column books: the half-page high, four-column wide ad looks almost the same as the full half-page ad (See Figure 7-1). It's 20 percent cheaper. The fact that a column of listings that customers will be looking through always appears with it on the page—which is not the case with a full half-page—only enhances its value.

The dollar bill size ad—the triple-quarter-column (TQC) I mentioned earlier—stretches across three columns, and looks much like the double half-column (DHC), which is

Figure 7-1 Half-page ad compared with four half-column ad.

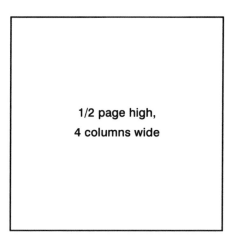

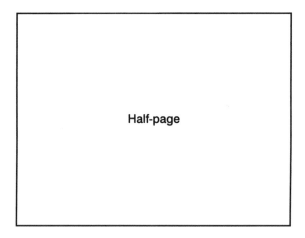

a half-page high and two-column wide set on its side (See Figure 7-2). It can't be guttered, and both often end up on the same page.

In four-column books, the distinctions between ad sizes are greater. Ads perceived as "just about the same size" are

Figure 7-2 Triple quarter-column ad compared with double half-column ad.

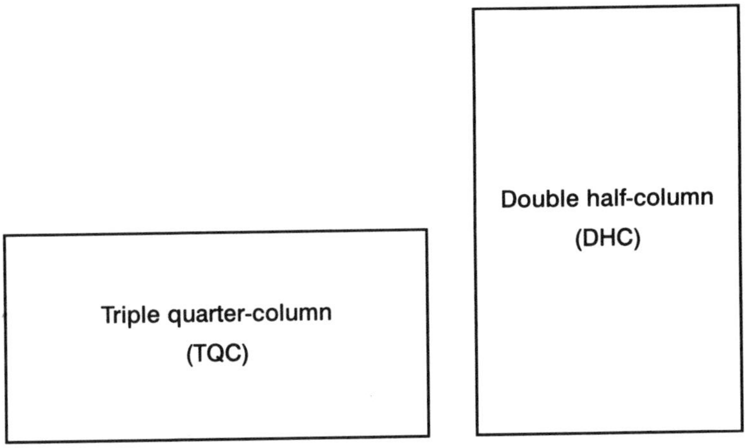

harder to find.

Still, is the half-page that much more visible than the triple half-column, which is a half-page high and three columns wide (See Figure 7-3)?

And when available:

- The double three-eights column is a cheaper version of the quarter-page ad (See Figure 7-4).

- The least noticeable reduction in either four- or five-column directories is the small version of the double quarter-column ad, which is actually only one-fifth (sometimes three-sixteenths) of a column high, but very similar in appearance (see Figure 7-5).

Figure 7-3 Triple half-column ad compared with half page.

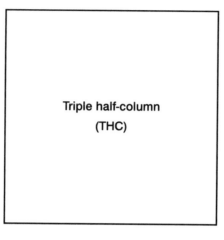

- An ad one-sixth of a column high by two columns wide is slightly less expensive than the one-third-column ad and slightly more expensive than the quarter-column ad. But because of its two-column width it is the best tiny display ad I've seen (see Figure 7-6).

Figure 7-4 Double three-eights-column ad compared with quarter-page ad.

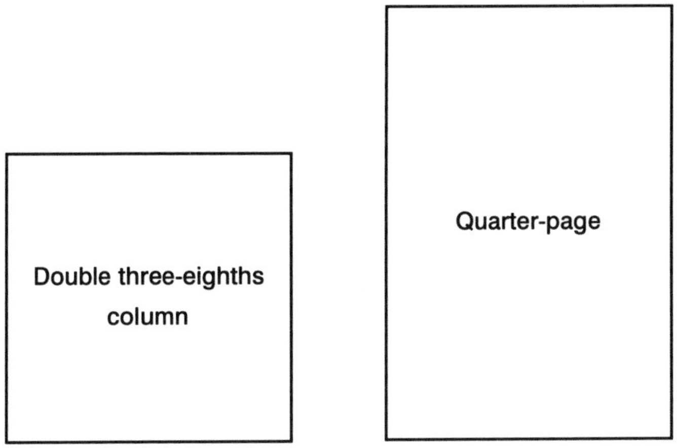

Quarter-page

Double three-eighths
column

Figure 7-5 Double fifth-column ad, double three-sixteenth-column ad and double quarter-column ad compared.

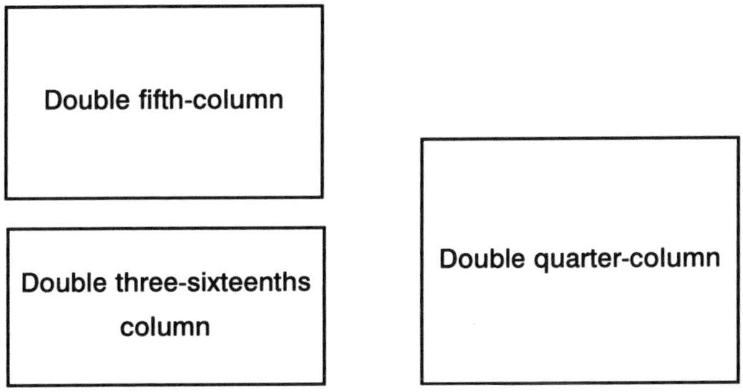

Double fifth-column

Double three-sixteenths
column

Double quarter-column

Size and position. Position and size. Always know what you are getting for your extra money and what you are losing when you cut back. In either case it could be a great deal OR very little.

Figure 7-6 One-sixth column high by two columns wide ad compared with one-third-column ad and one-quarter-column ad.

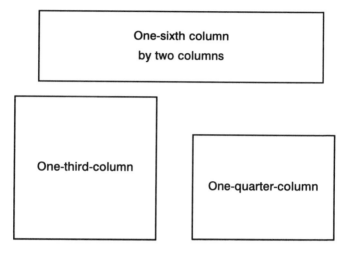

Color

Nobody responds to an ad because of the color in it. But a good use of color can make them see the ad first, or at least sooner. It can give the ad an earlier shot at the consumer. White knockout can be a particularly effective grabber.

"But what happens when there're a number of color ads on the page?" you may ask.

When a few similarly-sized ads are in color, the color photos tend to stand out first, then the most arresting uses of spot color. All else being equal, ads with the most color, the brightest color and with different uses of color are usually the ones that catch the eye. Obviously the more color is used, the less any individual color ad will stand out. Still, magazine ads are almost all in color, and the colored ads are generally more effective than the black and white.

Solid black, thick, dark and large—simple or with creative grey screening—can be nearly as powerful as single-color ads. But color photographs and the best spot-color ads usually overwhelm black and yellow ads. People always say that if phone directories ever become all color, black would come back into its own, for the sheer contrast and novelty, the way black and white commercials stand out on television today. But that would only work if black and yellow ads were so rare that they became a novelty.

All that said, color is no magic wand. It's just one more tool in the bag—or more accurately, one more set of tools— one more set of options. The old adage was that size and position were always more important than color. Increased color options have made color more effective in competing for visibility with ads that are placed on the same two-page spread. But all else being equal, a small color ad still doesn't convey the same positive implications that a significantly larger black and yellow ad does. And even the best color can't compete with ads on an earlier page.

Weigh the benefits of using color against the benefits of putting the additional money into increasing the size of your ad. Would it be enough, or almost enough, to take you to the next size up? If so, how large would that be and where would the ad fall within your heading? If the size you could get isn't much different and the placement not much better, consider the color.

The smaller your ad the more it needs extra visibility. Since the additional cost of color is figured on a percentage basis, the smaller your ad the less expensive it is to use color. Still, color can only help your ad be seen. After that, it's up to the ad itself to earn the call. Color won't do any good if the ad isn't large enough to provide the information the consumer is seeking or if the very size of the ad is telling him you're too small for his purposes.

And before you commit to any color option, first check the color in the directory. It can be very different from what's in the sales visuals the rep shows you.

Color can put more bullets in your gun: it gives you new ways to get your ad seen. Just make sure it's the most effective way you could use the extra money on you ad.

Multiple Display: Becoming Your Own Competition

Publishers allow advertisers to buy multiple display ads under any given heading using the same company name, and if you start using additional names you can sometimes go on forever. Some advertisers buy ads of the same size at the same time to try to billboard the ads together. This is risky. They can't be sure of where either will fall on the page. Some years, the page break might even fall between them. Other advertisers get different size ads to have one in the front and a second in the back of a large category. More frequently, a business with multiple ads will use different business names and/or different images and products in each. They become their own competition and learn the thrill of underbidding themselves when price shoppers call both ads.

Multiple display is not something you try until you know just how effective the classification is going to be for you. Personally, I would never even consider it until I reached the point where the money I had to spend would no longer significantly improve my first ad in either size, placement, or visibility. Better one effective ad than several marginal ones.

In-Column Ads For Your Present Customers

The more display ads there are within a classification the less effective in-column ads will be. But suppose you just want to be there for your loyal customers—who don't forget you, who are seeking you by name—and maybe a few referrals and a few of those around the neighborhood who're just looking for anybody close. You're either not much interested in new business or you generate it in ways besides Yellow Pages. Then, obviously, you go in-column, no matter what size the heading.

Since you're looking only for people who are looking for you anyway, you don't need to grab their attention, and you don't need much of an ad. A regular alphabetical listing can get lost, but they'll find a bold listing: Name, address and phone number.

Remember, many of those who use the Yellow Pages never even look at an ad. And purchasers looking for a specific firm when they go into the book buy from that firm the vast majority of the time—maybe 80 percent to 90 percent. Still, with just a bold listing you are going to lose a few of those looking specifically for you. A few will be tempted away by competing ads.

A small in-column ad can reduce that temptation. It makes you easier to find and gives you the chance to provide the information these people need—the information that can let them know they don't have to turn to one of those display ads to find what they want. Make the in-column large enough to add your well-known logo, and you gain all the recognition associated with that. If the logo is famous enough, it might even attract some attention away from the displays, especially if you put it in color. You'll even get a few calls from people who've never heard of you before—far less than with a competitively-sized display ad, but a lot more than with a bold listing.

Most directories now offer superbold type for simple in-column listings.

AAA LEASING
274 Forest St...........................555-1110

If everybody goes superbold can super-duper be far behind? Besides cluttering up the page and looking like heck, a superbold listing costs more than a small in-column ad, which, even if you have nothing to say, gives you more room on the page. Unless, of course, you have a really long name. Some publishers allow you to combine a superbold listing with an in-column space ad. Your business name at the top of the ad becomes superbold rather than just bold, and you have the ad underneath to tell your story. For a few dollars more than the price of an in-column ad, or a superbold listing by itself, you have the best of both worlds.

A superbold listing in red is as expensive as a small color in-column ad but it gives you more red and a larger typeface than you could get in any in-column ad. You won't be able to give people a reason to call you (besides your name), but your name will be far more visible than it would otherwise be. So the question becomes, "Do people need a reason to call you other than your name?"

In-Column Ads Competing With Display

A well-designed quarter-column or three-eights-column display ad can be extremely effective under a heading where it's competing against other ads the same size. But suppose that's all you can afford and it's going to be stuck at the end of a category like *Chiropractors, Travel Agencies & Bureaus* or any other classification where it would be competing with page after page of large ads and maybe two other pages of ads the same size?

I know an advertiser who tried to make one such ad work by adding the copy, "The money I saved on this ad is passed on to my customers." Clever. But nobody read it.

What could you do for the same money in-column? And where would that put you within the heading? Obviously, in a heading without a lot of display ads, a big enough in-column ad can compete with displays for visibility on the basis of size alone. Only "big enough" would probably make it more expensive than a more flexible display ad.

Smaller, cheaper in-column ads can also draw new and uncommitted consumers even under well-developed headings. Just make the ad so simple that it becomes a sign, a banner. Make all the lettering as big as it can be, including the phone number. It usually has to appear in small type across the bottom, but just because you can't make that any bigger, doesn't mean you can't repeat the number as large as possible inside the body of the ad.

A simple ad like that, maybe an inch and a half or two inches long, with every word large and bold, can be nearly as visible as a display ad. In red or another spot color, it could

even be one of the first things seen on the page, especially if the product, service or location you've highlighted is just what the customer is looking for. You haven't told him much, and you don't look like one of the big boys, but you will get calls for emergency drain opening.

When I was working for GTE, I always considered their in-column 11/2 inch ad in red one of the best values in the Yellow Pages. Of course, as more people in a given category use them like this, the less effective they're going to be.

In terms of image or prestige, your in-column ad is bigger than the listings around you. And since some of the largest national companies in the directory advertise only in-column, the unspoken message is, "this is all the ad I want or need." The tiny display tells customers you'd like a big ad, but this is all you can afford. If you don't believe that, imagine General Motors or Xerox with an in-column trademark ad, then try imagining them with a little quarter-column display ad.

In-column banners work even better if you have a name—or you set up an alternate listing for a name—that places you toward the very front of the heading.

There might be ten or fifteen pages of plumbers with huge ads, placed by size and seniority. All of them would kill to get to the front of the category. In-column, Aardvark

Plumbing sits right up there with display ad number one. If Al Aardvark buys the biggest, most colorful, most visible in-column ad he can afford, he'll still only be paying a fraction of what others are paying many pages to the rear. (Unless you're at the very front of a large heading, if you'd be spending enough in-column to buy what in that heading would be an effective display ad, buy the display instead.)

An in-column sign is not a full, detailed Yellow Pages ad. The headline doesn't have to be a specialty like *Emergency Drain Opening*; it can be more generalized, like *Complete Travel Service*, or *Pest Control*. And you can add a *little* more copy toward the bottom—even in the 11/2 inch size—and more as the ads get larger. But keep it as little as possible. If you try to crowd in the buying information you'd put in a display ad, you won't have a sign anymore.

Anchoring Your Display In-Column

Even if you've decided on a display ad, that doesn't mean you can forget about the in-column listings. "How about a second ad for those people who only look in-column?" the old-school Yellow Pages reps always ask. These guys work on commission, remember. Also remember that, under a well-developed heading with a number of display ads, most people looking alphabetically in-column aren't up for grabs anyway.

Still, always check where your name comes in-column. As we just discussed, placement towards the front of the heading—or sometimes toward the rear if your display is in the front—can be an opportunity for a second cost-effective sign- or banner-type in-column ad. But you can afford to wait until next year. Or the year after. When you know how well this stuff is going to work for you. And then only if the extra money you pay wouldn't significantly improve your display ad in size, placement, or visibility.

So what would you like to do in-column this year? To go along with that big display ad?

Nothing?

Sorry. You've got to have your business name listed—anchored—alphabetically in-column or you can't have a display ad under the heading. If somebody is looking for you alphabetically by name they have to be able to find you. This is a directory, right? An anchor listing is like any other listing except that under your name address and phone number is added a phrase like "see our ad this classification," or "see our ad page 224." Some publishers include the cost of an anchor in with the price of the ad, some even give you a bold listing, but most charge extra for the anchor.

Your anchor can be your one "free" squint-print listing. It can be another regular, semi-bold or bold listing that you buy or an in-column space ad of any size. You can not, however, anchor your display with trademark ads, custom trademarks, or trade name listings. If you have one of these and a display ad, you still need an anchor.

If an old-school Yellow Pages rep tells you that you need a second ad in-column for all those people looking for you alphabetically by name, tell him that they can find a bold listing. If you can get a bold listing in red at a reasonable price you might pop for that.

If you really do believe that a number of customers will be looking for you by name who:

1. Won't follow instructions to "see our ad page 224" and

2. Without certain information will either

   a) Go to someone else's ad instead of the one you have on page 224 or

   b) Make nuisance calls to your business,

all of which is possible, then splurge. Shoot the works. Get yourself the smallest, cheapest, in-column ad you can get away with. In most cases that will be the half inch, the ad that averages less than the price of a bold listing with an extra line of copy.

Other In-Column Opportunities

Some names and alternate listings put businesses in front of the alphabet. Others put the business where the customers will be looking.

Perhaps you've changed the name of the business. You'll want an alternate listing for those customers who'll be looking for the old name. The same goes if the business has a couple of different names, or, as is often the case with professional firms, if clients might be looking up the names of one or more partners, checking the listings for Dr. Watson or Dr. Roberts instead of West Webblesford Chiropractic Clinic.

Often there's a common confusion in spelling. Geoffrey's Jungle Gym should be listed under Jeffrey's as well or it is going to be hard to find.

The right name can also put you where the customer will be looking for the product or service you have to offer. Riverdale Volvo's alternate listing, Volvo of Riverdale, helps in both the white and the yellow pages of the directory, since alternate listings appear in both.

An alternate listing is the same as any other: alternate name, followed by the address and phone number. Unless you add an extra line, it makes no reference to the original name of the business. You can also buy cross-reference listings in either the yellow or the white pages: "Volvo of Riverdale—see Riverdale Volvo." With no address and no number.

On the subject of names, if you don't have one for your company, try to pick one that's simple and memorable and that describes what you do. "Discar Inc." may sound modern and impressive, but every listing—every sign, every mention—of "Discount Auto Repair" is an advertisement. The alphabetical advantages of "Aaron's Discount Auto Repair" we've already covered.

Co-Op Advertising

The best way to keep your Yellow Pages costs down is to have somebody else pay for the ad. Manufactures and distributors offer, literally, billions of dollars a year in advertising co-op money, as much as 40 percent of which goes unused. About 1,000 of these companies—companies, like RCA and Redkin, Pentax and Panasonic, Yamaha and Unisys, Georgia-Pacific and Ford—will co-op Yellow Pages advertising.

The programs vary. Many manufacturers focus on trade-mark and trade name ads, which we'll deal with in the next section. Others rebate to you for advertising anywhere from 1 to 5 percent of your net annual purchases—monies which may or may not be earmarked for phone directories. Others simply pay for part of a certain size Yellow Pages ad. The company purchases the ads nationally and bills you if you qualify and wish to participate. Or it has you buy the ad locally, then either reimburses you or pays its share directly to the publisher.

A typical display ad co-op program for authorized dealers might specify:

- The manufacturer pays 50 percent of the price of the ad for any display ad up to a quarter page. If you want a larger or more colorful ad, you pay for anything above 50 percent of the price of a quarter page in black.

- The ad may appear only within a certain classi-fication.

- Specifications for art and copy must be followed exactly. A copy of the proposed ad must be sub-mitted to the manufacturer's ad agency by the directory publisher.

- No products or brand names competing with the manufacturer's can be mentioned, listed, or shown.

Though your Yellow Pages rep can often be very helpful with co-op, don't leave it to him or her to be aware of the pos-sible co-op opportunities for your business. Check with man-ufacturers and distributors you deal with to see what—if any-

thing—they offer. If you're to implement the program locally, they can tell you the restrictions and provide you with suggested or required art and copy.

Co-op programs vary radically and so do requirements.
Make sure you understand both. And make sure you understand who is ultimately responsible for which portions of the
bill. In most cases, the entire bill will be sent to you and the
entire responsibility will be yours—just as it's your responsibility to meet the co-op requirements. If your ad doesn't
qualify or if—for whatever reason—the manufacturer doesn't
come through with the co-op dollars, you'll be required to pay
for all the contracted advertising yourself.

Manufacturers may specify that you may buy only into
your dominant local telephone company's *Core* book. But suppose you're sure another local book is getting better usage, or
at least getting high enough usage that you don't want to be
left out. Tell them. You're the person on the scene. They may
allow you to switch books or split the money between the two.

Or you may know that in your local area, the heading
they specified isn't the best one for their product. They
should be flexible. But get approval beforehand.

Often you'll have enough freedom—even using the
required art and copy—to be able to design what is essen-
tially your own display ad. You want to do that whenever possible. After all, you're putting out good money here too. Don't
just add your name to their ad unless what's best for them
coincides exactly with what's best for you.

Sometimes—not often, but sometimes—co-op can cost
you more than it saves. If Cheapy Camera's restrictions are so
tight that you're advertising nothing but their product, you'll
get no calls for anything else you carry. And even consumers
who do get excited about Cheapy might end up buying from
Irving's across town, because his ad played up his same day
service, his extended warranties, his evening hours and his
10-day trial exchange. All of which you have too, but had no
room to mention.

National Trademarks and Tradenames

With the national trademark ad (or custom trademark ad), the manufacturer or distributor—the brand name—pays for both the ad *and* the listings underneath it[2]. Or they might just buy the ad and allow local dealers to get their own listings. When they do neither, local dealers occasionally purchase a trademark ad for the brandname themselves.

More and more frequently, national trademark ads are closed, meaning that only authorized dealers are allowed to list under them. The dealers don't even get to choose whether to be in bold or regular type. When a trademark isn't closed, anyone can list. Anyone. Your Yellow Pages rep often won't know which trademarks are which.

Sticking your name under a national trademark ad, or

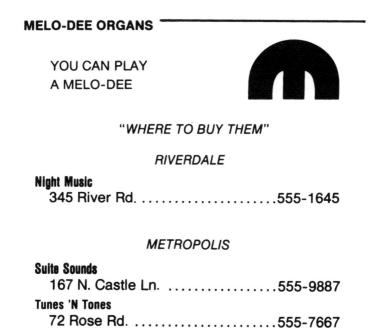

MELO-DEE ORGANS

YOU CAN PLAY
A MELO-DEE

"WHERE TO BUY THEM"

RIVERDALE

Night Music
   345 River Rd. 555-1645

METROPOLIS

Suite Sounds
   167 N. Castle Ln. 555-9887
Tunes 'N Tones
   72 Rose Rd. 555-7667

---

[2] Sometimes they bill back part of the cost to those who list underneath.

trade name listing, is a cost-effective way of taking advantage of all the advertising that brand name does. If your customers are likely to be looking for that brand by name, you want to make sure that, if you can be, you're listed in-column underneath it.

If you are authorized—say you're a Kodak dealer—you should have received a letter from Kodak telling you how to order your listing, usually through an ad agency. No letter? Contact Kodak, not your Yellow Pages rep. If your rep takes your order and the trademark is open, you'll get listed no matter who you are, no matter what your relationship to Kodak or its dealers, but if it's closed, when the book comes out you won't be there—not if you're the number one Kodak dealer in the nation.

In most directories, manufacturers and distributors can now get national brand-name display ads—the display ad equivalent of trademark ads. Like the trademarks, brand-name displays are devoted solely to the manufacturer's or distributor's product. But brand-name displays are always purchased nationally, and the manufacturer or distributor always controls which local dealers are listed in the ad.

To save some aggravation about open trademarks ads, consider this example: Calvin's Farm Emporium sells Jumbo tractors. Jumbo doesn't have a trademark program. You couldn't sell a Jumbo for green stamps in any normal town, but in Riverdale, Jumbos are the tractor of preference. Yuppies drive them to the health spa instead of BMWs. Since Calvin is allowed to use the Jumbo name and logo, he takes out a trademark ad for Jumbo in the dominant local phone company's Riverdale directory—$98 a month plus $14.95 for the Calvin's Farm Implements listing underneath the caption *Sales and Service*. (It should have read "Calvin's Emporium" not "Implements," but Calvin never got around to changing the company name with the phone company.)

Calvin's arch-enemy, Buster Brewster of Brewster Truck and Trailer, also sells Jumbos. When the directory comes out, Buster sees the trademark, and next year, he lists under it too, for $14.95 a month. Calvin's paying for the trademark; Buster pays only for his listing. What makes matters worse is that the listings are alphabetized. Brewster Trucks and Trailer actually comes first.

The following year, Alphonse—Alphonse's Autos: Used and More Used—jumps into the first spot. Alphonse has a couple of old tractors to sell. Maybe he had a Jumbo there once, maybe he didn't.

If you buy a trademark for a brand name locally, anybody can list under it. Some publishers try to restrict it to authorized dealers, but don't count on that. The good news is that if somebody else buys a trademark ad locally you can list under it for the price of the listing. You can also list under any open national trademark. Of course, you can't tell by looking whether a trademark is open or closed. So chances are, if you try to list under a trademark ad for Ford, IBM Typewriters, or RCA Television you aren't going to get in.

If you have a national brand you repair, rent, carry parts for, sell used or rebuilt, buy, or whatever, you should consider getting a trade name listing. The trade name, as you remember, is just like the trademark ad except without the ad. It's just the brand name, the caption and the listing.

COOL-AIRE AIR CONDITIONERS
AUTHORIZED SALES & SERVICE
JIM'S CLIMATE CONTROL
1798 Wallace Rvdl........................**555-4447**

You can't buy one where there's a trademark ad for the same product. And trade names can also be bought nationally and closed. But they're somewhat less likely to be.

Since they cost about the same as a simple listing, they're an excellent low cost way to reach the huge numbers of brand name owners out there. If, for example, my Alpha

Romeo breaks down, I'm liable to be looking for service under Alpha Romeo, right? And if you check the heading, *Automobile Repairing & Service*, you'll see trade name listings for most of the major brands. Only a few of the advertisers listing under them are authorized.

When more than one advertiser buys a trade name listing, the actual brand name is printed only once, followed by the captions and the various businesses. Captions for authorized dealers come first.

Check the in-column listings for all the major brand names you deal with, or at least, those your customers are likely to be looking for. Under some of them you might have almost no competition. Others might not even be in the book. In which case, your cheap little tradename listing makes you the local expert and gets you the call every time the product is looked up by name.

Ad Sharing

Another way of sharing costs and getting a bigger ad than you could normally afford is a kind of local co-op. If you or you and your partners own several different businesses of the same type, you can share an ad. You may have to add phrases like, "in partnership with," "under same management," or "three locations to serve you," but the type can be as small as you like. Just don't divide the ad into completely separate compartments. That defeats the purpose of the larger ad, and some publishers won't allow it. Thin lines that don't entirely divide the ad are no problem.

That said, if you have a full page ad and first position under the heading, you may want your shared ad to look like two separate ads. You become your own competition, and the customer who's calling the first few ads under the heading will be calling twice. Even when your publisher doesn't allow you to completely divide the ad with thick lines, you can still give the top half of the ad a completely different look from the bottom half, creating the illusion of two distinct ads. You might, for example, do the top of the ad with black letters and artwork against the yellow background and do some or all of the bottom half in reverse (the background shows through the letters and artwork and the area around them is inked).

Making Money— Minimizing Risks, Maximizing Profits

Figuring Your Return—Two Questions

Before you decide what ad to buy under your main heading in your *Core* book or, when the time comes, under any other heading, in any book, it would be nice to know how much money that specific ad would bring in. Unfortunately, you can't know that.

Next year, however, you will have a much better idea than you do now.

You *can* be certain how much the ad will cost each and every month. As to what it will earn, you have to make your best, educated guess, based on two things:

1. What is your average customer worth to you?

2. How many of those Joe Averages is the ad likely to bring in?

When you decide on an ad of any significant cost, you're betting that it's likely to bring in a lot of those average customers. By now you should have a pretty good feel for the potential of the heading you're considering. If you don't, you haven't done enough research. Go back and do it. Checking out the heading doesn't take long, but a lot of advertisers won't bother to.

Often the reasoning runs: "How can I go wrong? As the salesman says, the Mayberry directory reaches a population of 161,000. That's an awful lot of customers."

Maybe and maybe not. Let's take a look. Before we go any farther though, let me caution you. The following is for demonstration purposes only, done by a trained professional under controlled conditions.

Kids, do not try this at home!

Ready? Okay, here goes.

Harry's in the llama vacuuming business. He's already a big success in Metropolis, where he had the biggest ad in the *Core* local phone book for the last several years. Last year he opened a second store in Mayberry; population 161,000. The adult population—those 20 or over—is in line with the national average, about 60 percent of the total. In this case, conveniently enough, that happens to be 100,000, virtually on the nose.

One hundred thousand—that's an awful lot of customers. Only most people will not stick a dirty llama in the backseat of the Volvo and drive more than five miles to get the vile thing vacuumed, no matter how much they like Harry's free braiding and pink ribbons. Of that one hundred thousand people, no more than eighty thousand live within his five-mile market area.

Llama industry figures reveal that only 15 percent of the population will use a llama vacuumer in any given year. So Harry's active market is twelve thousand people. From his own records, he knows that about one third of llama owners go through the Yellow Pages when they need a vacuumer. That's four thousand customers. For the last couple of years, however, three different phone directories have been servicing Mayberry. Last year when he first opened the new store, Harry talked to all of them, and got everybody's facts and figures. One book was preferred by 92 percent of Riverdalians, the second was preferred by 73 percent and the remaining 68 percent swore they would give up their lives and their sacred honor before opening any directory but number three.

I warned you not to try this at home.

Harry ended up simply adding the new address to his ad in the Metropolis book, which was expanding to overlay Mayberry. He spent the rest of his advertising budget on iridescent llama collars. Unfortunately, hardly anybody in Mayberry used the Metropolis book—not, at least, to find something local like a bank, a bakery, or a llama vacuumer. And by the time the llamas needed grooming their fur covered up the name on the collars.

Since then Harry has talked to a lot more people about the various directories. He made a few phone calls and decided to try the Mayberry phone company directory—the *Core* book, the only one they put out. His best guess—and guess it surely is—is that it's getting 75 percent of the usage. Seventy-five percent of 4,000 potential customer is 3,000.

Of course, all these 3,000 customers aren't his yet. Some of them are loyal patrons of other firms, just using the Yellow Pages to find a phone number: customers who won't be swayed by other ads, no matter what the inducement. Some of the 3,000 are Harry's own satisfied clientele, already looking for him. Harry figures about 60 percent of the 3,000, about 1,800, are committed or—initially at least—will just go to whomever is closest to them. That leaves 1,200 customers up for grabs—1,200 uncommitted customers looking through that category each year trying to find a place to go. Harry doesn't know it, but that number includes some of his former customers who have forgotten him or who are just shopping around once again.

So he's paying to reach a mere 1,200 customers. That doesn't sound much like 161,000 does it? I'm not saying that for your business there are 1,200, 120, or 12,000 customers up for grabs for every 161,000 in population. I'm certainly not saying you should try this type of calculation. In fact, I'm saying you shouldn't. You won't get numbers accurate enough to make it worthwhile. What I am saying is, don't let the big population, circulation, or usage numbers the publishers toss around wow you. Check out the headings for yourself just as we've discussed.

And by the way, to Harry, 1,200 is better than 161,000.

"These are *customers*," he says. "They aren't necessarily my customers yet, but they are customers—not prospects—ready to buy. Cash in one hand, dirty llama in the other." And if you knew what Harry makes on an average llama . . . .

Hedging Your Bets

As I said, no matter what kind of a feel you get for the heading, no matter how much research you or I or anyone else does, no one can ever be certain how well an ad will work. You have to take your best shot with your ad, but you want to be darn sure while you're taking that shot the ad doesn't lose you money.

To maximize your potential profit at the minimum possible risk, ask yourself:

How many of those average customers we talked about does an ad—or a listing, a size increase, or a color-enhancement—under the particular heading you're considering have to generate each and every month to make a profit: so each and every dollar you spend there *nets* you more than a dollar in return?[1] If you're in a seasonal business, the ad might have to net enough during that season to cover the whole year.

You want to be as sure as possible your ad will make you something, that the only chance you're taking is whether or not it will make you as *large* a profit as you had hoped.

What Your Average Customer Is Worth To You

So what is your average customer is worth to you? Or even better, what is the average customer who'll be looking

[1] Remember that. Particularly with color. It may cost you 25, 50 or 75 percent more, but it doesn't have to generate 25, 50 or 75 percent more business to be profitable. It simply has to net you more than it costs you.

under the particular heading you're considering worth to you? If you're like most businessmen you probably have a pretty good idea already. If you don't, take a few minutes and work up an estimate. A rough one is fine, but if you're going to err, err on the low side.

It's easy enough to determine how much Joe Average spends. (You know your gross, you know your customer count.) How much do you net from what he spends, after subtracting everything it costs to service him? Be sure to include in all your costs, goods and labor—*including your own labor*—and assign each customer a share of your fixed costs like rent, utilities, salaries, etc. If, for example, you average 200 total customers a month, add on 1/200 of your fixed expenses before calculating the net.

Figure what your average customer is worth to you, net, but remember he's worth more than that. When you do your job right, new customers come back. They also refer their friends, who in turn refer *their* friends, starting a snowball effect. And word-of-mouth advertising is more valuable than any you can buy.

Also remember that every customer your Yellow Pages ad brings in is helping to pay your rent and utilities and those other fixed costs you assigned him—costs you'd have whether you advertised in the directory or not. Under this formula, if you break even on the ad, you're actually making money, because the ad is also paying part of your expenses. What's more, because of your fixed overhead, the more customers you generate, the greater the percentage of profit you usually realize on each.

Say you operate a cut-rate drill press boutique. Your drill presses sell for $1000 apiece. They cost you $400 each and you shell out an additional $100 per press to file off the old serial numbers and add new ones. Your fixed expenses, rent, utilities and help come to $2000 a month no matter what. Normally, you sell five machines per month, so each customer has to cover one-fifth of $2000 or $400 in fixed operating expenses.

So that gives you $1000 (selling price) minus $400 (cost) minus $100 (filing) minus $400 (fixed expenses).

This means your average customer is worth $100. With five of them you get $500 a month to live on.

But suppose you're a real go-getting, high-powered type and you take out a $150 ad in *Industrial Fantasies Magazine*. That month you sell 10 drill presses. You still gross $500 a machine after filing off the numbers. Your fixed overhead of $2000 stays the same, of course, but now each customer only has to cover one tenth of that ($200) not one fifth ($400).

$500 minus $200 means your average customer is worth $300 dollars to you.

This month you take home $2850 (10x300 = $3000 less $150 for the ad), and little Ralphie gets to wear shoes.

There are times when costs go up as business expands. If you have too much of an increase in drill press sales you'll have to rent more space at a much higher rate than you're paying now. You'll also have to pay more overtime since it's nearly impossible to get part-time help.

Of course you can also increase the net value of your average customer—and therefore your profits—even without increasing the number of those customers by developing add-ons to your basic sale, by highlighting your more profitable products and services, and by adding new ones. If you're maxed out on space and/or staff, consider products and services that can be contained in the space you have and covered by people already on the payroll. Harry, for example, added llama permanents and dye jobs—both could be done during a standard vacuuming—dramatically increasing his already exorbitant profits without overtaxing his staff or floor space.

Betting a Sure Thing

You know what your average customer is worth. Divide that into the price of the ad (or listing, ad increase, or color-enhancement) you're considering under the particular heading and you'll know how many of those average customers it has to bring you to keep from losing money.

If the ad is $400 a month and your average customer nets you $50, then you know it's got to bring you—or at least prevent you from losing—eight customers every month to break even. Figure nine to be sure.

If I was making what was for my business a significant investment, I wouldn't go with the ad unless I was virtually certain from my research that it would draw the nine new customers, and considered it very likely to do much better than that. I'd also apply the same standard to any ad increase, additional listing, or color-enhancement: virtually certain it will break even and reasonably sure it will make good money. The point is to minimize potential risk and maximize potential profit, especially if this is your first year under the heading.

CHAPTER 9

More Than One Ad? Other Headings, Other Books

There are supposedly more than 4,200 possible Yellow Pages headings to advertise under, including, *Psychic Mediums, Oils—Animal & Fish, Powder Puffs, Animal Eyes—Artificial* and *Luminous Products*. The average city directory uses between 1,500 and 2,000 of them.

Check out every heading that relates to you just like you did your main heading. It's not as difficult as it sounds. You've gotten most of the information you need from the calls you've already made, and secondary headings tend to be much smaller.

Go to the directory's index. Where does it refer consumers who are seeking the kind of products or services you're selling? If some logical headings don't seem to be there, make a note to ask your rep about them. They may have been left out simply because no one else thought of them. One or two might be cross-reference headings, which you can't advertise under but which your rep can have included in the book at no cost to you. If, for example, you have a truck driving school, you'll want to be certain *Driving*

Instruction—Truck is in the directory, telling users to "see *Truck Driving Instruction*," where your ad actually appears.

When eventually you do talk to your rep, have him run through his related-heading book. That should cover any other possibilities you may have forgotten. If it's in the headings book, he can list you under it.

If you find a potentially worthwhile heading that's been left out of the directory, you won't need an ad or even a bold listing—just a regular one. You won't have any competition there. For a negligible cost, take a chance—just as long as some of your customers are likely to be looking there.

One thing though, about the headings book: some Yellow Pages sales trainers call it, "the money book" because it makes the reps money by revealing more places to sell more ads. Don't get burned by this stuff. Checking out all possible headings does not mean buying ads under each of them or even listing your name under each. Many you'll be able to dismiss out of hand: People who'd be looking under that heading won't be the people whose business you're trying to capture. And just because you offer a product or service doesn't necessarily mean you should list under it. Do you want that extra trade under *Screens—Door & Window*, since you hate making them and only do so, at a loss, as a service to your high-paying custom door clientele?

Some trade associations advise members to select two or three headings and ignore all the others. Granted, if your budget is extremely limited it's better to be effective in one or two categories than ineffective in four or five. But if your customers are referring to a heading you've ignored, you're losing money, not saving it. When Roger Peugot of Roger the Plumber looked in his local directory in Johnson County, Kansas, he saw that nobody else had any significant advertising under *Water Heaters*. He placed a small display ad promising same day service, and "the phone just rang off the wall."

That's why you check out even the secondary headings: to find out if they're worth taking a chance on, and if so, to what extent. In some cases you may want a good-size ad; in others just being there with a simple bold listing or the tiniest in-column ad is enough. Such small ads and listings should always refer consumers to your larger display ad for more information. "See our ad under *Llama Vacuuming*." If you have several good-size displays, refer readers to the heading most pertinent to the one they're in.

When you're checking headings, also check the guides that sometimes follow certain headings, such as restaurant guides broken down by type of cuisine, and legal, dental and medical specialty guides. People looking there are looking for exactly your type of business. And you have less direct competition. Maybe your publisher offers "24 hour services" guides. Or—if the directory covers a large area—business guides broken down by location. In the Consumer Review Systems, Inc. study I mentioned earlier, over half the respondents said they turned to location guides first when such guides were available.

And don't forget the free listing the publishers give you under your main heading. Once you cover it up with advertising, even just a bold listing, you're entitled to move the free listing elsewhere. It's perfect for trying out a heading you're not sure of, where not too many others are listed. See if you get any calls. If you do, put something more significant there next year and move the freebie somewhere else. No calls? Move it anyway. See what happens there. What the heck, it's free.

But what happens when you've checked all the headings, and the best one for your business—one you're certain your customers will be madly turning pages to find—doesn't even exist. How do you get a new heading into the directory? It's simple: Tell your rep. Or you can tell me. Or your mother. She's got about as much chance of getting it into the book as anybody else. Bring it up anyway with your rep (your Mom and I are much too busy). He'll know the procedure for your particular publisher. Miracles do happen.

Heading Jumping

If you advertise under *Florists—Retail*, publishers insist that you actually sell flowers, and the ad you run there must be predominantly about the flower business. That seems pretty straightforward—few plumbers are all that anxious to advertise among the florists anyway. But how about balloon delivery firms? They're seeking the same customers the florists are seeking. A small, simple balloon ad under *Florists—Retail* could offer an interesting alternative to every other business there, and a lot more people look under *Florists* every month than under *Balloons—Novelty & Toy—Retail*.

It's been done and with success, though most directory publishers will require the balloon people to devote a certain percentage of their ad to flowers.

Advertising under a classification where you supposedly don't belong is called heading jumping. Aluminum siding companies under *Painting Contractors*, drug stores under *Physicians & Surgeons, MD*, savings and loan associations under *Banks*, florists under *Funeral Directors*, (the balloon guys haven't discovered this one yet). I've also seen termite inspectors under *Real Estate*, optometrists under *Opticians—Dispensing*, house painters advertising under *Real Estate Loans* and credit repair services under *Attorneys*. These are exactly the kind of thing heading jumping rules are supposed to prohibit, but the rules aren't always enforced.

Optometrists under *Opticians—Dispensing* may seem hard to understand, since optometrists undergo more rigorous training than opticians. It's hard to understand, that is, until you realize that the *Optometrists* classification is usually filled with large ads selling glasses. *Opticians—Dispensing* on the other hand tends to be a small category, with smaller ads selling glasses. It comes right before *Optometrists*, often on the very page where *Optometrists* begins. Thus an *Opticians—Dispensing* ad of whatever size will come before any *Optometrists* ads. And optometrists often do have opticians on their staffs.

Sometimes it's not even a question of stretching facts all that much. With some publishers, *Video Tapes & Disks— Dealers* comes right before *Video Tapes & Disks—Renting & Leasing.* Most video stores do both, and usually the big ads are under the first heading, even though most stores make far more from rentals than sales. In some of these books, most video ads, even for video tape rentals, are under *Video Recorders & Players—Dealers*, which comes before either category.

This type of situation is not that common. All of these headings and several before them start with the word, "*Video*," and that's what people are looking for. They probably just page through until they spot the ads they're seeking. (Most publishers now use a heading like *Video Tapes & Disks—Sales & Renting* for video rentals and have dropped the tape dealers heading altogether.)

Even aside from the ethics, heading jumping is danger-ous. The house painter who advertised under *Real Estate Loans* was not a happy man. And though it may be satisfying to sneak in front of your competition, you don't want your only ad isolated a page or two in front of everybody else— page or two away from where your customers are looking. And you never know how the pages will break.

White Pages

If a customer is looking for you in the white pages he'll find you as long as he knows the alphabet and how to spell your name. So make sure he can spell your name, or at least that he can find it the way he'll try to spell it. Actually we've already covered this. The alternate listings you're getting for your in-column Yellow Pages listings—to cover spelling con-fusion, multiple business names and names of various part-ners—appear in the white pages as well.

Sometimes a national brand name, like State Farm or Farmer's Insurance, will provide—or at least co-ordinate—

white page listings under their name for all their local outlets. You deal with the national company on this, as you would to list under its trademark ad in the Yellow Pages.

The consumer is probably going to find you in the white pages no matter what size your listing is, but that doesn't stop the directory publishers from trying to sell you advertising there. Nowadays, you can buy all kinds of ads. Of course, your regular squint-print listing is free. But your customers will have to search through the alphabet a bit more to find you. The theory is that if you make it easier for them, maybe next time they'll look for you in the white pages where you have no competition.

In my more generous moods, I buy that logic to the extent of a bold listing. Bold listings do stand out, and they mark you immediately as a business. They're also easier to read, which is a service to your customers, and should be a definite consideration if much of your clientele is old, with poor vision. But assuming that the normal type size for white pages listing is adequate (which is not always the case), bold listings aren't as important here as they are in the Yellow Pages.

If, however, you live in Riverdale and own the Riverdale Diner, trying to find your number in two or three pages of Riverdale listings can be like hunting for a silver marble in a ball bearing factory. With a bold listing, you can be found. If the confusion is with a competitor, you can even grab a few of his calls. Riverdale Rooter probably loses calls every day to Riverdale Drain Cleaning right above them alphabetically. With a bold listing, Riverdale Rooter will be seen and probably be called first. Under these circumstances, you might even consider a white page superbold listing.

RIVERDALE ROOFER
127 W. Maurice.................555-1812

White page superbold listings can be the first thing someone sees on the page. They are also much more expensive than bold listings—in some cases without being a great deal larger. Directory publishers say they give your business a first-class image. But unless people are having a lot of trouble finding your name or several of your main competitors are on the same white page you're on, or you're spending so much money in the Yellow Pages that the amount you spend here to try to train your customers to look you up in the white pages is insignificant, then in most cases you should put the extra money where it will do some real good—like in your pocket. If they're looking for you in the white pages, you've got the call anyway.

Companies with large TV budgets that advertise "Find us in the white pages," often go superbold. Usually, they already have giant Yellow Pages ads—often several under one heading—but are simply trying to keep the customer away from the competition lurking there.

Superbold *can* be extremely effective, if your name is one of many similar names all in the same business, like Subway Sandwiches or Herbalife dealers. If you're competing with businesses that list under the same brand name or share the same franchise name—and the superbold listings in your white pages are significantly larger than the simple bold listings—consider going with the superbold. And/or consider adding color.

If you have a reason for buying superbold, a bold listing in red is just as effective and cheaper. Few publishers offer them. Other publishers will color your superbold with red or yellow or some other color to make it more visible and more expensive.

Intermediate sizes, "mini-superbolds" do the same job as the bigger, black-only superbolds for less money.

You can usually add a line or two of ad copy to your listing, whether it's regular, bold or superbold, if there's something you need to tell your customers like directional information or special hours. You may want to include your fax number, e-mail or Web site address. A more recent break-through allows you to buy real ads in many white pages, space ads under your name or banners of various sizes across the top and/or the bottom of the page.

However, just because the technology exists, that doesn't necessarily give you a reason to use the ads.

Well, let's see. Reasons:

1. Your publisher offers the type of banner ad that runs every six, seven or eight pages throughout the white pages so people thumbing through the directory will see your ad over and over again. This type of banner provides first-rate creative (name recognition) advertising, offering exceptional exposure. It's well worth considering . . . if you can get one. Since the same ad runs over and over again, every few pages, availability is extremely limited.

2. Your competition is on about the same page as you are. He buys an ad, so you have to buy one in self-defense. Or you do it first to steal his calls.

3. There are so many red, yellow and green super bolds on the page that yours is lost in a sea of plaid and people are having trouble finding you.

4. You have vital information that you have to convey to the customer immediately. Either your publisher doesn't offer extra lines, or you can't put it all in just a line or two. However, the customer is just about to call you anyway. You aren't about to lose his business to Matson, Barbara, 555-2010 listed just above you or Maurow, Edwina M., of 1901 Mainline Road, just below. And if your customer was looking for additional information about your business, he probably would have looked you up in the Yellow Pages in the first place.

5. You're just advertising for exposure like you'd advertise on the back of a bus stop or inside a magazine. And since you've been searching for a way to gear your advertising to the kind of people who look under *M* in a telephone directory, this is the perfect vehicle.

6. You have more money than you know what to do with.

Are these the best reasons I could come up with? Okay, how about these?

Suppose Karl repairs Volkswagens, but he isn't an authorized dealer, so he can't list under the Volkswagen name in the white pages. Some publishers allow advertisers to place their banner ad wherever they want. Approximately. (Or Karl could set up an alternate listing virtually certain to appear on the Volkswagen page.) His ad reads, "Karl's Bug House: Volkswagens our specialty," and so on. If the publisher does get it on the right page—instead of just the approximate page—everybody who looks up Volkswagen will see it.

Or suppose when a lot of your competition lists under the same brand name, you put in a white-page ad instead of just a superbold. Who's going to get the lion's share of the benefit from the national advertising?

At least until somebody else puts an ad in, too. Then another somebody else. So you'll need a bigger ad. Then they'll go bigger. Then you. This may sound familiar.

Bottom line: There aren't now and there won't ever be nearly as many people looking under any specific name in the white pages—say, Volvo—as they will be looking under the appropriate heading in the Yellow Pages, in this case, *Automobile—Repairing & Service*. And virtually all white pages users already a have a firm in mind.

There aren't really that many white page customers up for grabs. If you can steal a few, great; but don't start throwing a lot of money at this stuff.

One last thing. Just like in the Yellow Pages, in a telephone company book your white page listing will appear exactly as you gave your name to the phone company (and independents usually buy their listings from the telco). If you're an attorney, a doctor or a certified public accountant, be sure to have "atty," "MD" or "CPA" placed after your name. These designations don't cost and they make your name easier to distinguish from those of us who are mere mortals.

And be certain everything is accurate. I wouldn't phone the listing in. Telephones do not bring out the best in telephone companies. Joseph A. Bank Clothiers, Inc. called and asked its phone company to drop the "Inc." from its listing. The next year the listing appeared as:

Drop Inc.
   3384 Peachtree Rd 262-7100

Don't Say I Didn't Warn You

When you're evaluating headings and ad sizes, and thinking about all the money you're going to make, there's one more question to keep in mind: How much business can you actually handle? As Roger Peugot says, "The worst thing is to put too big an ad in and not be able to take care of the business it generates."

There is such a thing as too many calls. You might be able to cream them and take just the most profitable, but you don't want to develop a reputation of turning down work. And you certainly don't want to pay for advertising just so you can refer business to your competition—not unless you can work out a way to make that pay.

A Touch of Flexibility

By now you'll have a good idea of what you want to do and what it will cost. At least in your primary directory. You don't want to bust your budget, especially if you've never charted your Yellow Pages response before. But don't scrimp at the expense of effective advertising either. When you total it all up, keep in mind that the choices you made were made to make you money. If you do have to go back and cut, cut secondary headings first: One effective ad is better than any number of ineffective ones.

At this point in the process, nothing should be carved in stone.

It might be an old salesman's prejudice but I would wait until the appointment with the rep to finalize decisions. You might even make up a list of questions to ask. Then listen to what he has to say, pick his brain, talk to him. Take what he has to say with all the grains of salt in the world, but listen. It doesn't cost anything, and some of it might make sense. After all, reps talk to people about Yellow Pages advertising all day, every day.

Directories From Other Markets

By now, you've seen how much territory other business-es in your industry serve, and how many businesses from out of the area advertise under your headings in your local *Core* book. Should you be advertising in somebody else's local book? First of all, is the market right for your kind of busi-ness? Does it have your kind of customers? The rep will have demographics or you can get them from the Chamber of Commerce beforehand. How are similar firms already there doing?

Second, could you serve the market? Would it be cost effective for you drive 20 miles to put a roof on a home in Smallville or to hire a crew to cover that market? Nowadays you can always put in remote call forwarding so your Smallville ad can have a prefix that looks just as local as the guy in the town square. But if customers have to come to you? Is there some inducement you can use to get the Smallvillians to drive the 20 miles to buy their draperies from your Riverdale store?

Too often advertisers toss money into foreign directories with no real chance of a draw. A plumber who's obviously from out of town is going to be seen as slower, a contractor or a gardener as more expensive. And no Smallvillian is going to drive all the way to Riverdale, past five or six shops that look just like yours, simply to help you pay for the gaudy multicolor ad you put in his local phone book. You have to give him a darn good reason: cheaper prices, a far better selection, perhaps a product or service that's unavailable in Smallville. If it's something not available locally and your business can be handled over the phone or through the mails you might want to put in a toll-free number.

If you can't look local, ask yourself, what would it take to get Smallville residents to deal with you? Can you offer it and still make a profit?

Sometimes you can even turn a disadvantageous location into an advantage. If anyone in Smallville is actually looking for someone in Riverdale to do whatever it is you do—if they commute there for work or for other shopping—a small, simple ad highlighting **Riverdale** could do the trick. If the clientele is there, that is. I've seen a lot more ads based on this particular logic fail than succeed.

If you discover a directory overlaying both Riverdale and Smallville—one that's so strong you'd be getting into it anyway as a secondary local directory—test the market with that the first year. Otherwise, simply go with the *Core* book of the dominant Smallville phone company, the former telephone company monopoly there. If that doesn't draw for you the rest won't either. Remember, however, the dominant phone company in your area is not necessarily the dominant phone company in Smallville. The Smallville book your telco rep is selling may not be the directory of the dominant Smallville phone company.

Concentrate on one heading the first year, the one most likely for the market, probably your main one. If your ad will look local, with a Smallville number, you can, if you feel the need, research that heading for that specific directory. But if your ad looks like it's for a business from out of town, there's no way to get an accurate feel for what kind of response such an ad might draw in that particular market under that particular heading. The best you can do is examine the book. How many other obviously Riverdale businesses advertise under your heading and similar ones?

Take a chance on foreign directories only after you've set aside the funds for your primary local book, which is, of course, your main concern. Obviously, this doesn't apply to businesses whose markets already cover extended areas, where books from any number of areas might be as important—or almost as important—as their local directories and should be treated as such.

Buying Secondary Books in Your Area

If you're not considering a secondary directory in your local area you can skip the next section. Go get a snack. If you are considering a secondary directory—independent or telco—try to see the rep, get prices, and do your homework before you make the final commitment on your *Core* book. (Independent reps usually come around first anyway, but with a phone company *Neighborhood* book, you'll probably want to set up a preliminary appointment—so you can compare its *Neighborhoods* from the last two years—instead of just getting prices and the other info you need for your *Core* book over the phone.)

Never sign the contract with a secondary directory on that initial call. If you're still interested in the book, have the rep come back later, after you're certain of what you're going to do in your *Core* book. The only time you should sign with a secondary book first is when you've missed the *Core* book and you want the secondary directory to tide you over until the next year's *Core* book publishes.

If for some reason you have to commit to your *Core* book before you can evaluate a secondary one, don't be too concerned. You know what you have to spend in the *Core* book. Spend it as planned. Examine the secondary book when you get the chance. If it checks out well, and you've still got money to play with, spend a little. If not, you'll be adjusting your program next year anyway.

Becoming a National Account

Businesses that need to advertise in a number of different directories over several states can become national accounts. This means that with one contact—through a national Yellow Pages Agency—their ads can be put in almost any directory in the country. Authorized Yellow Pages agencies (called CMRs, for Certified Marketing Representatives) and publishers who also function as CMRs can be found in your local phone book under *Advertising—Directory & Guide* and *Advertising Agencies & Counselors*.

Qualifications to be a national account vary according to the organization functioning as your agent. But according to the Yellow Pages Publishers Association definition, you must be in:

1. Twenty or more directories published by at least two different publishers,

2. In three or more states, *and*

3. Seventy percent of your Yellow Pages advertising must be outside of your primary state.

In some cases, you can qualify as a "regional national account" even if all your advertising is in your home state. Regional qualifications typically include:

1. Being in eight or more directories,

2. In two or more DMAs (Designated Market Areas), *and*

3. No more than 70 percent of your Yellow Pages advertising can be in any one DMA.

The agencies help you work up ad copy and layout. They also provide syndicated directory usage information, and research on markets covered by over 6,200 directories, with demographics broken down by age, sex, income, education, housing and occupation, concentration of industry, and so on.

They can also provide copies of your headings as they appear in specific directories.

When each book publishes, you're billed for the entire year, but the bills for the different directories are consolidated so you receive just one monthly bill. Some agencies even cut their commissions and sell the advertising cheaper than you could buy it locally. But make sure they aren't also cutting services you need.

Copy, Art & Layout— Designing Better Ads

Designing the best possible advertising is crucial when you're buying big, expensive ads: If you're spending thousands of dollars a month you want to make sure you have the finest, most eye-catching ads possible. And the smaller your ad—or ads—the more vital ad quality becomes, because you're competing against those with superior size and placement.

We'll start with display ads and take it point by point, deciding on the image you want to convey, including the necessities of headline, name, and phone number, selecting artwork and illustrations, and covering the various copy elements and how to use them most effectively.

We'll discuss what your ad must have, what it can't have, what it should have, what it might have, and why. We'll cover borders and ad layout and type selection using a system that should allow you to design ads that are easily better than 90 percent of the ads in directories today. We'll discuss designing with red, spot color and full process color, and finish up with in-column ads.

The first ad or ads you'll be designing will be for your *Core* book. After that, if and when you decide to go into any other directory, no matter what variations you may make in size, copy or design, the vast majority of the work will already be done.

Who Would You Call and Why?

Go back to your *Core* directory. Turn to your main heading? Who would you call and why? Try to be as objective as possible. If you can't be objective about your competition—and your own ad if you're already in the book—turn to that similar heading you used before or to the other directory from the nearby city. Or look at the Yellow Pages headings you've used as a consumer. Who did you call then? Why? Pay attention when you use the directory in the future.

Show your main heading to some of your customers and ask their opinion. Which ad did they see first? And if they knew nothing about any of the businesses, which ad would they call first and why?

Expert Help and You,
the World's Foremost Authority

The reason no one can tell you how much better one size ad will pull over another is that no one knows what you're going to do with that size. And bad advertising can actually cost you business.

Way back in 1974, in *The Business Owner's Advertising Handbook*, Alvin Boyd called Yellow Pages ads "the most neglected [and the] ugliest . . . in the business world." He added that under no circumstances should you allow the publishing company rep to have anything to do with creating your ad, "if you value your image."

Things have improved since 1974. The reps are more professional and more knowledgeable. The ads aren't nearly as ugly. And in the words of one highly-respected Yellow

Pages art director, "There's still a high level of crap in the books."

Your Yellow Pages rep designs ads all day long for the very directory in which your ad is going to be competing for visibility. How much eye-catching originality can he bring to it? Especially when he has to talk you into upping your ads, close the sale, write up the contract, develop the copy and design the ads, all before his next appointment.

If you're big enough an advertising agency might handle your account. Or, if you can afford it, you can hire a graphic artist for a set fee to do your artwork and layout, creating a total look for your ad. Maybe you're near a university with a good commercial art department and you can get a student who works cheap.

None of the above means you can skip the rest of this chapter on ad design. Stay with me step by step, just as if you were doing the whole thing on your own.

Layout artists know pretty—they might even know eye-catching—but they do not know Yellow Pages. Ad agencies make their money on commissions paid by newspapers, magazines, radio, and TV. They make nothing on a local Yellow Pages ad. They don't spend a lot of time studying the medium or talking clients into spending money there. And magazine and newspaper ads are not Yellow Pages ads.

Manufacturers and distributors—even if they don't offer co-op—will often provide you with ready-made ads. These ads can be great sources of artwork, borders, even layout ideas. But, as I said earlier, always make the ad your own—an ad for your business, not their product.

Trade groups sometimes have copies of Yellow Pages ads that worked for others in your industry.

But even if you do get help: Nobody cares about your Yellow Pages advertising like you do. Nobody else is nearly as concerned that it brings in customers. No one else will take the time with it you will. And nobody else has your expertise in one critical area.

Image.

Your ads should reflect the image you're trying to develop. And better than anyone else you know (or you darn well ought to know) the aim of your business, your market niche, the need you're trying to fill, whether you're trying to provide the lowest prices, the quickest service or the most convenience.

In short, you know who you are or, rather, *who* your business is. You know the customers you're trying to reach, the people who your image and your ad must be geared to attract.

Since it's often the first impression a potential customer gets of your business, your Yellow Pages ad *is* your image. Treat it accordingly.

Your Yellow Pages Image

To develop an image you need consistency and purpose. Though your copy will vary of course, every single ad in any directory should convey your image to the consumer. And all the design elements—borders, layouts, illustrations, color—have to help carry out that image.

Use the same typeface or customized imprint for your name and the same logo in all your ads. Use the same slogan as long as it's appropriate.

Many businesses even give all their ads—everywhere, whether in newspapers, direct mail, billboards, the Internet, whatever—the same general look. Using similar layout and design, each piece reinforces the others—building an identity and increasing recognition. Instead of a collection of different ads, you have an ad campaign. The look is maintained until it fails or until familiarity dims its effectiveness. Then a new one is developed—usually incorporating many of the elements customers have come to recognize. You don't spend years developing a slogan and then toss it out without a heck of a good reason.

In general, frequent Yellow Pages users tend to be better educated and more affluent than the regular population. They listen to more radio and watch less TV (or claim they do). We haven't talked that much about demographics of directory users because Yellow Pages users vary so greatly from heading to heading. You know the kinds of customers others in your business get through the directories. You know whether or not these are the customers you're looking for. That's most of what you need to know about your local Yellow Pages' demographics.

Your Yellow Pages image has to be consistent with the image of your business in general, but, if necessary, tailor that image to accommodate the specific type of customer you want and expect to get from the phone book. Or tailor it to avoid customers you don't want. Are you after the shoppers, those who'll buy strictly on price? Or the customer who's seeking quality and who's willing to pay for it? or the guy who makes one call from the Yellow Pages as opposed to 5 or 6 or 20? Are you trying to lure in families? Or top executives? Women? Long-term contracts or one-shot jobs? Commercial, industrial, residential, or all three?

Maybe you just want to open your image up. The folks at Industrial Strength Beauty Supply always dealt strictly with professional hairdressers. But now, their Yellow Pages heading research tells them that with a few small changes their ad can also bring in the average Josephine—and even Joe—as well.

What to Say, How to Say It

Your Yellow Pages ad might look like your other ads, but it shouldn't read like other ads. Remember, people looking in the Yellow Pages are often already sold. They know what they want. They're trying to figure out where to get it, and they're looking for the information they need to make that buying decision. You tell them you make hair grow on cue balls. You don't have to give reasons why they might want hairy cue balls. If they didn't want them already, they wouldn't have looked under *Cue Balls—Hair Restoration*.

You do have to tell them that you put hair there fast, cheap, in over 30 colors, and your work is guaranteed. In other words, you tell them why they should patronize you: what your business offers them, and how you, your products and services are different from all the rest. You know the customers you're aiming for, you know what they're seeking, what they need, why they buy, how they buy and when they buy.

What do you offer? And why should the consumer call you instead of the big red, blue and green ad on the opposite page? What can you provide that your competition can't?

The Yellow Pages user is seeking information. Make her search as easy as possible. Provide her with as much information as she needs to decide to call. And remember, everybody doesn't call for the same reasons. In an M/A/R/C study done for the Ketchum agency, people rated detailed ads as the second most important feature in a directory.

The information in your ad should be honest and, for the most part, it should be factual. Don't try to be funny. Humor varies too much from person to person. Remember all the bad jokes you've read in this book.

Be factual. But provide a little sizzle with the steak, too. Put yourself in the consumer's place. What problems are your customers concerned with? What will dealing with your business do for them? How will you—more so than your competition—make their lives easier, healthier, safer or happier? Often what businesses are really selling are dreams, comfort, and protection. How will dealing with you provide them with fun, approval, status, true love or a date for New Year's Eve?

Be careful with this. In a study done by Oglivy & Mather, over 70 percent of the respondents thought that advertisers insulted their intelligence. Don't make that mistake. But I do want you to see your ad from your customers' viewpoint. What are the *benefits* of doing business with you? The old adage is true: Features describe but benefits *sell*.

The single most amazing discovery I've made as a consultant to thousands of Yellow Pages advertisers of all sizes is this: When I ask my clients, "Why should someone do business with you instead of your competition?" The first answer they give—the main benefit to the customer, the most important piece of information they have to convey about their businesses—is almost never found in their Yellow Pages ads. Make sure it's in yours.

When you consider "who your business is," providing the sizzle often comes naturally. A picture of a happy, attractive-looking couple says a lot about the dreams a health club can fulfill. If he's got bulging muscles, she's dressed in a spandex handkerchief, and they're gazing lustfully into each other's eyes, that speaks to one set of dreams. Cover them in designer sportswear, make them thin, fit and contented and you speak to entirely different desires.

Still, never forget this is a directory, a reference source. Unlike any other form of advertising, when people go to the Yellow Pages they're doing it because they want to read the ads. They're looking for the hard, factual information. If you don't provide it, they'll look elsewhere.

First, of course, you have to get their attention. You might not be competing with magazine or newspaper articles, but you are competing with other ads, sometimes page after page of them. That means competing for visibility and readability. Make yours more inviting to read.

Originality Without Effort, or Talent—Doing it My Way

Make the ad easy to see, appealing and eye-catching. Originality can help. If your ad looks like all the other ads on the page, how can anyone choose among you? How can anyone even notice yours? The Semolina Original International Pastas chain got close to 500 calls a month for two of its restaurants simply by printing its menu instead of the standard Yellow Pages ads its competition was running.

One expert puts it, "The greater the contrast, the greater the pull." And you do want a different look. Yet, not so different as to be confusing. An ad can be so clever or even so beautiful that the sales message is lost.

If you're a graphic artist, it shouldn't be too difficult to come up with an original, yet professional look.

Professionalism is vital. Too many directory ads have a home-made air about them. Your rep will tell you that you can look as big as anyone in the Yellow Pages. What good does that do you if your big fat ad looks like it was put together by a big fat three year old?

If you don't happen to be a graphic artist—if, like me, you have the artistic ability of a big fat three year old—consider yourself fortunate. You won't get ink all over your fingers, and you just might end up with a better ad. We're going to get our originality the old-fashioned way: We're going to steal it.

Designing Your Ad—Step One

Find a blank piece of paper to use as a copy sheet. That's the easy part. The hard part is finding a ruler. Draw a box the size and shape of the ad you've selected for your main heading. It doesn't have to be exact, just close.

Later, if your rep talks you into a bigger size or your husband or wife talks you into a smaller one, the design and copy elements can be easily transposed. You may, however, want to add or edit for the new size.

If you need more than one ad, create a separate copy sheet for each one, display and in-column.

Got your empty box or boxes? That's nice. Now put them aside. Dig out that list of copy points with products, services, departments, and various other reasons for customers to call you instead of the other guy.

It's time to break up that list into separate lists. One for each ad you've decided you need—display *and* in-column. One list for each copysheet. (If you have any copy points specifically geared for a particular secondary directory—perhaps a book from another area or a *Neighborhood*—you can make another short list for them, and put it aside for now.)

Remember the overall look—border, name, logo, art, etc.—for all your ads may be the same. The sizes may or may not be the same. But the copy must be tailored for each specific heading. That may mean almost entirely different copy.

It may mean nothing more than a change of headline.

Usually, your main heading, *Furniture Dealers—New*, covers every aspect of your business. Your other ads under *Beds—Retail* and *Carpet & Rugs, Dealers—New* are more specialized; customized for those whose needs you can narrow down considerably.

Only when exactly the same aspects of your business are of exactly the same importance to the different consumers looking under different headings, should you run exactly the same ad. If you sell only beds, you may run the same ad under *Furniture Dealers—New* you run under *Beds—Retail.* A fitness center's *Health Clubs* ad could be identical to the one under *Gymnasiums.*

As we cover each of the following elements, add what you need to the appropriate lists. We'll be talking a little about how and where these elements might appear in your ads, but for now that's just to start you thinking, to help you get an overview. No sense laying anything out until we've gathered all the pieces.

Screaming Headlines

Your headline is what your ad screams to the world. It's the biggest, boldest type in the ad, and it tells the reader that this is where to start reading. Only use the name of your business as the headline if that's the most important copy in your ad. Chances are it isn't.

The headline has to be the grabber. So unless your business name has the recognition to do that—to grab the reader into the ad and get him reading—or unless it's descriptive of what you do and what he's looking for, your headline should be something else; something that will sell what you're selling.

If customers only call you every six years, they probably won't remember your business name anyway. Of course, if all your business is referrals or you're as well known as Roto-Rooter, you'd be a foolish not to use the name you've spent so much time and money promoting as a headline.

The Yellow Pages Publisher Association says your headline shouldn't merely repeat the name of the heading. Directory users know what heading they're in or they couldn't have found your ad. Still, if nobody else is doing it, a headline that categorizes the whole heading—"*Drain Opening*" under **Plumbing—Drains and Sewer Cleaning**—can grab people paging through the book even before they spot the caption at the top of the page. There's nothing wrong with giving them what they're looking for.

Whatever is most likely to attract your kind of customers to your ad should be your headline.

24 HOUR EMERGENCY SERVICE

Printing While You Wait

Bedding you can dream on.

BALLOONS

Catering with Elegance.

PET ODOR SPECIALISTS

It could even be your location. Are you closer than anyone else to the majority of your potential customers? Again, check your heading. Look at the headlines you're competing against, what they say, how big they are and where in the heading they'll be. What word, phrase or short sentence will give you the biggest advantage?

"FREE" is good. As in Free Consultation or Free Delivery.

Many advertisers headline questions. Questions lead readers into the ad seeking answers.

Roof Leak?

INSURANCE CANCELED?

Linda Utsey of BellSouth Advertising & Publishing suggests that if you ask a question, answer it right away.

Roof Leak?

Call Seal-Fast.

The period at the end of the sentence strengthens it. In this case that makes it even more of a command.

One of the best headlines I've ever seen was for burglar alarms systems. It read simply:

Security.

The headline is usually placed across the top of the ad— or at least the top of the copy. It doesn't have to be, but this is the strongest copy in the ad. This is where you're telling people you want them to start reading. Be wary about putting weaker points above it; they might never be read. We all read from top to bottom, left to right, and backtracking takes an effort.

Put your headlines onto the individual lists of copy points you've been making for each ad.

The Last Necessities—Name and Number

Now add your name and phone number to the lists. More than once I've finished designing an ad with an advertiser, only to discover that neither one of us remembered to put in the name of the business.

Your name should be large and bold in the ad; in the same typeface or imprint you use everywhere else. If you aren't doing the lettering of your name in any special way yet, this is the time to start. Make a note to ask your rep to show you some of the typefaces he has available. Or ask if he can have his artist work up a custom imprint for you. However, you won't have the control you'd have if you hired a private artist, and you won't get the individualized attention. But you won't get the bill either. Few Yellow Pages publishers charge for artwork, and if they do it should be minimal. Just make sure you see spec art on it beforehand or at the very least ensure that you're getting a proof of the ad and that you can change the cut on the proof if you're not happy. Keep readability in mind as well as image when providing the examples and/or instructions. Too many business imprints are so artsy they need to be deciphered, not read.

You'll find firm names get stuck all over Yellow Pages ads: top, bottom, center—even running up and down the sides. Think about what benefits you might get from linking your name with your headline, which is, after all, the piece of copy you most want to be associated with.

Many advertisers put their phone number at the bottom of the ad, but it certainly doesn't have to be there. It does have to be prominent, especially if that's what your potential customers are looking for. If it's important enough, you might even make your number large enough to be the first one they see on the page.

Ideally, your phone number should be where your readers end up. When they've been drawn into the ad, started reading at the headline, followed the flow of the copy through all your important points and are ready to call, they should be at the phone number. In the story of your ad, the headline is the start and the phone number is the conclusion. But it should be big enough so that no matter when they stop reading they can spot it immediately.

Many advertisers stick their number in a box. A good portion of the boxes are reversed or have drop shadows—you know, like Superman letters. It draws attention to the number; that's why everybody does it. Some ads are so overcrowded that without the box you couldn't find the number. You may not want a box. Your ad may be cleaner and more readable without it, and just that much different from everybody else's. Wait and see. But if you need one, use it, especially if few people under your heading are.

A firm with two telephone numbers is a bigger firm. At least that's what the ad suggests. Put your second number—the one you want called less—to the right of the first, where it will be read second.

Your second number can even be your home phone if someone's there to pick it up. Train that person to answer with the name of the firm. Normally, few people will call during non-business hours, but be aware that by putting in your home phone you are making yourself fair game. People certainly will call in an emergency.

If you go out of business, your billing will probably continue until both numbers are disconnected.

In many fields, a specific after-hours number can generate business:

After eleven call:
555-1100

nights and holidays
555-1101

Some firms play down the service and make the after-hour number much smaller than their regular one. Others provide nothing more than an answering machine or voice mail, or a message bureau, which in a true emergency might contact them.

Custom phone numbers with words instead of numbers are easier for customers to remember.

Flying to San Francisco? Dial 1-800-I FLY PSA.

For a non-smoking room at Quality Inn, it's 1-800-228-LUNG.

When Purolator began using the Road Runner and the number 800-BEEP-BEEP, calls went up 40 percent. (Yes, BEEP-BEEP is eight numbers, or letters, but after the area code and the next seven, the computers don't care what keys you push.)

Yellow Pages users don't have to remember a phone number very long. It's right in front of them. Custom numbers are inexpensive: a set-up fee, then a few dollars a month. But you get a custom number for your other ads—TV, radio, newspapers—where people are likely to forget the number before they get around to making the call. Don't get one just for the Yellow Pages. By the time they need you again, they'll probably have forgotten it anyway.

Still, if you do get one, don't just put "call LUV-BOAT" into your ad. Aside from being excessively cute, it's not immediately recognizable as a phone number to anyone scanning the ad. And people don't like searching the phone dial or keypad for the letters. So if you use a custom number be sure to include the numerals, clearly visible above or below the letters.

A second number—*for current specials and up-to-date prices call*—hooked to an answering machine or voice mail lets you create your own "talking Yellow Pages ad," giving consumers timely information neither you nor your competition can put in a year-long printed ad. And the calls are counted automatically for you. A Web site address, of course, can link customers to even more information; your site, for example, might detail your entire inventory.

On the subject of call-counting, the simplest way to evaluate the response to a Yellow Pages ad is to have just one number in the ad. A number you use nowhere else. Whenever it rings, bingo! You know where the call came from. We'll be covering other, more sophisticated ways to gauge response, but when you have a single ad—and you're in a phone-in trade—nothing is easier than a dedicated line. If you have multiple lines in a hunt group, you can use the last number and have the phone company stop calls from rolling over onto it.

Put your name and your number or numbers onto your lists. And your Web site and/or e-mail addresses if you have them.

But We're Not Quite Finished

Well, that's it. Those are the necessities. Headline, name, and phone number. Everything from this point on is optional. Optional and more or less vital, depending upon your business.

The first option is your address.

Adding Your Location—Why and Why Not

Your address should be prominent if your customers will be coming to you. Readers usually expect to find it along the bottom of the ad. Make it easy for them, unless you have a particularly good reason for putting it elsewhere. Some former customers will remember only where you are, not who are you.

If you're at all difficult to find, add a directional line. The points of reference should be as well-known and as obvious as possible. Help out those newcomers and tourists:

1123 N. Broadway, Suite A
(Behind McDonald's in the Broadway shopping center)

1675 East Lost Drive (on the corner of Main)

If it's more complicated, put in a directional map. Keep the map simple—two or three main streets, possibly a landmark or two, and your location. On a separate piece of paper from your copysheets and your lists, sketch the map, as you want the artist to draw it. If you have several locations be sure to include them all, with maps as necessary.

The bigger the area your directory covers, the more important your location will be to potential customers. And if yours is an advantage jump on it.

Some service businesses, which go to the customer instead of the customer going to them, are better off leaving out the address altogether. If it's not as local as some of your competition, people assume you'll charge more; they don't know you do half of your business in their area anyway. "People want the local guy," says plumber Terry Johnson, "who'll be around if anything goes wrong. Who 'probably won't hurt me.'"

When his telephone company put Terry's non-local address in one book three years running, calls to his Dial One A.A. Johnson Plumbing, Heating and Air Conditioning, Inc. dropped from forty a day to four, even though he'd been in the area for six years, and had in fact started his business there.

If your address is obviously in a residential area, or if you're afraid people will drop by and discover you work out of your garage, or you just don't want people to know where you live, skip it. Or use the address of your answering service, or a partial address:

Main St.

Corner of State & First.

Or even just the town, if that's an advantage. In general though, having a local, accountable address is at least a small selling point. Not having an address never is. Most addresses are neutral sounding. The customer doesn't know if you have a five story building or a shack in the back yard.

But if you have a good reason for leaving your address out, few who read the ad will even notice it's not there. Fewer will care.

In some cases, which vary from state to state, you'll be required by law to give your location. Usually, it's when you're picking something up and taking it with you. Legislatures feel that if you come for little Jimmy in the nursery bus in the morning, his parents ought to have a fighting chance to find you should they decide they want him back, come sundown. A few publishers require addresses—or the name of your town—in all ads. Small print and creative placement are usually as effective as complete omission.

Illustrations and Photos

If you have a great illustration maybe it should be the grabber for your ad. The focus. If you think it can out-pull your headline, make it prominent enough to do so—to actually pull the reader into the ad and then turn them over to the headline.

When the illustration is the focus, consider placing it across the top of the ad or on the left-hand side—possibly even stretching it from top to bottom on the left. Again, the idea being we read from top to bottom, left to right. You draw them into the ad with the artwork; that should lead them to the most important copy, the place they are to start reading—

the headline.

Whether it's the focus or not, chose your illustration or illustrations carefully. Don't clutter the ad with too many. If the picture is actually worth a thousand words, put it in. If not, find one that is. Keep it—or them—simple, effective and large. Large enough to differentiate your ad from the others in your heading, all of which may be saying just about the same things. Most Yellow Pages artwork is too small.

Though one major illustration usually pulls better than several smaller ones, in some businesses you might want to actually show a number of the different products—or types of products—you carry. This gives an immediate impression of the range or the specialization of your line, an impression that a general heading such as *Rental Service Stores & Yards* or *Concrete Products* fails to convey. If I'm looking for a backhoe or a particular kind of awning, I'm going to notice a picture before I ever notice the words. In some of these businesses, more than a few customers will recognize what it is they want when they see it, but won't have a clue to what the darn thing's called. How many types of industrial doors can you name?

Multiple illustrations like these are usually more effective if you treat them as a unit, arranging them in one part of the ad so they draw like a big picture, rather than scattering them throughout. Two large balanced illustrations or groups of illustrations—one on each side of the ad—also work well.

And if a picture faces one way or the other, it should be into the ad, to draw the reader's vision inward to what you're saying, not outside where the competition lurks. If it doesn't face in, have your publisher's art department "flop" it.

Lots of illustrations show part of their subject, not the whole thing. Nobody notices when a drawing of a car doesn't show the bottom of the wheels. But stick that car in an ad and surround what is there with yellow space and suddenly you've got a car with very flat tires. Head and shoulder and upper torso shots look natural, but extended arms with no hands do not, nor do heads that vanish above the forehead. Sometimes these illustrations look natural against a border, but more often the subject looks like an amputee.

Above all, your illustration must fit the image of your business you're trying to convey—must appeal to the people you're trying to reach. I just opened a directory to **Opticians**. One firm billing itself, "the alternative to optical mediocrity," depicts a finger shoving a contact lens into an eye. Makes you want to stick with mediocrity.

The world does not need more 1930s Yellow Pages cartoon figures. But a *carefully chosen* cute or even humorous illustration could hit just the right note for your ad. Just be sure that it is the right note, and doesn't detract from the total effect you're trying to achieve.

If you have a logo use it. A distinctive logo can unify all your advertising. It's also a memory refresher for your customers. If you have a great logo—maybe the one piece of professional art you've ever had done for your business?—how about blowing it up, using it as your illustration, and perhaps even building your whole ad around it?

The most effective logos and illustrations are like a politician's daughter: clean, prominent, and simple. Originals should be high-contrast, without lots of detail or shading, though some shading is acceptable. Line drawings reproduce best, particularly black and white line drawings. When you aren't sure if what you're providing is truly camera-ready—ready to be photographed and printed as is—give the publisher the option to, "re-draw if necessary." If it is camera-ready, the cut (the artwork) can be enlarged or reduced within reason, but the proportions must stay the same. Enlarged or reduced *within reason*. A business card or letterhead logo blown up to three or four times its normal size starts decomposing around the edges. Any small image stretched too far does. You need a good-size original for a large illustration. On the other hand, a large image over-reduced loses detail. Avoid illustrations, except for your logo, in small quarter-column or three-eighths-column display ads. They usually end up looking like somebody squashed a bug on the page, and they take up too much room.

Manufacturers and distributors can provide you with plenty of camera-ready line drawings and photos of their products. Your rep will have a cut book with pictures appropriate for your business; you can also buy cut books at any art supply store. And the directory publishers can stick any noncopyrighted drawing from any of their recent books into your ad. Their art department should also be able to come up with something reasonably close to any simple picture you supply that won't reproduce well. And they will often develop logos. (A Yellow Pages artist created Western Exterminator's famous logo. See Figure 10-1. Speaking of squashed bugs.)

Figure 10-1 An enduring example of the work of a Yellow Pages artist.

Source: Western Exterminator Company. Reprinted with permission.

Use your publisher's art department as your own. Once again, be sure you can change the cut on the proof if it doesn't work out.

Do you want to use a photograph in your ad instead of a line drawing? A couple twisting away from each other, arms crossed, jaws clenched, for that divorce attorney ad? A gorgeous friend turning heads on the street for your beauty parlor? Your recently remodeled hotel rooms? A satisfied customer riding on the new Jumbo Silver Cloud tractor or a party of delighted children bouncing on your moon jump? Perhaps the engaging smiles of your multi-ethnic associates? You?

A photo of your charming self is especially effective when your product is intangible and you and your competition all offer basically the same services. In other words, when what you're really selling is yourself. People like to see the insurance man they called for a phone quote. And who wouldn't want an advance look at the chiropractor or the dentist he's entrusting his spine or his molars to?

Nothing conveys a more specific image than a photo, (especially a color photo). It can illustrate a problem, it can depict your product at work or the results of using your product or service. It can show who you are, what you do, or the benefit of what you do. And the wrong photo may be the surest way to kill an ad. Use your head, not just your pretty face. Nobody wants a doctor who looks like a high school kid or an escapee from a geriatric institution. You can find both in your local Yellow Pages.

Some advertisers use photos of their showroom or warehouse. If you're in a business known for its instability, what gives a better impression of stability than a building? Otherwise, unless it's particularly impressive or a well-known landmark everybody will recognize, I'd use something else. And just because you recognize it doesn't mean other people will. I drive by buildings every day that would be plain old storefronts if I saw their picture in an ad.

When Doctor John sticks his cheerful self into his Yellow Pages ad, the picture is usually run background and all, edges squared—a box. It's like a formal portrait hanging inside the ad. Print his image without the background, silhouetted against the yellow of the page, and Doctor John himself is in the ad, not his portrait. It's a different, warmer, image. For photographs you don't want to look like portraits—and especially for people in action, buildings, cars, and other inanimate objects—having the publisher remove an insignificant background can help integrate the picture into the ad, freeing it from its box and bringing it to life.

If you build your ad around a photo, it's usually better to allow room for most of the copy beyond the borders of the photograph. Copy superimposed on a photograph can be difficult to read, and the smaller the type the more difficult it becomes.

To be printed in the Yellow Pages, a photo has to be turned into a halftone. In a black and white photo, all the shading becomes black dots against the yellow paper. The larger the dots the darker the area. Subtleties are lost. Good Doctor John can end up looking like Jack the Ripper. And when it comes to color photos, though there are several processes used to duplicate color images in directories, none of them reproduce the full range of possible colors. The colors in your original are not necessarily the colors that will end up in the book.

When considering photographs, always check the current directory. What are the predominant colors in your ad and how are they reproduced there? Is that going to ruin the effect you need? For that matter, are any of the photos acceptable—black and white or color? There are still a few publishers out there incapable of anything more than mugshot smudge. The problem is compounded because the photo that appears in your proof may be considerably better or worse than the ultimate reproduction in the directory. And you can't rely on the publisher to tell you what will work well and what won't.

One of the finest attorney ads my company ever designed was for William Berg, a top northern California personal injury lawyer. A major directory publisher assured us the ad was well within its specifications, and "there couldn't possibly be a problem with the kind of sophisticated processes we employ." The proof was gorgeous. But when the first directory Berg bought into hit the streets, the ad looked like it had been soaked in motor oil. That, the publisher explained, was a fluke. The second directory was another fluke, which couldn't possibly happen again, now that they were on top of the problem. We abandoned using the ad in that publisher's books after directory number four, returning to the simple, idiot-proof, black and grey reversed ads that we'd used the year before.

If you do decide to use a photo, your directory publisher may have a library of stock images that you can tap. But if you're submitting your own shots, make sure they're glossy prints, sharp and clear with lots of contrast. If the subject of the shot is dark, the background should be light. If the subject is light, the background should be dark. Originals should be large enough that they don't have to be blown up to twice their size for the ad.

Color originals don't reproduce well in black and white. The reds and greens and blues that stand out so well in color become indistinguishable grays. If you have a color shot you absolutely can't resist using in a non-color ad, run it through a photocopier. That'll show about how it'll reproduce. If you're happy with the results, chances are that the print will work. But you're still taking a chance.

You may think you have just the shot you need lying around somewhere or that you can shoot the picture yourself, especially if it's just a simple shot of a person or a product. My advice is to spend the money and have your photo done correctly by a professional. Then, do not bend, fold, spindle or mutilate it. Don't write on it. If you want it cropped—only part used in the ad—indicate the part to be used on the edges not on the picture itself.

Ask your rep to return the original of any picture you supply, but do not expect to see it again. Always keep a copy, preferably the negative. If you want to run the ad anyplace else, they won't be able to duplicate the photo from a halftone in the Yellow Pages.

Never give away any camera-ready art without a copy of

equal quality.

And if you use a photograph of anyone besides yourself and you don't enjoy being sued, have them sign a model release, granting you the right to use their face in your ad. The same goes for any photo that someone else might own the rights to.

Slogans—Rhyme and Reason

A good slogan is more memorable than your everyday, garden variety business name. In fact, studies show that using your business name in your slogan helps your customers remember the name. If you can, mention your product or service, too. Your slogan also helps create your image and helps your Yellow Pages ad make its point.

Most slogans stink.

"*We clean it like you've never seen it,*" could be any of a thousand companies, in any number of different professions.

If you're trying to come up with a slogan think image, image, and image. Action verbs, rhythm, rhyme, puns, and words with similar sounds all make the slogan easier to remember, but don't shatter image for the sake of any of them.

"*Nobody sucks your sewer like a Secord Sewer Sucker,*" shoves specific information straight into memory, which is exactly what you want. But don't expect to attract the carriage trade or little old ladies.

Within the ad, slogans are often set in italics and/or quotes so they stand out. One theory says that quotes around copy make it more believable. If you want to use a slogan, spend some time on it. What you're doing is summing up your entire enterprise in a single phrase. Think *image* and think *meaning*.

Bite Your Tongue—Restrictions and Qualifications on Your Claims

Different publishers have different restrictions on the way you can make certain advertising claims. Most of those restrictions and qualifications I'll mention specifically as we go along. But with over 200 different Yellow Pages publishers, it's impossible to touch on every one. And enforcement can be haphazard and erratic. As a general rule: If your claims are honest, without intent to mislead, you should have no real problem with any qualification the directory companies might require.

Beyond this, most publishers won't accept:

- Ads they consider vulgar, indecent or offensive.

- Ads attempting to discredit the competition.

- Ads that "refer to race, creed, color or national origin in any way that could be considered prejudicial against another."

- Ads promoting dangerous drugs, promising cures or offering free treatment. This does not prohibit "free consultation," or "free examination" offers.

- Ads "inconsistent with a rigidly constructive advertising practice." Translation: "anything else we don't like."

Because of federal law, you can't use pictures of stamps —foreign or domestic—unless you're advertising is aimed at stamp collectors. Paper money can't be reproduced at or near actual size, and bonds and savings stamps can't be depicted at all. Use of the flag and military insignia is supposed to conform to whatever regulations—state and federal—are in effect in your area. The restrictions and qualifications are to protect publishers from legal action. They also protect you. You can often get past them, but are you sure you want to?

Reliability and Quality

Many people who see your ad in the Yellow Pages will have never heard of you before. That's why firms stress their reliability in any of a number of ways.

Since 1967

Locally owned and operated

Under new management

Family owned. (Anyone impressed by this
obviously has never met my family.)

15 year's experience

I had one tree service owner who added the experience
of everyone in the company together. To me, "85 years experience," painted a picture of a 103 year old man shinnying up
giant trees, hacking feebly at the upper branches.

Some advertisers use the Christian fish symbol. This
may generate trade from other believers. And I have heard of
non-born-agains calling, figuring such firms might be more
honest. It can also causes a backlash, as in: "who cares about
your religion?" Other consumers are wary of sermons: "I want
my car fixed, my soul isn't broken." "Black owned and operated" and "minority owned" are similarly two-edged phrases.
You know your community. Use your best judgement.

Your years in business, your experience, both are reassuring. Substituting how long you've been a Yellow Pages
advertiser—which some publishers encourage—promotes
their business more than yours.

Are you or your employees specially trained or certified?
"Factory trained?" Directory companies often require that
you specify what factory. Whether it's GM factory trained or
the Rotten Rebuilt factory.

"Certified," "Licensed," "Registered." If whoever certified, licensed or registered you is a government agency, you
don't have to name them. If it isn't, you may be required to
make it:

A.A.C.T. Certified

Registered with L.I.S.P.

If you are licensed include the license number in all your
ads (listings—name, address and phone number are usually

not considered ads). It's impressive and state regulations often require it, especially for various contractors: building, electrical, heating, air-conditioning and refrigeration, etc. Such legal requirements for advertising your business are your responsibility. Your rep may or may not know about them, and he has no way of knowing if the number you give him is from a contractor's license or a fishing license. But it's not his livelihood on the line; it's yours. You can see what other firms are doing, but if you have any doubts check with your state attorney general's office.

If you're a mover of household goods your ICC number must be included in every Yellow Pages ad of half-inch size or greater.

Are you bonded or insured? People want to know that when you fall off their roof they're covered. Often the words, "bonded" or "insured" are sufficient. Some publishers require that if you use such terms you be more specific about the coverage, for example:

Insured against property damage

All employees fidelity bonded

Do you offer a guarantee or warranty? Great. But never put in "fully guaranteed" or "unconditional warranty" or even just "guaranteed" by itself, not even if your rep will accept it. Your customer could drop his jeep out of a plane and then expect you to fix your "fully guaranteed" axle. When his sink backs up ten years later—hey, your ad says you guarantee your work.

Instead use: "Ask about our limited warranty," "our conditional guarantee insures all repairs." The words, "conditional" and "limited" qualify it. Here again, your rep and your Yellow Pages publisher should know and protect you (and themselves) from trouble, but of course they might not.

The logo of a trade, professional or business association or society you belong to can have the impact of a seal of approval, particularly if consumers have actually heard of the group.

The size of your firm, the number of branch offices, stores or warehouses, "over 5,000 different models to chose from," "over 9 billion served," even the obvious expense of your large Yellow Pages ad—all these imply reliability. That's why every piddling little bank in the country keeps telling us how big they are, and why their lobbies look like Mussolini's train stations.

One roofer put a box in the middle of his ad. Inside it said: "Our list of 200 satisfied customers supplied on demand." And every year he updated the number. And presumably the list, though I don't know if anyone ever bothered to ask for it. The offer itself was enough.

A short, particularly impressive testimonial quote can be similarly reassuring. Or perhaps you've won a civic or industry award. Be prepared to verify any quote to your sales rep.

The higher the price of what you're selling, the more important reliability and quality are.

If you have quality—in the products you carry, in the services you provide—don't hide it. Show it in your image, talk about it in your slogan and your copy.

If you're not reliable—if your work is shoddy, if you're selling junk—even a huge ad won't keep up with your customer turnover.

Just What it is That You Do?

What type of trade are you looking for? Retail or wholesale? Men or women? Commercial or consumer? Industrial or residential? We touched on this under image, but often you should specifically mention it within your copy, as well.

Of course, you already have all your pertinent services, products and departments on at least one of your lists: anything that's a significant part of your business or you think can become a significant part of your business. If somebody is looking to get their swimming pool re-tiled and you're the only one of eight contractors who mentions it, who are they going to call first?

Do you offer any product or service that's new or

unique? Or new or unique to your area?

Don't assume that just because all tile contractors do all the same things that your customers know that too. The Berry Company quotes a study in which over 60 percent of the respondents said that if an ad didn't mention a product they assumed the company didn't sell it. The figures for services were even higher. And over 70 percent said they wouldn't call to find out. They assumed, "if you don't say it, you don't do it."

Obviously, such results depend upon the type of business and the particular product or service we're talking about. If a family dentist doesn't mention he fills cavities, less than 70 percent of those who see his ad are going to assume he doesn't. But how about laser whitening or bleaching?

Readers are attracted by ads that offer exactly what they're seeking, and also by ads that offer a full range of relevant products and services. That doesn't mean you have to offer to do anything imaginable to any appliance ever made. Rather, it means that if you only deal in Kelvinator refrigerators, you'll get more calls if you inform consumers that you service and repair all models; that you have a complete stock of parts on hand, both new and rebuilt, along with free advice for the do-it-yourselfer; that you sell new and re-conditioned refrigerators; that you buy used ones; and that you accept trade-ins.

Fake-Food Farms advertises, "All your plastic fruit needs," so it must carry the lucite watermelons I need, right? (Probably, though if somebody else actually mentions them Fake-Food Farms could lose out.) And since Marty's Meats says they butcher and dress quail and ducklings, I can go there on the way home from work and kill two birds with one stone.

Sorry. The good news is that's the worst joke in this book and now we have it behind us.

Let consumers know about the other products and services you offer in all your ads, no matter how specialized the particular heading may be. You don't have to go into a lot of detail, though you might if you have the room and the heading is closely related to your other business. Often a quick phrase will do.

"All your furniture needs under one roof" in your small **Beds—Retail** ad tells the reader that, aside from all the bed stuff you've told him about, he can also shop for dining room sets when he comes in. If you add, "see our ad under **Furniture Dealers—New**," he might even do it.

Completeness of inventory—selection, variety, special types, immediate availability—these are things the customer wants to know. "Over 20,000 different types of blinds." "56 acres of cars."

And if your business changes with the seasons, don't forget that your ad has to serve you year round.

On the other side of the coin: do you have a specialty or an expertise within the broader range of what you do? Something you're famous for or you'd like to become famous for? A couple with a Dodge and a Volkswagen decided to patronize Quick-Fix Automotive after finding them under **Automobile—Repairing & Service** and reading, "Expert care on all makes and models—foreign and domestic." But in the same ad, the line that drew Jonathan Smythe-Jones was: "British Cars Our Specialty." We all accept generalists who have a specialty or two. We can even envision a huge firm encompassing specialists in any number of areas. Just understand the image you're trying to project and don't dilute it trying to be all things to all people.

You have to know who you're trying to attract. Remember the problems GM had when it began trying to sell Cadillacs to filing clerks and Chevrolets to bank presidents? Quick-Fix Automotive realizes that a certain percentage of Jaguar snobs won't consider Quick-Fix because they also work on Dodges and Volkswagens. And because of the name Quick-Fix. (One of the very things that attracted the young couple.) They know others will see "British Cars Our Specialty," figure that's what Quick-Fix is really all about, and take their Fords elsewhere. But Quick-Fix isn't looking for the snob trade, and they know their specialty brings in far more business than it costs them.

Major Brands

I could have covered major brand names when I talked about reliability and quality. After all, that's what people think, or at least hope, they're buying when they buy name brands. Do you sell or service major brand names? If GE appliances are a good part of your business—or you'd like them to be—put them in the ad. If people can't get them locally anywhere else, put them in. If you're an authorized Whirlpool dealer or service center, a lot of people with Whirlpools are going to be looking for just that. Fortunes are spent promoting these brand names; hitchhike on that money. Do you deal in all major brands? If you work with only two, billing yourself as "John Deere and Jumbo specialists" shows expertise and reduces nuisance calls. "John Deere and Jumbo exclusively," is even stronger. It also tells tractor mechanics who might not service John Deere and Jumbo that you're not a competitor. So they can refer customers to you without fear of you encroaching on their other business.

In your ad a couple, even a few, famous logos—if they're sharp, clear, famous logos—are often easier to identify than the written names. But eight or ten logos of assorted sizes and type styles—no matter how famous—are a headache looking for a home.

Never use any logo, trademark or slogan you're not legally entitled to display. Even brand names are copyrighted. And directory publishers have restrictions about their unauthorized use. If you're authorized, find out what restrictions, if any, apply on how the name and logo may be used. But even if you're completely independent of the brand name, you can usually refer to those products you deal in if you insert a qualifying phrase first. In other words, listing the following might be considered unauthorized use of the brand names:

Volvo

GM

Alpha Romeo

Saab

Mercedes Benz

But you can say:

Experts on:

Volvo

GM

Alpha Romeo

Saab

Mercedes Benz

Other such phrases include:

Specializing in

New and Used

Parts to fit

Service & Repair on

And of course there are innumerable other ways of saying the same thing.

More Selling Points, Services, and Helpful Phrases

One of the advantages of a small business is the personal service it can offer and the flexibility of that service.

Putting your store hours in the ad is a necessity for retail shops: the exact times, not just the days. It doesn't have to be huge, just easy to find when someone's looking for it. But your hours can also be a real selling point, if you're open when some or all of your competition are closed.

Do you accept credit cards? Usually it's clearer to use their logos than their names.

Other helpful phrases include:

24 Hours

Emergency Service

24-Hour Emergency Service

1 Day Service *or* Same Day Service

Self-Service

Rush Jobs

No Overtime Charges

Free Estimates

Free Consultation

Free Phone Consultation

Free Initial Examination

Free Demonstration *or* Free Home Demonstration

Free Installation

Free Training

Free Delivery *or* Free Pick Up and Delivery (Be sure to specify within what area you deliver and/or pick up, even if you cover the whole area of the directory. "Limited area," can be enough.)

Free Parking *or* Plenty of Free Parking

Free Anything (If strings are attached be sure to mention them.)

Do you offer credit? Easy terms? Immediate credit? No down payment? In-store financing? Don't forget the qualification, "on approved credit." (O.A.C. is often enough.)

Ease of returns sell. "3 day free home trial," "Ask about

our trial exchange program," "Money cheerfully refunded," under whatever the circumstances may be.

"Call for appointment" or "For immediate appointment call" are phrases that go above or in front of the phone number. They're requests for customer action, for a response to the ad. "Call" phrases can also be linked to selling points. "Call for fast, friendly, reliable service," describes how pleasant and convenient dealing with you will be. "Call today for Free Spinal Examination," actually gives the customer something of value for making that call.

No Appointment Necessary

Open Eves., Sat., Sun. by Appointment

Air Conditioned

Toll-Free Number

Collect Calls Accepted (Far inferior to using a toll-free number)

Order by Phone. (What could be more convenient to someone looking in the Yellow Pages? If you take phone orders, it's a good point to emphasize.)

Order by Mail

Are you close to public transportation? How close? Do you accept insurance? Workers' Compensation? Under what qualifications?

"We accept most major insurance plans" or "We accept most major insurance plans as full payment for services rendered." Many chiropractors use a variation on: "Recognized by most major insurance companies. Your condition may be treated at little or no cost to you." Be advised that some consumer watchdog groups may consider some of these phrases misleading. Obviously, you want to use them only if you can do so without being misleading.

Copy like "Mention this ad for a special gift" or "Ask for Mike for an additional screen door discount" provides another easy, though crude way of charting your ad response. It also stimulates the customer to call. Some publishers don't allow it.

Do you have wheelchair access? Your rep can put a wheelchair logo in your ad signifying that. If you have a large handicapped population in your area, you could be the only one telling them they can get into your store.

Do you rent tools or offer advice?

Do you provide warranty service for major brand names?

Do you require reservations or advance notice?

If the directory covers a large area, you might want to be explicit about the area you serve:

Serving the entire Santa Clarita Valley Since 1776

Serving the entire Smallville, Mesopotamia, Riverdale area

You may be in Riverdale, but you're telling the people in Smallville and Mesopotamia that they're well within your normal service area as well. Ideally, with a service business, you could have a local exchange for each of the three areas in the ad and no address. Then you're as local as anybody and probably bigger.

If—even without the local exchanges—you get calls from the Smallville and Mesopotamia area, for whatever reason (within the same directory it's quite likely not a toll call and the only other carpet cleaner in Smallville is a drunk and the one in Mesopotamia insists on taking the carpets back to the shop), a simple phrase like this can get you more calls. And give you an edge over others in Riverdale who haven't made it explicit that they cover those towns.

What do your customers want to know? What questions do they ask most frequently, and shouldn't the answers be in your ad?

Are there slow times you want to build up? Certain customers you'd like to encourage? You can offer student discounts, "early bird" prices, family night or Tuesday afternoon specials for lefthanded redheads? If you offer senior's discounts and your publisher has a senior's program be sure to have them include the logo. Nowadays most publishers also allow you to put prices in your Yellow Pages ads. If low prices are what you have to sell, this can be a big advantage. Just be absolutely sure that the price that gets into the ad is correct (which of course means getting a proof), and that it's a price you can live with for the entire year.

When You're Speaking of Price

Even if you can't or don't want to say, "Seat covers $49.95," you should be aware that many buyers use the Yellow Pages to shop price. You can let them know that if they're concerned about price, you're the one they should be talking to.

You can talk about spending less, saving money, low cost, tiny profits, mini-mark-ups, bargain basement, cut-rate, rock-bottom, slashed prices, and so on. "Wholesale," if you are. "Practically wholesale," if you aren't. "Discount," is acceptable, though publishers usually won't let you talk about the percentage of discount: No, "20 percent off" or "35 percent cheaper."

"Well," you may say, "let's just tell everybody I've got the cheapest prices in town."

You don't want to do that. And there's a good chance your directory publishing company is nice enough not to let you.

Superlatives That Aren't Really Super

Most publishers have regulations about superlatives, claims about being the cheapest, the best, the largest, having the most of whatever you have the most of. "Lowest prices in Montana," "Fastest cures of any psychologist in town," "Largest selection of artificial ears in three states." If you can verify it, of course, you can say it. But you'd better be specific and accurate about what you say. "More service bays than any shop in Riverdale." "Number one in sales volume of any Chevy dealer in Nevada." An exact, verifiable statement leaves you in the clear with consumer protection agencies, and discourages the competition from suing you.

If you have a clear-cut, obvious and verifiable advantage over your competition, tell people about it. Otherwise avoid superlatives. If you're merely claiming lowest prices, somebody can always beat you on a price or two.

The way some Yellow Pages reps suggest you get around using unverifiable superlatives is simply by softening the claim:

> One of the largest selections around.

> Our slogan is, "Lowest prices in town."

> We believe we give the best haircut in Manhattan.

Better to re-think the whole idea.

Lowest Prices in the Known Universe— Bringing Your Hot Air Down to Earth

Many advertising claims are empty and unimpressive, and we're not just talking about superlatives. It's especially true in the Yellow Pages. "Best deals around," "Huge volume," "Low, low prices." "Greatest selection." Many directory publishers even allow certain superlatives on the grounds that they're "accepted by the public as puffery." In other words, nobody believes them anyway.

Hot air doesn't have much impact. You've got to bring that hot air balloon down to earth. And don't just bring it down, tie it down—securely. Claims should be graphic and specific. If at all possible rooted in a hard concrete fact the reader can visualize. Use numbers if you have them. The most impressive ones available. How big are you? "Over 7,500 different models." "More than 800 installations a week." "109 major brands."

"36 miles of overstocked aisles," has a lot more impact than "visit our huge warehouse."

Quality? "98 percent of our members renew every year." "Three years without a customer complaint." When I was growing up, a local furniture store used, "47 years without a sale." I could never figure out how they stayed in business without selling anything, but at least it's not some lame generalized claim that any store on earth could make.

Be vivid. "Save enough on your roof to re-paint the house." "Last year, 17,987 car buyers shopped us last."

Commitment—or apparent commitment—also pounds the point home. "We will meet or beat *any* advertised price in Omaha," "Get your best price, then call us," and even the relatively timid, "We challenge anyone to beat our prices."

If you can't be factual and concrete and don't want to be committed to promises you might not be able to keep, then try the dramatic. "Prices so small they're almost invisible," is at least better than, "Low, low prices," "Compare our prices," or "Shop our discount showroom and save." Consumers will allow you a little poetic license to make your point. But wild and extravagant claims meant to be taken seriously, won't be.

Give yourself a b.s. quota. A limit of one per ad—at the most, two—on claims that aren't tied down with hard facts. "7,500 different models," is factual. "Invisible prices," no matter how vivid, is still b.s. Be factual, informative, useful, accurate and honest. That, however, as we will see, doesn't mean you can't be descriptive.

Your Copy Points

That's the tour of possible copy points for your ad. You've added those you're interested in to your list or lists. Now, if you haven't already, assign each copy point a value, ranking them by importance. I use asterisks: *.

* Unimportant or slightly important

** Below average

*** Average

**** Above average

***** Vital

You know—or you certainly should know—the customers you most want to attract from the Yellow Pages. You also know the most profitable part of your trade. And the fastest growing. What about new products or services that need promoting? Make your rankings with care.

Slashing Your Copy

Eliminate anything you don't need from your list or lists. How often is the same basic idea covered in several different ways on the same list? Note where one phrase might cover several copy points without losing meaning, especially for those points of below average importance.

Specifics are more vivid than generalities. But in a Yellow Pages ad that may mean, "Over 200 different types of heavy equipment, from lawn mowers to pile drivers," and a list of your fastest movers, rather than naming all 200 types.

Decide at which point in your ranking system copy points become "possibles"—worthy of including if they don't overcrowd the ad, but not otherwise.

Slash. Because now it's time to create an ad—an ad that's easier to read than the others in the classification. Which means uncluttered. Ads crammed full of tiny type are an effort to read. Nobody needs to make that effort in the Yellow Pages. There are too many other ads.

White space—yellow space—sells like nothing else you're going to put into your ad. It makes the ad readable. Without white space nothing stands out. The more there is, the more each line of copy is emphasized.

A storage company went from an eighth-page ad to a half-page. It put its name large across the top, the address and phone number large across the bottom. It stuck the rest of the copy from the small ad just as it was—same exact size—into the middle of the half page ad, surrounded by white space.

In general though, the less you have to say, the bigger everything can—and should—be. Not, however, to the point where the ad becomes cluttered because of print size.

Terry Johnson, a founder of Dial One, talks about checking out your heading with the squint test. "Take off your glasses or just squint," he says. "Then decide which ad you'd pick. That's the one that'll get the calls."

The ideal Yellow Pages ad would be as readable as a billboard. Of course, ideals aren't always possible. I've just spent page after page on possible copy to put in your ad. Potential customers want and need complete information about your business and you have to provide it—as simply, as clearly and as readably as you can.

You've been improving your potential copy all along. Dreaming up an improvement here, borrowing another there. Now it's time for even more refinement. Keep your copy points short—in keeping with your image, but to the point—in familiar language. Don't try to sound formal. Use simple sentences and phrases, even single words or a list of words and phrases. Eliminate unnecessary words.

Say what has to be said. But say everything as clearly, simply and briefly as you can: "We develop your passport photos in three minutes or less," might become "Passport photos in 3 minutes." Do you have a good reason for, "We rent our cars by the day, week or month." The whole ad's about car rentals. How would, "Daily, Monthly, Weekly" read?

None of this, however, means that you have to turn a potent sentence like, "When you need quality refinishing, you need McMurphy," into a telegram. Not unless the telegram is more effective for what you're trying to do. The tone of your words is another building block of image. "Thirty-seven exquisitely authentic Victorian suites" is—for the right business—far more powerful than "37 old-style rooms." Making your ad factual does not mean making the facts sound uninviting.

Go over your list. And over it. Refine, refine, refine. When you do start laying out your ad, each copy point you include should be more meaningful than anything else you could have put into that space.

Don't worry if you don't make much progress. You will.

The process will continue as you assemble your ad, when you work with your Yellow Pages rep, even on the final proof. If you're smart you'll be making improvements and refinements for years to come. Slash away. Be as brutal as you have to be. If a sentence, a phrase or a word isn't going to make you money, kill it.

Don't Quit Yet

Don't wait for your rep to assemble all the elements we've gathered. It's time to try to turn the raw copy into a productive ad. This is the most intimidating part, the creative part, the part many people believe takes magical expertise beyond their abilities.

Don't be intimidated. You run your own business, don't you? And this is business. You can learn this—just like your rep learned. Probably better. After all, your sole concern is making the ad work, not selling more ads. There's no big secret to designing good Yellow Pages ads. Just a little hard work and a pinch of creative imitation. Less creative people than you have mastered the art. Less creative people who haven't mastered it are selling Yellow Pages ads in major markets today.

You have nothing to lose. You're going to go over the whole thing step by step, point by point, with your rep anyway, taking any suggestions that make sense. So no matter what, the final product has to be at least as good as any ad you'd have if you didn't try.

In reality, it will be many times better.

Work on your ad gradually, painlessly. An hour today, an hour tomorrow. No pressure, just put in your time. That's 99 percent of creativity: putting in your time. You'll be surprised with what you come up with. And of course, what you bring to that meeting with your rep can be as rough or as finished as you like. But the more you know and the more you can tell him about what you want, the more likely you are to get just that.

So stick with it.

Borders

You start by picking out a border. Every Yellow Pages display ad has a border.[1] As with every other element in the ad of course, it has to fit your image and the total effect you're trying to create. Sometimes anything more than the most rudimentary border will detract from, rather than add to, that effect; you get all your visibility—and your originality—from what's inside the ad, not from what's around it. Generally, if the interior of your ad is compelling, go with a weaker border. The less compelling the interior the greater the need for a stronger, more visible border.

You can select a standard border. It doesn't have to be fancy. Once again, check your competition. A fine line border can make your ad stand out from a field of dark, thick borders. A thick, dark border from a field of thin, frail ones. Corners can be squared or rounded or even turned inward for added visibility.

Not enough visibility? Perhaps you need more originality?

A graphic artist could design several custom borders for you and let you take the one you like. You could get a book of cuts from an art store or a computer program and pick one out. Or you can go to any telephone directory and chose from thousands and thousands of borders. If nothing in the first book suits you go to another. You'll have millions of borders to choose from. It shouldn't take long at all to find one perfect for your ad, with the visibility you need. Be a sport and use books from the directory company that's publishing your book. Cut out or make a copy of the ad, noting the page number, the year and name of the directory, and save it for your rep.

So you have the work of thousands of graphic artists at your disposal. Just avoid copyrighted material. The ad you get your border from doesn't have to be the same size as the one you're buying. The publishers can adjust.

Look through the directory. Decide on a suitable border.

[1] If you've decided on in-column ads only, you can skip this section.

Could any graphic artist offer a better selection?

For a border customized for your particular business—flowers for a florist and a radiator for a radiator shop are two of the more trite—you may have to look in several directories. Or just tell your rep what you want and let the directory company try to work up something for you. Better still, find a picture that'll convey to their artist the kind of thing you're looking for. Or if you can draw, rough something out. The more exact the picture and the more precise your instructions the better (when it comes to artwork, however, some publishers have a far greater capacity for getting you what you want than others).

You can even use your illustration as part of the border. Or have it bursting through, out of the top or the side.

Just don't chose any border so flowery or ornate that it distracts from the copy or makes it difficult to read. Your border should call attention *to* your copy. And remember, the border does take up space *within* the ad. It isn't extra room, over and above the size you're paying for. A border's worthless if it doesn't leave you the room to say all you have to say.

Have several ads? Your border—or borders—must work in all your headings. If it's a thick one you might have to consider a slightly slimmer version in the smaller ads. Weigh the need for extra room against how much those ads could use the increased visibility of the full thickness.

Once you've chosen—and of course it may not be your final choice—pick up your copysheet and mark off enough space around the edge of the ad box to accommodate your border. Save any samples in a safe place for your rep.

If you have instructions you want to put on the copysheet where you won't forget them, stick them off to the side of the page, inside a circle. Circled words are directions, not to be printed. Of course, since this is just a worksheet, you don't really have to be too concerned with such niceties. If your rep forgets a circle on his copysheet, your ad may read: "Create a border in the shape of Texas, with drop shadow along Rio Grande and western panhandle." That's why we have proof sheets.

Reverses and Screens

When considering a border, be aware that part of your ad, your headline or logo, even some of your copy, can be *reversed*. With a reverse, instead of black (or colored) letters on yellow, the letters are the yellow of the page, showing through the inked background. A reverse can be a continuation of the border or a separate area or areas inside the ad.

Using solid black—in thick, dark patches, sharply contrasting with the yellow lettering—is nearly as powerful as using a single spot color. Publishers who can do entire ads of solid black reverse sometimes charge a premium for the extra visibility.

Some publishers limit the amount of an ad which can be done in any solid color—black or otherwise. Sometimes it can be only 10 percent of the ad, sometimes 25 percent, sometimes 50 percent. But if the reverse is screened—converted from solid color into colored dots against the yellow page, which can create a variety of shades—it can cover more of the ad. Screens are used to provide the shading in artwork and border designs. And when used with imagination, screens and graduated screens that go from light to dark allow for an almost unlimited number of creative effects within an ad.

Reverses stand out on the page and add emphasis. But they also take up more room. Only large type should be reversed—and not that much of that—or it becomes difficult to read. Which means you probably don't want to reverse the main body of your copy. No matter what the publisher allows.

For extra clarity, letters can be outlined (see Figure 10-2). Heavy black or colored print can also be used against a screened background of the same color, though care must be taken that the screen doesn't print darker than expected, making the letters difficult or impossible to read. Reversed artwork must be simple, of high contrast, with no detail.

Figure 10-2 Examples of Yellow Pages type treatment.

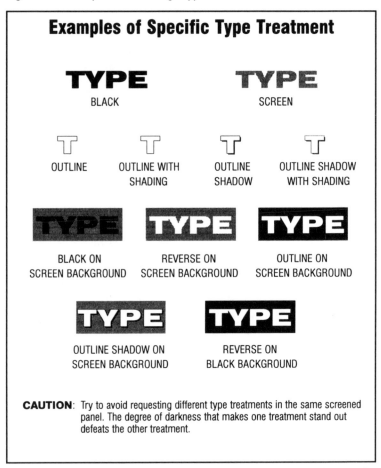

Source: Reprinted with permission of the copyright owner, Southwestern Bell Media, Inc., who reserves all rights herein. Further reproduction is not permitted.

Laying it All Out

Now that you have your border, all the elements are ready and waiting. All you have to do is to arrange them in a neat, eye-pleasing, visually-interesting way—not long paragraphs of copy, but short sentences, phrases and words, as well-spaced as possible. The more information the reader can pick up at a quick scan the better. Think of a billboard.

When it comes to layout, logic is more important than creativity. Remember, we read from top to bottom, left to right. You want to lead the reader through the ad, from point to point, without confusion. It's like you're telling a story—the story of your business.

Think in terms of flow. If you put your finger on the focal point of the ad, the spot where your eye is initially attracted, you should be able to move it—as your vision would be drawn while reading—through all the important copy, without picking up your finger and without doubling back. Try it on a couple of ads in your directory. How many times do you have to pick up your finger? Once? Twice? Five or six times? Too many Yellow Pages ads are assembled randomly, with no flow, making them an effort to read.

Try it on the ad shown in Figure 10-3.

When we talk about flow, we're basically talking about copy flow. But in Figure 10-3, as is often the case, it's the illustration that first pulls you into the ad. Then you see the headline—"Caught in the web of legal confusion?" That

Figure 10-3 Display ad with inverted "U" eye flow, ∩.

Caught in the web of legal confusion?

PERSONAL INJURY
AND AUTOMOBILE ACCIDENTS

NO RECOVERY • NO FEE
NO CONSULTATION FEE

823-9642
Call Anytime!

Dean
&Solen
ATTORNEYS AT LAW

Over 30 years experience in the courtrooms of Broward County.

1121 Metropolis Blvd, Suite 102, Delville

brings you to "PERSONAL INJURY." You move down through the phone number, the name, and finally to the address. Eye movement through the ad is in an inverted *U*: ∩.

In the ad in Figure 10-4, we're pulled in by the "ARRESTED?" headline (with the name linked to it). That carries us to "High Bail?," then down though the body copy to the phone number. The general pattern is ◺.

Figure 10-4 Display ad with diagonal flow.

Diagonals work well as grabbers. But that means a single strong diagonal piece inside the ad—a screened banner, an illustration or a piece of copy. Imagine how hard the ad in Figure 10-4 would be to read if the whole thing was set diagonally?

In Figure 10-5, the copy moves in an *I* pattern. The headline's the focus. Then the two balanced pictures channel the reader down through the various points to the information across the bottom.

The "Weather-Guard Exteriors" ad (see p.94) grabs you with a reversed headline. Then, "20 years experience," and down, making a ⌐. Obviously copy flow and the positioning of the illustration or illustrations in your ad couldn't be more interdependent.

Linda Utsey and the people at BellSouth Advertising & Publishing have done extensive research on Yellow Pages lay-

Figure 10-5 Display ad with "I" pattern eye flow.

out. The four general flow patterns in these examples— ∩ ,
⌒ (often N), I, ⌐ —represent four of five successful flow
patterns they've isolated as typical in Yellow Pages ads. The
fifth is the most common, the straightforward top to bottom
ad, with focal point—either illustration or headline—on top
and copy following underneath. This doesn't mean the flow
of your ad has to follow one of these models. It doesn't. And
remember, they are only broad outlines: Things like additional lines of copy in a diagonal, double lists within a down-
stroke or centered lines across the bottom don't alter the general movement of the flow. But these basic patterns do work
and they can work for you.

The more crowded an ad has to be, the more important
good flow and an orderly layout become. It's all right to
reverse or somehow box off a name, a headline or other key
pieces of copy for emphasis or to help achieve a well-thought-
out "look." But your ad should be a unified whole, not a collection of fragments and compartments.

Misplaced blocks of copy, and lines drawn completely
across the flow of the ad can stop the eye and free your readers' attention to wander to your competition. Allow their
vision easy access from one part of the layout to another.
(Occasionally, an advertiser's copy absolutely must be so
dense that *partially* dividing it into segments makes it more
readable, not less.)

Pick up your first copy sheet and the appropriate list and
give it a try. What's your focal point? Is it your illustration?
Where does it go? Across the top? Left? Where? Mark off as
much space as you want it to occupy. Think a moment about
how it's going to look at that size. Try to have the action heading into the ad, toward where the copy will be. Label the
space.

If your illustration came first, your headline must be
next. Are you linking your name to the headline? What goes
after that, your slogan? The main body of your copy? Then
your phone number? Put them in.

Any room left? Don't worry, everything takes up much

less room when it's set neatly in type. Much less. Still, being able to hand letter all your copy into the ad size you've chosen is a good way to make sure you leave white space. That doesn't mean that whatever you cram in is going to look great once set in type. This is your model; try to make it as accurate an approximation as possible.

If your printing is such that you really have to write your copy outside the ad box, allocate and label the space the way you did with the illustrations. Remember that the printers will get the copy you give them into the space you're buying. But it would be nice if it was large enough that it could be read by human beings—even those with poor vision.

Want to start over? Find a straight edge, draw a box.

Layout II

The ad should be balanced. That doesn't mean you have to center each line of copy, just that the various elements, and therefore the overall look, should be in balance. Not perfectly symmetrical; just not lopsided. It shouldn't look like something is missing from the upper left, or that the bottom right is weighted down with words.

If you are centering all or part of your layout, beware of the dreaded jagged-edged look. When too many lines of copy—one after another—are simply centered it's both boring and hard to read. (See Figure 10.6).

Directories everywhere are full of this stuff.

This doesn't mean that centered layouts are bad, or that you shouldn't center any lines of copy. Even several lines in a row. Just don't overdo it. Obviously, there's an almost infinite amount of ways you can position copy within your ad. Don't settle for dull.

Have Another List

Lists—in all shapes and sizes—are one of the great mainstays of Yellow Pages layouts. It's hard to find a way of presenting large blocks of information that's much easier to read. For example, take the ad we just looked at. Simply jus-

Figure 10-6 Ad with all copy centered.

tifying related lines flush left makes them far more readable, like a page from a typewriter (see Figure 10-7). Better still, see Figure 10-8.

The bullets highlight the individual points. The most important points come first. With double lists, the left side will be read first. The more important items belong there. Items in each list only have to be generally the same length. For an odd number of items, the final one goes underneath in the middle.

Figure 10-7 Ad with related copy set flush left.

Centering a line of copy across the top adds unity:

SALES—SERVICE—PARTS

- lawn mowers
- chain saws
- backpack blowers

- hedge trimmers
- weed whackers
- portable generators

- outboard motors

Figure 10-8 Ad with related copy set with bullets.

Related points can also go flush right:
continental breakfast
heated pool and spa
free color TV
weekly & monthly rates

No bullets on flush right lists. Bullets before the copy over-emphasize that jagged edge. After the copy, they look backwards. Copy that is flush right doesn't work well for double lists:

continental breakfast	night porter on duty
heated pool and spa	valet service
free color TV	medicated flea baths
weekly & monthly rates	most major credit cards

Also avoid it for large amounts of copy and/or complete sentences:

Try our exclusive, fully automatic system
Eliminates soap residue, odor, and spiritual imbalance
Fertilize all your follicles and purify your psyche
Monday through Saturday, by appointment only

Lists can take any number of forms, as long as they work within your flow.

SANYO

SONY

ZENITH

PHILCO

Or:

PUMPS   TRUCKS

GENERATORS

LIFTS   LOADERS

ET CETERA ET CETERA ET CETERA ET CETERA

Type Style, Sizing and Emphasis

The type styles in your ad should be clear and readable—relatively straightforward and not overly ornate or fancy. And consistent, of course, with the image you're trying to project.

Here are some examples of common typefaces:

This is Times Roman.

This is Futura Light.

This is Bodoni Italic.

This is Helvetica.

This is Garamond.

This is Gill Sans.

The possibilities are endless.

Every type style is available in a number of densities—from light to medium to bold and heavy bold—as well as in an italic version. And each of those thicknesses comes in a variety of different sizes.

This is 9 pt. Futura.

This is 9 pt. Futura Light.

This is 9 pt. Futura Medium.

This is 9 pt. Futura Bold.

This is 9 pt. Futura Extra Bold.

This is 9 pt. Futura Medium Italic.

This is 10 pt. Futura.

This is 10 pt. Futura Light.

This is 10 pt. Futura Medium.

This is 10 pt. Futura Bold.

This is 10 pt. Futura Extra Bold.

This is 10 pt. Futura Medium Italic.

This is 12 pt. Futura.

This is 12 pt. Futura Light.

This is 12 pt. Futura Medium.

This is 12 pt. Futura Bold.

This is 12 pt. Futura Extra Bold.

This is 12 pt. Futura Medium Italic.

Yellow Pages reps often recommend that advertisers leave the selection of type style and size to the publisher's art department, the people who'll be putting the final ad together.

To a certain extent they're right. Many advertisers select so many different typefaces for their ad they end up with a visual blizzard. And if you do specify exact type sizes, the publishers have to give you what you asked for, and it may not work once everything is put together. Even a professional has trouble eyeballing an ad in rough form for type size.

But how can a layout artist guess the type styles that best suit the image you're trying to build? And how can he determine the proper size and weight—the correct emphasis—for the different copy points in your ad without knowing how important each one of them is to your particular business? And all plumbers aren't the same: They aim for different clientele and they stress different services and different copy points.

My recommendation, then, is to select a single type face. Get an idea of what you want from the directory, show your rep where you got it in the book, and tell him you want something as close to that as possible. Understand that the publisher may not be able to provide an exact match. Though the typeface came from their directory, an advertiser may have supplied it to them in a camera-ready ad. If you want to use a type style from a source besides your publisher's directory, provide a sample and instructions to make the match as close as possible.

Your selection should be the main typeface for your ad. But tell your rep you do want a second, compatible typeface used too. Two type styles over and above your name imprint—each with a number of possible thicknesses in a number of sizes—provide all the variety you need for any one ad.

Don't pick out the second typeface, and don't indicate which lines are to be set in which. Leave that to the professional in the art department.

As for size and boldness: If you emphasize everything,

you emphasize nothing. Varying type sizes and boldnesses tells the reader what you consider important and how important you consider it—whether it's a section of copy or a single line within a section, as in:

custom
AUTO UPHOLSTERY
all domestic makes & models

It also makes your ad more readable. But related copy of the same importance—for example, items in a list or the main body copy of the ad—should usually be the same size and weight.

Indicate which copy you want to be the largest. Indicate any you want to be large, small or tiny. Or "large as line above," "smaller than above," or "same as above." Which lines do you want bold, which heavy bold, which especially light?

Most Yellow Pages ads are set in all capital letters. Nothing wrong with that. But using capitals and lower case letters—"Ask about our limited warranty,"—is one more way you can stand out from the herd. And, according to most experts, it's also easier to read, as long as the type size is adequate. It's certainly what we're most used to. Lists and short phrases are the best places to use all caps. On some lines you may want the main words capitalized, as in, "The Pants of a Lifetime."

Indicate any preferences you have about capitals on your copysheet.

Indicate anything *to be set in italics*. Use italics sparingly, once or twice per ad.

In other words, tell the art department what's important to your business—put in any size and/or boldness variations you're sure the ad needs. Beyond those specific commands let them do their job and use their expertise. In that way, you can combine their strengths and yours.

You don't have to mark every line. On those you do mark, you don't necessarily have to indicate both size and boldness. You don't have to determine a normal or average size type.

Just tell them which points you want to emphasize more than the average, which less: be it "large and bold," or simply "small." With these requests, plus the general idea they'll get of how the ad should look from the final copy sheet you prepare with your rep, you can safely let the art department, "size and set *all* copy to best advantage."

If you've been planning on getting professional help with you ad—or if you're really concerned that you know exactly what your ad will look like and you don't trust your publisher's art department—now is the time to bring the professionals in. You know what you want to say, about how you want to say it, what needs emphasis and what doesn't. An ad agency, a graphic artist and/or a copy writer, or simply a good print shop or typesetter—depending upon your budget and the level of help you want—should be able to give you anything from camera-ready typesetting (be sure they allow room for your border), to a fully-designed ad, at a very reasonable cost. And the ad will be a heck of a lot better than if you'd just dumped the job in somebody else's lap in the first place. Get estimates. Use the Yellow Pages. It's a small investment, compared to what you'll be spending to put the ad in the directory this year and in the years to come.

Or you can use the publisher's art department, which is free. If you're in a couple of different major publishers' books, you can put both art departments to work and get yourself a choice.

Color Design
Spot Color

If you have decided to use spot color—separate areas of red, green and/or blue (and/or black)—design the ad with that in mind. You don't simply splash it on later in a random effort to increase visibility. You use color to help build the image you're trying to achieve, to help set a mood, perhaps to carry out a color theme you've established in your business or your ad campaign. And with different color usages evoking different feelings, be certain the way you're using colors is consistent with the message you're trying to deliver.

According to one very candid art designer for a major publisher, blue and red contrast, conveying excitement. Blue and green give a quieter, more sophisticated feeling; and red and green, "look tacky as hell together." The green ink that publishers use is often a very dull olive, poor for lettering.

There are numerous other opinions about particular colors. "Blue, for instance, does not go well with eating," says Ann Telthorst, senior product manager with Pacific Bell. "Other than blueberries . . . there are no blue foods. It's not within our realm of familiarity, and is simply not inviting in that context." Telthorst adds that blue connotes security and stability, green is relaxing and calming and "red evokes a stimulated psychological response. People tend to eat and spend more in a red environment, so it's great for restaurants." She also says that using red, blue and green together creates a carnival approach which may not be appropriate for your particular business.

There are those who don't like any Yellow Pages red. One supposed expert on directory advertising for medical firms claims that red reminds their patients of blood and pain. You can take this for what you think it's worth. She recommends that health-care advertisers avoid red ads. Clients of other types of businesses, of course, enjoy being reminded of blood.

I'm no color expert, but my own opinion is that it's the final result that creates the particular emotion, and I suspect that many of these colors can be used to help create any number of differing feelings.

Beyond the image and mood considerations, you obviously *do* use spot color to increase visibility and to highlight key selling points and important copy in your ad. And if you have a blue logo that you've been using in all your other advertising for years, it's certainly going to be more recognizable in the Yellow Pages in blue than it would be in black and yellow. Just as long as the blue or the blue screen that ends up in the directory is at least a somewhat similar shade to the shade of blue you've been using in the logo.

Do not underuse spot color. Publishers sometimes like to keep down the amount of color in their books by getting advertisers to use small touches of color, "a spot of blue," "a hint of red." You aren't paying all that money for a hint, you're paying to be seen.

Don't scatter color randomly throughout the ad. Balance it, and try to move the reader's eye from color to black to color as his vision passes through the ad. A thick colored border adds unity as well as visibility. When it comes to visibility, solid blocks of color and dark screens—particularly in conjunction with white knockout—tend to be far more effective than paler screens. They *tend* to be more effective, but never discount the benefits of creativity and originality.

Don't use spot color in small print, it's hard to read. Only large letters should be reversed through color. You can use it on illustrations. But not on a small one or one with fine detail. You still want a black and white original of course—the publisher just prints it in colored ink. And never use spot color to reproduce a photograph, for that you need

Color can be a powerful aid in helping you sell your products or services, so when using it, consider the following associations:

- **Blue connotes**: stability, strength, cleanliness, health, water, comfort, professionalism and coolness.

Suggested headings: cleaners, janitorial services, air conditioning equipment/systems, physicians or hospitals, swimming pool services, plumbing, psychotherapists, or attorneys.

- **Red reads**: danger, romance, style, excitement, urgency, heat, pain, and spicy.

Suggested headings: burglar or fire alarm systems, locksmiths, florists, auto dealers, party supplies/services, towing, heating, chiropractors, and restaurants.

- **Green suggests**: safety, growth, freshness, new life, environment, money, and relaxation.

Suggested headings: insurance, gardeners and landscape architects, restaurants, nurseries, recycling centers and services, banks, motels, or rest homes.

Source: Pacific Bell® Smart Yellow Pages® ADvisor, September/October 1995. Used by permission.

to go to process (full) color.

Some publishers don't allow you to have different spot colors touching one another. They require an eighth or a sixteenth of an inch separation, and any given line of copy or piece of art must be entirely of one color or another. If that's the case, be sure to keep it mind as you design the ad. Otherwise the colors won't always line up correctly.

Process Color

With process color, you have to start with a good glossy color photograph or slide, or a high-quality colored drawing. Some publishers allow you to use pre-printed material from magazines or brochures if it's exceptionally clear and sharp— if, of course, you have the right to reproduce it. Pre-printed material must be sized as is or reduced, never expanded. Photos or camera-ready illustrations should never be blown up more than 200 percent, if that.

As I said before, the color processes that directory publishers use vary, and so do the publisher's requirements. Some publishers will allow you to fill the entire ad with a process color photo or photos; others will limit you to 50 percent. Some allow you to superimpose copy over the image (something you do with care, with limited amounts of copy, using good-size lettering and making sure the background won't hide or obscure the print). And, of course, different color processes reproduce different colors differently. That's why some advertisers submit two or three photos and let the experts pick the most promising.

In any case, I would never commit to a process color ad without first having a spec ad produced. Otherwise the end result may be far different from what you expect. Tell your rep you want a creative, integrated use of color. Then be sure to compare the color in the spec ad to what's actually in the book.

More Emphasis

Other ways of adding emphasis to copy include:

enclosing it in boxes,
bursts:

bold underlining:

the aforementioned drop shadows (Superman lettering),
having the lettering condensed—short and fat—or
extended—tall and skinny,
varying the size or boldness of a
word or **an entire phrase** within a sentence.

Use all this with restraint. None of this is what I meant
by creativity.
And:

N	H	C	V
E	A	O	E
V	N	P	R
E	G	Y	T
R			I
			C
			A
			L
			L
			Y

As Yellow Pages publishing consultant Dennis Rosen
says: whatever you decide to emphasize and however you
decide to do it, "do so to meet your ad's objectives, not merely to attract attention."

Taking the Time—Or Do You Really Need a Larger Ad?

Experiment. Layout takes work. Try it, then look at
what some of the ads that appealed to you are doing. See how
they flow. You have all the ads in all the phone books in the

library to use as models. Try it again. But don't just copy another ad, especially not one from your own heading in your own book. Don't laugh, any number of advertisers have told me they want an ad just like their main competitor's.

You can do better. Again, the more time you spend the better it will be. Try different arrangements, different flows. You don't have to write down every line of copy every time if you don't want to, just allocate the space, labeling the different elements with letters. Then when you get something you like, see how well it all fits.

Keep refining your copy. I've never known an advertiser who couldn't cut superfluous copy when told he needed a larger ad to say all he wanted to say.

Do you need a larger ad?

You can ask customers, employees, associates and friends for their feedback, creating your own low-budget marketing research and making sure that you've said what you think you've said—and said it clearly and forcefully. Sometimes this will lead to a profusion of different opinions, in which case, pick out two people you trust, two people who know what you're trying to do with your business. Tell them about the other responses you have received, and give their opinions the most weight.

And take heart. The first ad is the most difficult. If you have several to do, they'll get easier as you go along.

A Simple Test

When you think you're finished, when your finger and your vision glide through the ad like an eagle through the sky, try this test. Find an ad the same size, with about the same amount of copy. How big or how small is everything? How visible? Is that what you had in mind? Is it anything like a billboard?

If you can't find an ad that size with as much copy as yours among all the cramped and cluttered ads in the average Yellow Pages directory, send your ad—along with a large magnifying glass—directly to the *Guinness Book of Records*.

In-Column Design

After you have at least a rough draft of all your display ads for the directory, take out your in-column copy sheets and the appropriate lists of copy points.

There are no borders on in-column ads. Most publishers will limit you to one illustration to increase visibility, which should either be your logo or a reversed box with the word or two most likely to draw potential customers to your ad, e.g., "*Discount Repair.*" Remember, the logo or box has to be reduced to the size of the in-column logos already in the book. That leaves out photographs and anything with much detail, not to mention Visa, Mastercard and brand-name logos. If you want to refer to them, you have to write out the words.

For your basic space ad for a particular heading, the possible copy elements are the same as those for a display ad, but with less room, they must be selected and honed even more carefully. And what you need to say has a lot to do with what size ad you chose.

The next question I always get is: "How many lines of copy fit into any given size in-column ad?"

My answer is: "You can squeeze in as many as you want. But don't!" The more you say, the smaller everything will be. If you have to shoehorn it in, if you come anywhere near the allowable limit, you've said far too much. Either cut it down or go to a bigger ad. You're buying an ad to get your message across. The harder that message is to read, the less likely it is to be read.

Refine your list. You might even want your ad as simple—or almost as simple—as the in-column signs we talked about in Chapter 7.

Your name is preprinted across the top of the ad; your address and phone number usually have to appear across the bottom. In local telephone company books, name, address and phone number will all run exactly as you have them registered with the phone company. If you want them altered or left out, you have to change that registration. If it really is the headline (and your publisher doesn't allow the name at the top of the ad to be in superbold), your name can be repeated larger inside the ad. So, of course, can the phone number or even the address.

Layout possibilities are extremely limited with in-column ads. As with display ads, arrange the copy to lead the reader through the ad point by point, logically. You can and should vary type size. If the publishers allow it—most don't—use a different type style from the standard in-column ads around yours and consider using a reverse for the most important line of copy. Because everything is so small and most phrases will be short, use upper case—all capitals—for most of the ad. For readability, bullets are better than undifferentiated lumps of copy or long sentences. Remember: simple, clear, readable, balanced.

If your location is important, you can have a directional box inserted into the upper left-hand corner of the ad. Some publishers will let you put other information besides your location into the box. It's good emphasis, but only, of course, if what's in there is worth emphasizing.

If you use red, green or blue, the same restrictions apply as in the displays. And usually neither your name preprinted at the top, the small address and phone number line at the bottom, nor the thin border around the ad can be in color. The largest and most important items inside the ad should be.

When you've finished your in-column ad design, use the same test as with your displays ad. Check it against the same size ad with about the same amount of copy.

Do you need a bigger ad?

CHAPTER 11

The Salesman Cometh—The Final Cost

Once you've done your preparation for a directory, once you know what you want and where in the book you want it, it's time to call your rep for an appointment.

Courtesy is good business. (Even when dealing with the phone company.) When the time comes for your appointment, set aside enough time to handle your program. For your *Core* book, that means at least an hour, possibly two. Have somebody around who can deal with customers while you're busy. Anyone else who has to be in on advertising decisions should be there, too. If you can't keep the appointment, call; just as you'd want one of your customers to call you.

The salesman arrives—in a custom-made gray suit with a plastic pocket protector full of pens. He works on commission and possibly a daily quota. When I was with GTE, only the amount we increased advertiser spending—over and above what they already had—counted toward that quota, and any reduction in spending counted against it.

No matter how much advertising you've already decided on, your rep will try to sell you more. He may be right. If you haven't checked out your headings and sizes properly, you may need more. Even if you have, you may need more—but next year.

Testimonials

Your rep will come armed with testimonials, statistics, his directory and possibly spec ads, all of which are calculated to get you to spend more money. Testimonials are nice. They're attractively mounted and colorful. But unless the advertiser who gave the testimonial is in the same type of directory, under the same or similar heading, with about the same size ad and about the same amount of competition, it don't have much to do with your business.

I mean, you never really doubted that Yellow Pages worked well for somebody, somewhere, did you?

Lies, Damn Lies and Statistics

Yellow Pages publishers love statistics. Boy, do they love statistics. I've got boxes of them.

There are some excellent Yellow Pages studies. I've quoted some I feel are accurate, in particular, the on-going Statistical Research, Inc. surveys. With more competition and ever-increasing advertising rates, publishers need more and more reliable information to make their cases. Consequently, Yellow Pages research has improved greatly, especially on a national level.

That said, the numbers on the sales aids any given rep shows you might be something less than Pure Scientific Truth.

Say you're a heating contractor. Your rep points to a study of residential air conditioning, heating and refrigeration contractors done by a contractor trade group. Seventy-seven percent of the respondents spent over half of their advertising budgets on Yellow Pages. He might forget to add—he probably doesn't even know—the same study found 81 percent of the same people rated the leads they got from those

Yellow Pages dollars as "fair," "poor" or "bad." Most Yellow Pages publishers aren't going to tell you anything they don't want you to know.

Of course, in that particular study, "fair"—with 57 percent responding—was defined by the survey as "many good prospects, a lot of bid shoppers," which sounds a little more than "fair" to me. If the same study was done by Yellow Pages publishers, they could have just as easily told advertisers who had "many good prospects, a lot of bid shoppers" to check "good" or even "very good." Then the headline on the sales visual could be "72 percent of Air and Heating Contractors Rate Their Yellow Pages Response Very Good or Excellent." The actual response the contractors got from Yellow Pages wouldn't have changed in the slightest. Only the way that response was defined would have changed. If a newspaper advertising group competing with Yellow Pages had done the study, "many good prospects, a lot of bid shoppers," could have been defined as "poor" or worse.

Suppose your sales rep tells you 77 percent of the people in Riverdale use Yergic's Yellow Pages. That doesn't mean that those people use only that book or even use that book most often. If that were the case you could be sure he would say so—in those words. What he is saying is that 77 percent of those studied said they had used the book—or perhaps they only said they *would* or *might* use the book—sometime.

Individual publishers doing small-scale studies only release and promote those that make whatever point they're trying to make. You never know how many studies might have been conducted to get the results they show you. This is particularly true with surveys on sample directory pages, the "which ad would you call first" type. Call-count studies on ads with dedicated numbers are more reliable, particularly when backed by phone bills. But I've heard of at least one advertiser threatening to sue a minor publisher over an allegedly deceptive call count. The advertiser claims that a huge percentage of his calls were messages left on his answering machine at times when it could be expected that no one would be there. The callers either left no number or failed to call back after the advertiser returned their calls, and none of the calls ever turned into business.

To take any research seriously you have to know how it was conducted. Did some dispassionate agency in search of objective truth randomly call 10,000 people? Or did the publisher hire three high school kids at minimum wage who asked loaded questions to seven people and then got bored and faked the rest? Mail-out opinion cards on a new directory measure only the opinion of those who were interested enough in the directory—one way or the other—to return the card. Response cards stuck inside the directory mean that those who never open the book don't even see the card much less return it. Hence: "84 percent of those who responded to our survey loved Confabulated's New Improved Yellow Pages."

I've got a response card in front of me. On it is printed, "after examining [name of directory] and seeing what it has to offer, I can say, 'this is a directory I will use.'" Then it asks a couple of innocuous questions.

This is the best survey yet. One hundred percent of those responding are saying they'll use the directory. 100 percent. A great directory. Sign me up!

Science is a wonderful thing. One usage survey allegedly "proved" the strength of an independent book by recording responses that didn't specifically mention the phone company directory by name, yet obviously referred to it (responses like, "I use the Bell book" or "the big book") under "other directories." On the other side of the coin, many consumers think any directory given to them is from the phone company. If they aren't required to get out the book itself and identify it by name or color or cover picture, who knows what book they're actually using?

Other studies that reps cite can be ancient, conducted on old Bell System books that had no competition, books with smaller ads, and less-developed headings. Some of this "research" has been quoted in so many different ways over so many years that it's closer to rumor than reality.

Even reputable, up-to-date surveys can be misused. I received a call the other day from a highly-respected researcher. (I haven't referred to him or his work directly, but he has provided valuable background.) He was concerned about what other people might be doing with his figures, and wanted me to double check with him on anything anyone else attributed to his organization.

Good Yellow Pages research is being done—by reputable, reliable people. But if your rep starts grabbing numbers out of the air and flinging them at you, duck.

Monkey See?—Buying From The Directory

Your rep will show you your headings in the directory. More Yellow Pages ads may be sold because businessmen see their competition in the books than for any other reason. By this point you should be immune. But one more time: Competitive presence is a strong reason to investigate the heading, not a basis for a final decision, even if you're sure the competition knows what it's doing.

Publishers often offer "second ad free" or discount specials that require the second ad to be put under another heading. Secondary headings can end up with a lot of large ads. Telephone company *Neighborhood* books often give free or discounted ads to businesses who advertise in the *Core* book. Or you might see many of your competition in the first year of a low-cost directory. That, of course, doesn't mean it worked for them. They were taking a chance—as you are if you jump into next year's book without checking.

Truly ineffective books sometimes have "distress" headings. They'll renew ads free or at minimal cost so they won't have to show other prospective advertisers barren classifications. At least one minor publisher even offered to run some ads on a bizarre "pay-us-if-you-think-it-works" basis.

Occasionally, you may get a rep who tries to sell you more advertising by telling you how much bigger a competitor's ad will be next year. Be wary. Even if it's true, no reputable Yellow Pages publisher allows its reps to give out that kind of information. After all, you wouldn't want him telling your competitors what you're going to do.

Spec Ads

If you asked for a spec ad—a mock-up of an ad for your business—and often, even if you didn't, your rep will have it, probably much larger than expected and as colorful as possible. A spec ad is a source of more input. It is not—no matter how beautiful—a take-it-or-leave-it proposition. Any element you like can be adapted to your ad. However, if what you like is the gloss and the vivid color, that isn't going to reproduce in the Yellow Pages. And no matter how much of it you love, nothing from the spec ad should get into the final ad without careful examination. This is especially true for the copy, which—if you've had no input into the process—will simply be whatever you had in last year's ad. Remember, you don't have to buy a size or a color you don't want in order to get those elements you do want—unless what you really like about the spec ad is the size.

Listening for Publishers' Specials and Whatever Else You Might Hear

I've given you a lot of reasons not to change your plans and buy more advertising from your rep. Let me repeat the one reason you might buy more:

Because what your rep has to say makes sense.

So, listen to him. Take his words with all the salt you need. Ask questions. Make them tough, make them blunt. Demand firm answers. But listen. He might make sense. Yellow Pages advertising does work.

And, if you haven't before, find out about what specials he has to offer. With all the competition, Yellow Pages publishers often offer real deals. You could save money doing what you were planning on doing anyway, or spend the same amount and get a lot more for your money.

If you're advertising under only one heading, your publisher's special could give you a chance to try a second. Sometimes you can even split your bonus ad up and try a second and a third. Or you can put a second ad under the same heading. Maybe under an alternate name, stressing a different aspect of your business.

Here's the catch. Yellow Pages discount programs are usually geared to span several years. What may be free the first year will probably be 25 percent the next, then 50 percent, then 75 percent, and finally full price. The directory company is betting you'll keep the ad, either because it will work, or you'll get used to having it, or you'll be afraid to move it because now the competition is there too. (His ad was free as well.) If you sign up for a freebie (or any discount-price ad), be sure that as the prices go up the ad is still justified. You'll have records of what it drew. Take what's free. If it stops making you money, dump it.

Independent Yellow Pages publishers have also been known to pay co-op. If you stuck their logo in your newspaper ads, telling the world you could be found in the such-and-such Yellow Pages, the such-and-such Yellow Pages would pay for part of the ad. Don't expect much of this. What's almost as rare, but hardly nonexistent, are publishers who'll guarantee your advertising and rebate part of your cost if the ad doesn't generate a predetermined number of calls. So far this has been limited to a few smaller non-telephone company publishers.

While you're listening to your rep, listen to ascertain if he makes sense as you make up the copy sheets together. If he's going to be your rep in the future—or even if he isn't—he should be concerned that you get the best possible ads, and therefore the best possible results from his directory.

Cover Ads, Emergency Pages, Yellow Pages Magazines

Your Yellow Pages rep often has other print advertising to sell other than classified Yellow Pages advertising: ads on the inside and back covers, on tabs between sections, on the emergency number page, in the informational section and/or magazine section of the directory, and so on. None of this is Yellow Pages advertising. Rather it's like print advertising you'd do in any magazine, newspaper, or flyer. It's creative advertising: You're trying to increase your name identification and create or stimulate a need for your product. When the need suddenly arises—when they want to know where to find a mover or an electrician—nobody is going to open their phone book and turn to the zip codes and the seating charts. Not even if the person remembers that someplace in there among all the other unclassified ads they once saw your ad. Not when every mover or every electrician in Riverdale is within easy reach, alphabetically, inside the same directory.

The exception is the outside back cover, or the front cover when it's available. That should get so much exposure that, when potential customers want what you have to offer, they might remember your ad. And if they don't remember, they might stumble across it before opening the book. If the ad's big enough, that is. If it isn't lost among a bunch of other random ads, or if people haven't gotten so used to seeing it that it never registers, even as they pick up the directory and turn to your heading.

What's on the back cover of your phone book now? The front cover? That advertising pen on your pocket, what's the name on it? If you need what they're selling do you look in your pocket? Or do you just dig up the Yellow Pages? Then you turn to the back cover, right?

Anyway, with the possible exception of the outside covers, you buy non-classified directory advertising just as you would any other creative medium—to get your name and your message in front of the public.

But this ad gets into virtually every home and business, and it's there for an entire year.

A year's non-classified advertising in the telephone book is not quite the same as a year's coverage in the newspaper, which people read every day, or in a magazine they read every month. A lot of those who get phone books *never* look into the informational parts. Want to see something new? Open the back cover of your telephone directory.

For non-classified ads, you don't care how many people get the directory. You need hard information on how many of them ever get into the specific section your ad's going to be in, and how often they go there—not how many people say an emergency number page or a informational magazine is a good idea, or how many say they *might* use it.

If you can get information like that, which you can rely on, and if the cost per possible exposure stacks up well against other media available, consider an ad. But remember, unlike newspapers, magazines, radio, TV, billboards, and direct mail, this is still advertising that covers an entire year. You can't promote sales or seasonally hot items. You can't adjust for changing market conditions.

A recent innovation offered by most publishers does work much like direct mail. Your advertising piece is delivered in the bag with the new phone book. You can purchase the entire distribution area of the directory or just specific zip codes. Or you can sign up for just the secondary distribution, targeting newcomers—those without established buying habits—as they move into your particular area and sign up for phone service. It's a chance for your business to stand out from the direct mail clutter; of course you never know how many other ads will be in the bag with yours.

A much less interesting Yellow Pages related product that keeps popping up is the plastic directory cover. It's sold by independent companies that have nothing to do with Yellow Pages publishers. You buy an ad or a listing. Then, theoretically, everybody in the area gets a cover so they can protect their phone book. Presto! You're on the front the Yellow Pages. Great! Or it would be if anyone was concerned with protecting their directory, instead of scribbling numbers all over it. And if, of course, anyone wanted to use an ugly plastic jacket covered with advertising to do it.

I've never seen anybody who wasn't advertising on one using it.

Coupons

Your rep may also sell coupons, though sometimes he might not actually *sell* many of them. Coupons are often offered as an incentive to advertisers, either free or at a considerable discount. Sometimes the more ad space you buy the cheaper your coupon. So, many advertisers who have coupons in a directory may not be paying for them. When coupons are a fully-paid item, the price is often small—at least when compared to the cost of direct mail coupon distribution.

It's not that phone book coupons don't ever work. In some places, they've been quite successful. In many other places, however, publishers have canceled the program altogether. In one major market a directory that served a population of 1,600,000 had 42 coupons in it.

In general, consumers are not fabulously excited by coupons in their phone book. The marketing director for one large publisher says, "of all the things we could do, coupons would have about the least impact on the directory." The selection of coupons—especially in smaller areas—is sometimes so bad people never think of checking them before they buy. And often the coupons are unindexed or poorly indexed. Specific ones can be difficult to find.

Still, as an advertiser, when you're dealing with distributions of directory size it doesn't take a high return rate for a coupon to be successful. Especially if the cost is minimal. Some firms even use them as a tool for closing sales. After an in-home estimate, they ask for the phone book, tear out their own coupon, and give an instant discount.

The more you offer in your coupon, the greater your response will be—and the less you'll clear on each response.

Even for free you can go wrong. Your coupon will be in every telephone directory in every home and business in the city. This is not the place for anything that even vaguely resembles a loss leader. Your ideal offer must be good enough to bring people in—5 percent discounts don't impress—yet not so good you don't make a decent profit on each and every redemption. Otherwise, you could be out of business before you get a chance to correct the copy.

You must also determine what restrictions you need. Coupons are a great way to increase traffic during slow hours, but they waste time and cut profits when you have all the business you can handle. Should you restrict the days and hours? Or redeem them "by appointment only." Do you need limits like one coupon per customer, per party or per purchase? Does your discount apply to labor and parts? To everything in the store or just certain items?

Know exactly how long these coupons run. Can you honor your commitment for that long? Do you really want to? Does the publisher allow you to use your own expiration date?

Coupon users can be as careless about reading the fine print as businessmen are when they sign advertising contracts, and just as upset when they find out they aren't getting what they expected. Purchase requirements must be clear and prominent. You aren't doing this to create bad-will.

Now, suppose you aren't getting your coupon free or at a relatively inexpensive price. Suppose you're considering one, even though you'll have to pay significant money for it? First, ask your-

Yellow Pages Coupons

Businesses that tend to get the best rates of return on telephone directory coupons include:

Auto Parts Stores
Auto Repair Shops
Beauty Salons
Building Supply Dealers
Car Rental Agencies
Carpet Cleaners
Clothing Stores
Copy Shops
Dry Cleaners
Gift Shops
Hardware Stores
Hearing Aid Centers
Mini-Storage
   Warehouses
Muffler Shops
Nurseries
Office Supply Stores
Oil Change Services
Opticians
Optometrists
Pet Shops
Pharmacies
Photography Dealers
Pizza Parlors
Printers
Rental Yards
Restaurants
Sporting Goods Stores
Swimming Pool
   Contractors
Tire Dealers
Transmission Shops

self how much larger an ad, how much more effective could your Yellow Pages program be if you put the money you'd pay for a coupon into the Yellow Pages where it belongs? Where people could find you. Where you know people are looking for your type of business. Not in coupons, tabs or magazine sections either, for that matter. If you've done all you can do effectively in the Yellow Pages, in many cases you'll be eligible for a free coupon anyway.

If you have and you aren't, and you still have a few bucks left over, try a coupon if you want. But first call several current coupon advertisers—if possible with similar businesses—to find out how well the program works in your area. Next, check what the competition is doing to be sure you can meet or beat their offers and still make a worthwhile profit. Then, make sure the directory publisher's coupon logo will be in your display ads. The coupon logo gives people one more good reason to call you. The coupon itself should also refer consumers back to your Yellow Pages ad.

After all that, give it a try, but don't pay too much.

When to Sign on the Dotted Line

You've done your homework. You know what sizes you want and what you want to say in which headings. Then listen to the rep's spiel. Go over his related-headings book. Check out "foreign" (other area) directories he handles that you're interested in. Ask your questions. Do your ads.

Yellow Pages reps like one-call sales. But that's to his advantage, not yours. If you can finish your program during this appointment, go ahead. Oblige him. You'll get your proofs that much sooner. But don't be stampeded (even if this is really his second call).

Are you sure that when he turns in that final copy sheet you're going to get the ad or ads you want? If not, maybe you should have him take all your ideas and input back to his artist to work up another spec ad—at least for your primary ad. This second spec ad, in the size you've decided upon, gives you a chance to evaluate what your final ad should look like *before* you sign the contract.

Almost all directory publishers have spec ad capability. And no matter what they might tell you, there is almost always time. The more enlightened directory publishers want to be sure you end up with just the ad you want. Still, you may have to insist. (If, after insisting, you honestly believe that getting a spec ad before signing the contract and committing to the advertising isn't possible, at least be absolutely certain that you are getting that proof.[1])

"The book is closing tomorrow, Mr. businessman," your rep might tell you.

You know when the book is closing. You don't? Have him show you the close date on his rate sheet or on other pre-printed material.

"If you don't sign today you could lose seniority. And since our ads are placed by size and seniority . . . ."

Bull. A current advertiser can't lose seniority, no matter when he signs his renewal. A new advertiser who waits can only lose ground if in the meantime other new advertisers sign up for the same size ad under the same heading. How many of them are there likely to be?

DO NOT SIGN A CONTRACT until you're certain:

- What you want

- What ads and listings you're getting under which categories

- That you will be getting a proof for each display ad

- That you know exactly, to the penny, how much everything will cost and when you have to pay

---

[1] Don't confuse the proof with the spec ad. The spec ad comes before you sign the contract—to entice you to buy. The proof comes after you sign the contract—to show you exactly what's going to be in the directory. In most cases, you can't cancel the ad if you don't like the proof, but you will be able to do whatever fine tuning is necessary.

- What happens to your billing if you move out of the
  area or go out of business during the life of the
  directory

If your Yellow Pages program is handled by phone
instead of the rep coming out in person, there's one only difference as far as the advice in this book goes. Be even more
certain you know exactly what you're getting before committing to buy—whether by signature, fax, telex, recorded voice
or simply verbal agreement. And, once again, if doing your
program by phone is a problem, go into the publisher's office
or have them send someone out to you.

Contracts and Copy Sheets

Never renew your Yellow Pages program until you're certain you and your rep have covered every ad and listing pre-
printed on your Yellow Pages contract. And whether you're a
renewal or a new advertiser, find out what heading and directory each charge on the contract is for. It's not difficult. You
don't have to understand the ad codes, though they are usually on the contract if you need them. Just be able to turn to
the directory once it comes out and find everything you're
paying for. Make notes on your copy of the contract if you
need to.

Some Yellow Pages reps prefer to get your ideas and
instructions, then do the final copy sheets by themselves
later—in the evening in front of the TV, or in a few spare
moments the next day between calls. If your ad means that
little to you, why are you paying so much for it? Final copy
sheets should be finished and as close as possible to the form
of the final ad—before you sign them. Check them over carefully. Mistakes run for an entire year, and just might put you
out of business.

You should have at least until the close of the directory
to make additional copy changes. Find out for sure. And find
out the procedure.

Checking Proofs

Never let a display ad go to press without seeing a proof. Many publishers won't send them unless you ask. Ask. Again, this is a place to insist if you have to. You can't afford to let them cut costs here. How else are you going to see what you've bought before the book hits the streets?[2]

Usually, you can change copy on the proof—but not ad size or color—even after the close of the book. The advantage of finishing your program early is that you should have time to make extensive changes on the proof, including artwork, and if you have to ask for a second proof you may have time to get it. With any luck such changes won't be necessary. But just make sure that if they are you'll be able to make them. Let the competition rely on luck.

When the proofs do come and you've made your corrections, sign them and return them, keeping copies so you have a record of what you've approved in case something else appears in the directory.

In-column ads are fairly straightforward, little more than typesetting. Many publishers don't proof them, which is one more reason to get those copy sheets right the first time.

Know What You're Paying For

Since the Yellow Pages bill is usually tacked onto the phone bill (at least for the *Core* books), an amazing number of advertisers have only the vaguest idea of what they're paying.

Find out.

What are you spending—on each directory and in total—with this publisher? How much has it increased over the year before? Is last year's special program not so special anymore?

---

[2] If you buy right before the close of the book, reps from a few publishers might tell you it's too late to get a proof. Tell the rep in that case, it's too late for you to buy. If he packs up to leave without the sale, he's telling the truth. Decide if you want to be in the book bad enough to take a chance on going without a proof. With a reputable publisher you probably do.

When does the directory come out and when do your payments begin? How long do they run? Are discounts available for advance payment? When the life of the directory is up, can the publisher prolong it and keep charging you the monthly rate without printing or distributing a new book?

The figure on the contract is monthly, not yearly, but are you sure payments are monthly? If your bill is below a certain amount in any single directory—say less than $20 a month—some publishers will bill you for the whole year when the book comes out. Instead of $19 monthly, you have to pay $228 all at once. Even tiny ads in several books that publish around the same time could be a strain. Sometimes, if you make enough noise, they'll bill you monthly anyway. I just wouldn't want to count on it.

Does the publisher offer insurance to cover your losses if they mess up your ad? Consider insurance only if such a foul-up would be catastrophic. The error rate for reputable directory publishers is low, but you don't want to bet your business on it.

How long do you have to change the amount of advertising you've contracted for?

Changing Your Contract

Once you've signed the contract, if you decide to buy more advertising, it's not usually a problem—as long as the directory is still open. As for reducing or cancelling, publishers used to allow it until the directory closed. Many still do. With some the deadline is a week prior to close. Others may try to hold you to the dollar amount on the contract immediately, or make it binding within three or seven days.

The decision on whether or not to let you alter your contract is frequently left up to your rep. And when you cut your advertising, you cut his paycheck. Good reps will place customer service over a commission, but just in case, if you need to cancel or cut back, inform them by certified mail, so you have a record of when you made the request. If you have no luck with them then try their boss. If that doesn't work try *their* boss. Keep going up. Eventually, you might find someone to whom your relatively tiny advertising expenditure doesn't mean much.

Once the directory has closed, if you want to get out of your contract, better try the president. Of the United States. And work up. Actually, if you strike in the first day or two and your reasons are strong enough, you may have a chance. After that, the only way to get out from under your advertising is to cancel your business phone—and nowadays even that doesn't always get you relief.

CHAPTER 12

Tracking Your Ads, and What to Do When the Publisher Screws Up

Department store tycoon, John Wannamaker said, "Fifty percent of the money I spend on advertising is wasted, but I don't know which 50 percent." With Yellow Pages you can know; so you can capitalize on what works and you can junk or try to fix what doesn't.

Ad Tracking

The new directory is born into the world—distributed—anywhere from two to even nine months after you've developed your program. Your advertiser's copy should arrive beforehand. Make sure you get one for every directory you're in, especially for "foreign" books you wouldn't be receiving otherwise. You should get a full copy of the directory, so you have the entire heading and any other headings you may want to examine for next year. A single page with your ad on it is not sufficient. The publishers can afford to send you a directory. See that they do.

Before you start trying to determine how much your new Yellow Pages program is helping your business, allow a little time to make sure distribution is complete, and a little more time—another week or two—to let people start using the new book, instead of the old one with frequently-called numbers written all over the cover.

The most common way of gauging ad response is the seems-to-me method. The new directory comes out and, "it seems to me we're getting more calls." If you've never been in the book before, you could see a radical increase. But just how many calls is that, and for how much business? And for a continuing advertiser, the difference in the response from the quarter-page ad you ran last year and this year's three-eighths page is even tougher to estimate.

A sophisticated refinement of the seems-to-me method is the Herbert Hoover Memorial, Happy Days Are Here Again Variation. When the new directory comes out, you actually keep records of your sales volume and compare them to the same period last year. Of course, you have to adjust for the economy, normal growth of your business, weather, public taste, changes in your other advertising, changes in your merchandise and/or services, and perhaps the fact that your counter help have started to bathe.

Both methods have been used by thousands of advertisers over the years. Each has generated considerable business for bankruptcy courts.

Other simple ways of tracking have the advantage of actually working. An, "ask for Joe for special discount" or "mention this ad for a free whatever," will give a rough indication of the draw of an ad. Still, many people won't ask for Joe even for a free whatever, and some publishers don't allow such coded phrases anyway.

A dedicated number that appears nowhere else will accurately measure the response to an individual ad, or—if you assign a number to an entire book—to a directory. If you use a remote call-forwarding number, you'll get an automatic call count, though you'll also get a charge for every call. Still, a dedicated number works only if your customers always call first. And to gauge all their ads and listings, the average heating contractor or appliance repair shop would need more phone lines than a bookie parlor.

Which, come to think of it, is more lucrative and requires no advertising.

Occasionally, you can arrange for a directory company to meter a dedicated line for you. If you get a lot of calls it has one more argument for its advertising. It counts the calls automatically, and picks up the cost of the metering, and occasionally even the ad.

All these methods—even the first two—are better than nothing. But none of them determine how much business each individual ad and listing in each directory brings in. That's actual business—dollars and cents—not just calls, shoppers, and bad leads. Measuring response correctly isn't quite as simple as wasting money on unproductive ads, but it's a lot cheaper.

Quick and Easy Ad Tracking That Works

The tracking survey is simple—as little as one question. You train your employees to conduct it politely, efficiently, and you record the results. Some firms conduct separate periods of tracking—for example, three periods of one month each—scattered throughout the year. But you should also consider doing it all year long, questioning as many customers as possible, especially if you don't have a huge volume of frequent customers or if your industry has sharp seasonal swings.

If you always go out to your customers or if they *always* phone before coming in to you, do your tracking over the phone. If your customers come to you without always phoning first, survey them when they pay or when they sign the contract.

When They Always Call First

The phone survey is extremely accurate because if they're using the directory, it's open in front of them when they call. Your phone rings. You or one of your splendidly trained employees snatches it up on the second ring.

"Good morning," you say cheerfully. "Kennedy Carpet Cleaning. We clean it like you never seen it." At least your splendidly trained employees would have remembered the new slogan.

You handle the call. To track your Yellow Pages ads, you asks a single question at the end: "If you've got the phone book there in front of you, could you tell me what page of the phone directory you found our number on?"

Bingo! You know which ad under which heading in which directory your customer used to find you. Whether it was white pages or yellow. Whether the phone book was used at all. (If the caller's closed the book, ask the name of the heading they found you under, and—if you're in more than one directory—the name, picture or color on the cover of the book, whichever is the best differentiator.) If the answer happens to be a page where both your listing and your display ad fall, you can ask a second question to distinguish between the two: "Did you look at the big display ad with the drawing of the carpet Genie or the small in-column listing?"

Record the answer circled in an upper corner of the work order or estimate sheet, on whatever paperwork is going to stay with the job until the sale is closed. For radio dispatched service, this information goes out with the call along with the customer's name and address.

Later, after the sale is made or lost, the contact is recorded on that month's tally sheet. Simply log in the date, a check mark under the appropriate ad in the appropriate book and the result of the contact: the dollar amount of the sale or simply "no sale." Also record the zip code or the phone number prefix so you can pinpoint where your business is coming from.

Total your results monthly—or quarterly—and yearly. Next year you'll know exactly how well each segment of your directory advertising did, and when you make changes you'll be able to measure the effect.

To track all your advertising instead of just your Yellow

Pages, first explain to your caller that you're doing a short survey to monitor ad costs. You'll be surprised at how cooperative people will be. The initial question is: "Could I ask how you heard about us?" If the answer's the phone book, ask what page. If the answer is not the phone directory—even if it's "you were recommend" or "I've dealt with you before"—record the result and ask: "Did you look us up in the phone book before you called?" If "yes," ask the page number.

When They Come to You

Customers who come to you might not have to foresight to bring their phone books. Get a lose leaf binder and some of those clear plastic pages that go inside. Make a section for each directory you're in by using the cover of each directory (with a labeled tab for easy reference) followed by each page on which you've got advertising, arranged by heading.

You do the same basic survey, but after they've made their purchase. Ideally, the person who works the register or signs them to the deal can do it, recording the page numbers on the tickets or contract. Once again, you start by explaining what you're doing and that it will only take a moment.

Instead of asking the page number, have the customer identify the cover of the directory he used. Flip quickly through the binder from one cover to another. Don't waste his time. The *Core* book should be first followed by the second most likely directory, and so on. If you're in a lot of different areas, narrow it down by first asking where he's from. Few businesses whose customers go to them are in enough directories for this to take more than a couple of seconds.

When you've found the directory, confirm the ad he or she saw and record the result. (If you're under a number of headings arrange them in the order of their importance to your business, not alphabetically, so most customers will see the ad they called as soon as possible.)

With in-store surveys, it can be particularly difficult to question every customer or even survey every customer within a designated period. You may want to train your people to do the survey when they have time and to skip it when they're too busy.

Get as good a sampling as possible. The more people you question and the better the cross-section, the more accurate the results. But don't drive customers away doing it.

Surveys That Bring Customers Back In

Your employees should be polite. They should never insist when someone doesn't have time for their questions. Obviously, customers they see every day, can be marked "former customer—no directory" without asking. But everyone else they should ask. Your other repeat customers won't be annoyed. The most *they'll* be getting is two quick questions. They're far more likely to be impressed that you're doing it.

Still, you might want to reward those who take the survey with a small discount or a free something with the purchase of something else—a reward for helping you with your advertising. It should be a worthwhile offer that will bring them back to do business with you again, even if it's nothing more than a coupon you'd put in a newspaper ad and pay money to have spread across town.

For phone callers, who may be shopping around through different Yellow Pages ads, rewarding them with a discount on the very service they're calling to investigate can close the sale. "When our service man arrives, be sure to tell him you're eligible for the advertising research discount."

Your survey is making you money.

And "paying" for participation also allows you to make the survey longer, to ask anything else you want to know: What caused them to call your ad? Have they ever shopped with you in the past? How often do they use your product or service? What you could do to serve them better? Anything.

During the Year—Your Yellow Pages File

You make money by determining what advertising works and what doesn't. If you've got a bad ad, re-read Chapters 5,

6, 7 and 10. See if it can be fixed or changed to a more cost-effective size. If you can't fix it, kill it.

You also make money by continuing to improve the ads that do work.

You'll need a Yellow Pages file, with all your contracts and copies of proof sheets grouped by year and directory, and with the results of your tracking.

As soon as your old ad is finalized, everything in it should go right onto your new list of copy points for next year's ad. Keep it in your file or someplace else easy to get to. Maybe you only add one item a year, and that might be nothing more than a better way of phrasing something already on the list. Some years you'll add nothing. Keep your eyes open for better borders or type styles or illustrations. Read your trade magazines and newsletters, noting changes in the field. Watch your competitors' advertising. Compare yourself with them in price, service, selection, hours, and every other aspect of your business. Your national competition spend the most and have the most influence on the market. Sometimes you can capitalize on that. If Fantastic Sam's has created a market for family hair cutting, maybe you want to go after some of that business, especially if they aren't visible in your directory and no one else's ad is geared for that market.

When you travel, notice the ads in the local directories.

Watch your market. Are your customers changing? Listen to what they're saying. What do they want? What do they need? And what can you do about it? Maybe you'll come up with a product or service to add to your line. Or maybe you already have something you should be hyping more.

At least once during the year, go over your list—or lists—of copy points, even if you haven't added to it. Remove anything no longer important. Reevaluate your ratings. An item with four stars might only rate one now. Perhaps, since the piggery moved into the neighborhood, you're no longer selling much lawn furniture, but air purification systems are becoming a more significant part of your business with every breeze that blows.

Yellow Pages Gone Bad—
When They Foul Up Your Ads

Sometimes saving money means not paying full price for an ad that didn't turn out to be the ad you thought you were buying. If you find an error in an ad, first determine it wasn't your mistake. This is why you kept copies of your proofs. If what you have is something you signed for, something you should have corrected, some publishers might still give an adjustment. Especially if the mistake was so serious it should have been caught in their proofreading. But don't count on it and don't expect nearly as much.

If you can prove it wasn't your mistake, that doesn't mean you're going to get your Yellow Pages program for free for a year. The publishers will offer you a reduction in the cost of the single ad in question, based on the their estimate of how much the mistake diminished that ad's effectiveness.

Say the phone number is wrong. You're an exterminator. All your business comes in through the phone. You might get a 100 percent adjustment. Unless the telephone company could put an intercept or a referral on the number that was in the ad, giving customers your correct number, in which case you might get nothing.

An incorrect address could rate a very large adjustment for a boutique, but for a plumber it could be little or nothing.

Services omitted, copy errors, typos, artwork and layout problems might range anywhere from 10 percent to 25 percent.

It's a negotiation. They'll make you an offer. You scream that spelling Hisner's Kosher Catering as Hitler's Kosher Catering is worth more than a 15 percent adjustment. When Annie Gross had her name printed as Gross Annie in her house cleaning ad, she probably overreacted in the same way. Not to mention the therapist who somehow became "the rapist."

You make a counter offer. If it's reasonable they might accept it. Otherwise you fight on up the line, through managers and managers' managers.

Many businesses don't pay their advertising bill until the

issue is settled. They feel that gives the publisher incentive. Contrary to popular opinion, if your problem's with your local telephone company book and you don't pay for your advertising, they can't cut off your phone. Not as long as you pay the remainder of your phone bill.

Incidentally, while you're hassling with publishers, call collect if you can, especially if it's the phone company. Why make them rich while you're fighting to keep from being overcharged?

Eventually, unless you want to sue, you're going to have to reach an accommodation and pay your bill. That is, if you want to be in the directory the next year. In some cases, you might consider suing. Remember, however: "The directory company shall not be liable for damages resulting from omission or error in the advertising in excess of the price of that advertising, no matter how badly they screwed it up."

That's a standard clause in your contract. Basically, it says that no matter how much damage they do to you, your business or your life by ruining your ad—or leaving it out altogether—you can't collect for it. All you can get is a reduction on the price of the ad.

If your ad was left out of the book and you went out of business, not having to pay for an ad you never received is small consolation. Courts in several states have agreed—though in far more cases they've sided with the publishers. If you can show that the injury to your business significantly exceeds what the publisher offers, you might think about talking to an attorney. Understand, however, that the odds remain stacked against you.

Yellow Pages Cutting Agencies

Now that you're an advertiser, you might be approached by a "Yellow Pages agency," that will claim it can cut back your program without hurting your response. You give them a percentage, usually about half, of what you "save."

Like butchers, the more they hack, the more they make. Surgeons don't get paid by the pound.

CHAPTER 13

Last Words— Yellow Pages of the Future, and Turning Callers Into Customers

I wanted to call this chapter "Miscellaneous," but the editor thought that was a tad vague. Still, it's a place for everything that doesn't fit anywhere else. That worked for the New Haven Phone Directory, and it can work for me.

For example, did you know if a current advertiser can't be contacted by the close of the directory, the publisher automatically carries over the advertising for another year? Some publishers have contracts that allow for such "unable to contact" renewals. Others simply hope the advertiser will still want his ads and continue to pay for them, contracted or not. When in doubt, they don't want to cut someone out of the book who needs to be in.

As Miscellaneous as it Gets—Red Yellow Pages

• Individual directories are copyrighted, but, if you want your particular display ads to be covered, copyright them yourself. If you want your trademark, name imprint or slogan secure, register them.

- Don't just offer low prices. Service your customers too. Give 'em more than they expect. Customers drawn by price only will move on to anybody whose prices look lower.

- Never let anyone sell you a Yellow Pages ad on a cost-per-thousand circulation basis. Unless they want to give you cost per thousand for those who actually look under your heading of that directory.

- Beauty shop operators and realtors have both told me their Yellow Pages ads are a source of employees. Apparently, many beauticians and realtors let their fingers do the walking when they're looking for work. Since both work on commission, they call companies that do the most advertising and seem the most aggressive first.

- Just as you can upgrade your home number to a business number, many phone companies will let you downgrade it back if your advertising has run out and you aren't renewing. Some phone companies will even let advertisers downgrade—terminating their Yellow Pages billing—while current ads are still in the book. The advertisers must first prove they are genuinely out of business.

- In order to stop his Yellow Pages billing, one air-conditioning repairman in California used to disconnect his phone every September when business slowed down. Then he'd re-connect—effective in May when the directory published—in time to put the same ad in the new book. Several years he even managed to get the same phone number.

- Until recently, anyone who looked up ***Boring*** in the London Yellow Pages was instructed to "See Civil Engineers."

- Historically, one of the first indications of what was about to happen in the communist world was when GTE contracted with the People's Republic of China to sell advertising in a Beijing business-to-business directory.

High Tech Yellow Pages

Way back in 1986, in the first edition of this book, I talked about what was then called "electronic Yellow Pages:"

"Someday, consumers will be reading ads from computer screens instead of yellow paper, finding a company, ordering a product and transferring funds in an instant. Advertisers will be able to update their copy daily with prices and specials. Hourly, if they like."

"Buck Rogers will be living in a plastic dome on Jupiter."

The Buck Rogers crack was, of course, sarcasm, and I went on to cite predictions that it would be 10 or 15 years before such computer Yellow Pages were profitable to operate.

Now, of course, the Internet is a reality, and with it have come Internet Yellow Pages. And the predictions of the top experts remain the same: that it will be years before Internet Yellow Pages are profitable to operate. Right now, developers—many of them current print directory publishers—are positioning their electronic products with an eye toward that future. Many of their products are impressive. I can sit in my Santa Barbara home and find listings for every Mexican restaurant in Plano, Texas, along with full color pictures, menus, and detailed driving instructions for getting there.

But computer usage is hardly universal. Even if it were, how often are you going to fire up the computer and wade through the Internet trying to find a local plumber—when you can simply pick the phone book? As Charles Laughlin, editor the Yellow Pages Publisher Association's newsletter, says, "While those developing Internet directory products are working very hard to deliver value, most of the products out there still largely replicate the printed product—only they are more difficult to use."

Even if we were all on line, how many national electronic directories do consumers really need? No one knows which, if any, of the present crop will survive and prosper. Right now, those linked to a thriving Internet search engine—and therefore to a built-in source of users—seem to have the best chance.

As an advertiser, you buy or don't buy an Internet directory depending on usage, as you would with any other directory. And not national or worldwide usage. What do you care if the product had 17,000,000 hits from all around the world? You don't care about hits and you don't care about the world. You're a plumber from Edgewater, Colorado. What you need to know is how many times someone from the Edgewater area went into the system searching for plumbers—how many searches were made that would have led users to your business.

As things stand today, national advertisers are more interested in advertising on commercial Web sites than on Internet Yellow Pages.

The other prediction the experts made in our 1986 edition was that, even after electronic Yellow Pages were successful, print directories would remain with us—"until about 3049." I'll stick with that prediction as well. But I will add that in 7 to 10 years we may well start seeing significant advertising dollars coming out of print directories and going into Internet Yellow Pages.

Before the Internet, the previous wave of the future was audiotext. Audiotext is an enhancement to regular old print directories. It appears in three main formats. The first is *Talking Yellow Pages*: which simply means that the ads contain a coded number readers can call for current recorded information. The other two formats both feature audiotext messages sponsored by individual advertisers. *Consumer Tips* appear in selected Yellow Pages headings, and feature—you guessed it—tips for consumers. The *multi-subject information guide* format includes stock quotes, weather, horoscopes and other messages on a wide range of topics.

Sometimes audiotext is linked with a direct-connect service, so the caller can simply remain on the line and be connected to your business.

"Audiotext is a product that people put into the books with very high expectations and, in most cases, it hasn't performed to meet those expectations," said Dan Maitland, CEO of a major audiotext provider, in a recent issue of a Yellow Pages industry newsletter. Many audiotext services have been discontinued or severely cut back. Others, that continue, may be more a mechanism for publishers to differentiate themselves from their competition than hugely effective advertising vehicles.

Successful audiotext is expensive. Consumers first have to get in the habit of calling the service, which means heavy promotion. And what they hear when they do dial in has to justify the call. Too often "talking" ads merely repeat what's already in the Yellow Pages ad, instead of offering sale prices, specials, and up-to-the-minute copy the print ad can't provide. Consumer tips and information guides must be packed with information people actually want to hear.

Directory publishers who offer audiotext should be able to provide you with actual call-in figures. And if my ad were to appear *after* the recorded informative message—which is often the case—I'd also want the publisher to somehow convince me that people might actually hang around to listen to advertising after getting the information they called for.

Another aging Yellow Pages innovation that's still managing to hang on is the dial-in Yellow Pages. Consumers call in for a sewing machine dealer, and they're given one to four names of advertisers who are either in their area or who pay to be mentioned to callers from that area. In seconds, a dial-in directory can come up with a nearby Chevron station that takes Mastercard or a bakery open Sundays. Additional information beyond name, number and address is minimal, though a taped ad message is sometimes available, and sometimes the service does connect the caller directly to the business.

Advertisers can target the areas they want to reach. But it can be costly. Especially if they need to be in several categories and cover a large area. The service is even more expensive to provide than audiotext, and any number of them have folded over the years.

Once again, this is not a Yellow Pages substitute, but a separate medium. It's quick and convenient, especially for travelers, newcomers, people with emergencies, people for one reason or another without directories (perhaps they're at a pay phone), and consumers ready to grab any nearby business that offers what they need. But it's not geared for providing the kind of detailed information so many buying decisions require.

A caller can never tell if he's even been told about the business he'd have chosen if he'd used a complete directory with a full range of businesses and a full range of information.

And what about callers who want the phone number and/or address of a specific business? The dial-in directory either has to give out the numbers of advertisers and non-advertisers alike or refuse such requests altogether. People aren't going to continue to call if they can get a number for Al's Aluminum but not for Bill's Billiards or Harry's Hairpieces. So, if the service is building up the calls they're getting by providing a free alternative to the phone company's directory assistance, you don't have to be an advertiser to benefit.

"Whaddya Want?" When Customers Do Call

And lastly.

To a customer calling in, whoever answers the phone *is* your firm. If that person has to be an answering service, use a good one; you might want them to beep you and assure the caller you'll call right back. An answering machine won't do—far better to simply carry a cell phone. A voice-mail system that can automatically page you is preferable to an answering machine, but you're still going to lose calls.

You, or whoever answers the phone, should be all the things you want your customers to think your business is. You should be courteous and friendly, yet businesslike and competent. Answer the call by the third or fourth ring, using the name of the firm. A naked "Hello," or a "Yah," sounds like an operation that doesn't get a lot of business. And train your people to answer questions about all your products and services, especially those mentioned in your ads.

Every book on selling ever written tells you to get the customer's name and use it. But that means use it a couple of times like a human being, not every other sentence like a used car salesman.

Yellow Pages advertising—any advertising for that matter—can only get you the calls, the contacts. It's up to you to turn them into business. How much selling you normally have to do and what you have to do—setting appointments, getting the caller to come into your shop, taking phone orders—depends upon your type of business. The better whoever answers the phone is with people—the better they are at uncovering the caller's needs, making your case and moving the caller to the next step in the process—the more of those callers will become customers.

Just make sure you and your people always remember the image you're spending all that money to build. Remember it when you give information or set an appointment or make your pitch or close the sale. Remember it when you do the work and when you back up what you've done. If you actually are every bit the company you appear to be in your ads, you'll be your own best advertisement.

Appendix A
A Guide to Creating Your Advertising Budget

Plan Your Advertising Budget—A U.S. Small Business Administration Guide

By Steuart Henderson Britt
Chairman, Britt and Frerichs, Inc.
Chicago, Illinois

Summary

Deciding how much your advertising should cost—just how much should be invested in making sales grow—and how that amount should be allocated is completely up to you, the small business owner-manager.

Advertising costs are a completely controllable expense. Advertising budgets are the same means of determining and controlling this expense and dividing it wisely among departments, lines, or services.

This **Aid** describes various methods (percentage of sales or profits, unit of sales, objective and task) for intelligently establishing an advertising budget and suggests ways of applying budget amounts to get the effects you want.

If you want to build sales, it's almost certain you'll need to advertise. How much should you spend? How should you allocate your advertising dollars? How can you be sure your advertising outlays aren't out of line. The advertising budget helps you determine how much you have to spend and helps establish the guidelines for how you're going to spend it.

What you'd like to invest in advertising and what you can afford are seldom the same. Spending too much is obviously an extravagance, but spending too little can be just as bad in terms of lost sales and diminished visibility. Costs must be tied to results. You must be prepared to evaluate your goals and assess your capabilities—a budget will help you do precisely this.

Your budget will help you choose and assess the amount of advertising and its timing. It will also serve as the background for next year's plan.

Methods of Establishing a Budget

Each of the various ways in which to establish an advertising budget has its problems as well as its benefits. No method is perfect for all types of businesses, nor for that matter is any combination of methods.

Here, concepts from several traditional methods of budgeting have been combined into three basic methods: **(1) Percentage of sales or profits, (2) Unit of sales,** and **(3) Objective and task.** You'll need to use your judgment and caution in setting on any method or methods.

1. Percentage of Sales or Profits

The most widely used method of establishing an advertising budget is to base it on a percentage of sales. Advertising is as much a business expense as, say, the cost of labor and, thus, should be related to the quantity of goods sold.

The percentage-of-sales method avoids some of the problems that result from using profits as a base. For instance, if profits in a period are low, it might not be the fault of sales or advertising. But if you stick with the same percentage figure, you'll automatically reduce your advertising allotment.

There's no way around it: 2 percent of $10,000 is less than 2% of $15,000.

Such a cut in the advertising budget, if profits are down for other reasons, may very well lead to further losses in sales and profits. This in turn will lead to further reductions in advertising investment, and so on.

In the short run a small business owner might make small additions to profit by cutting advertising expenses, but such a policy could lead to a long-term deterioration of the bottom line. By using the percentage-of-sales method, you keep your advertising in a consistent relation to your sales volume—which is what your advertising should be primarily affecting. Gross margin, especially over the long run, should also show an increase, of course, if your advertising outlays are being properly applied.

What percentage? You can guide your choice of a percentage-of-sales figure by finding out what other businesses in your line are doing. These percentages are fairly consistent within a given category of business.

It's fairly easy to find out this ratio of advertising expense to sales in your line. Check trade magazines and associations. You can also find these percentages in Census and Internal Revenue Service reports and in reports published by financial institutions such as Dun & Bradstreet, the Robert Morris Associates, and the Accounting Corporation of America.

Knowing what the ratio for your industry is will help to assure that you will be spending proportionately as much or more than your competitors; but remember, these industry averages are not the gospel. Your particular situation may dictate that you want to advertise more than or less than your competition. Average may not be good enough for you. You may want to out-advertise your competitors and be willing to cut into short-term profits to do so. Growth takes investment.

No business owner should let any method bind him or her. It's helpful to use the percentage-of-sales method because it's quick and easy. It ensures that your advertising budget isn't way out of proportion for your business. It's a sound method for stable markets. But if you want to expand your market share, you'll probably need to use a larger percentage of sales than the industry average.

Which sales? Your budget can be determined as a percentage of past sales, of estimated future sales, or as a combination of the two:

1. **Past sales.** Your base can be last year's sales or an average of a number of years in the immediate past. Consider, though, that changes in economic conditions can make your figure too high or too low.

2. **Estimated future sales.** You can calculate your advertising budget as a percentage of your anticipated sales for next year. The most common pitfall of this method is an optimistic assumption that your business will continue to grow. You must keep general business trends always in mind, especially if there's the chance of a slump, and hardheadedly assess the directions in your industry and your own operation.

3. **Past sales and estimated future sales.** The middle ground between an often conservative appraisal based on last year's sales and a usually too optimistic assessment of next year's is to combine both. It's a more realistic method during periods of changing economic conditions. It allows you to analyze trends and results thoughtfully and to predict with a little more assurance of accuracy.

2. Unit of Sales

In the unit-of-sale method you set a fixed sum for each unit of product sold, based on your experience and trade knowledge of how much advertising it takes to sell each unit. That is, if it takes two cents' worth of advertising to sell a case of canned vegetables and you want to move 100,000 cases, you'll probably plan to spend $2,000 on advertising them. Does it cost X dollars to sell a refrigerator? Then you'll probably have to budget 1,000 times X if you plan to sell 1,000 refrigerators. You're simply basing your budget on unit of sale rather than dollar amounts of sales.

Some people consider this method just a variation of percentage-of-sales. Unit-of-sales does, however, probably let you make a closer estimate of what you should plan to spend for maximum effect, since it's based on what experience tells you it takes to sell an actual unit, rather than an overall percentage of your gross sales estimate.

The unit-of-sales method is particularly useful in fields where the amount of product available is limited by outside factors, such as the weather's effect on crops. If that's the situation for your business, you first estimate how many units or cases will be available to you. Then, you advertise only as much as experience tells you it takes to sell them. Thus, if you have a pretty good idea ahead of time of how many units will be available, you should have minimal waste in your advertising costs.

This method is also suited for specialty goods, such as washing machines and automobiles; however, it's difficult to apply different kinds of products to advertise and must divide your advertising among these products. The unit-of-sales method is not very useful in sporadic, irregular markets or for style merchandise.

3. Objective and Task

The most difficult (and least used) method for determining an advertising budget is the objective-and-task approach. Yet, it's the most accurate and best accomplishes what all budgets should:

It relates the appropriation to the marketing task to be accomplished.

It relates the advertising appropriation under usual conditions and in the long run to the volume of sales, so that profits and reserves will not be drained.

To establish your budget by this method, you need a coordinated marketing program with specific objectives based on a thorough survey of your markets and their potential.

While the percentage-of-sales or profits method first determines how much you'll spend without much consideration of what you want to accomplish, the task method establishes what you must do in order to meet your objectives. Only then do you calculate its cost.

You should set specific objectives: Not just "increase sales," but, for example, "sell 25 percent more of product X or service Y by attracting the business of teenagers." Then determine what media best reaches your target market and estimate how much it will cost to run the number and types of advertisements you think it will take to get the desired sales increase. You repeat this process for each of your objectives. When you total these costs, you have your projected budget.

Of course, you may find that you can't afford to advertise as you'd like to. It's a good idea, therefore, to rank your objectives. As with the other methods, be prepared to change your plan to reflect reality and to fit the resources you have available.

How to Allocate Your Budget

Once you have determined your advertising budget, you must decide how you'll allocate your advertising dollars. First, you'll do any institutional advertising or only promotional advertising.

After you set aside an amount to build your image (if that's in your plans for the year), you can then allocate your promotional advertising in a number of ways. Among the most common breakdowns are by: **1) departmental budgets, 2) total budget, 3) calendar periods, 4) media,** and **5) sales areas.**

1. Departmental Budgets. The most common method of allocating advertising dollars is percent of sales. Those departments or product categories with the greatest sales volume receive the biggest share of the budget.

In a small business or when the merchandise range is limited, the same percentage can be used throughout. Otherwise, a good rule is to use the average industry figure for each product.

By breaking down the budget by departments or products, those goods that require more promotion to stimulate sales can get the required advertising dollars. Your budget can be further divided into individual merchandise lines.

2. Total Budget. Your total budget may be the result of integrated departmental or product budgets. If your business has set an upper limit for advertising expense percentage, then your departmental budgets which are based on different percentages of sales in each area, might be pared down.

In similar businesses, the total budget may be the only one established. It, too, should be divided into merchandise classifications for scheduling.

3. Calendar Periods. Most executives of small businesses usually plan their advertising on a monthly, even a weekly, basis. Your budget, even if it's for a longer planning period, ought to be calculated for these shorter periods. It will give you better control.

The percentage-of-sales methods are also useful here to determine how much money to allocate by time periods. The standard practice is to match sales with advertising dollars. Thus, if February accounts for 5 percent of your sales, you might give it 5 percent of your budget.

Sometimes you might want to adjust advertising allocations downward in some of your heavier sales months, so you can boost the budget of some of your poorer periods. But this should be done only if you have reason (as when your competition's sales trends differ markedly from yours) to believe that a change in your advertising timing could improve slow sales.

4. Media. The amount of advertising that you place in each advertising medium—such as direct mail, newspapers, or radio—should be determined by past experience, industry practice, and ideas from media specialists. Normally, it's wise to use the same sort of media your competitors use. That's where, most likely, your potential customers look and listen.

5. Sales areas. You can spend your advertising dollars where your customers already come from, or you can use them to try to stimulate new sales areas. Just as in dividing your appropriation by time periods, it's wise to continue to do the bulk of your advertising in familiar areas. Usually it's more costly to develop new markets than to maintain established ones.

A Flexible Budget

Any combination of these methods may be employed in the formation and allocation of your advertising budget. All of them—or simply one—may be needed to meet your advertising objectives. However you decide to plan your budget, you must make it **flexible**, capable of being adjusted to changes in the marketplace.

The duration of your planning and budgeting period depends upon the nature of your business. If you can use short budgeting periods, you'll find that your advertising can be more flexible and that you can change tactics to meet immediate trends.

To ensure advertising flexibility, you should have a contingency fund to deal with special circumstances—such as the introduction of a new product, specials available in local media, or unexpected competitive situations.

Beware of your competitors' activities at all times. Don't blindly copy your competitors, but analyze how their actions may affect your business—and be prepared to act.

Getting Started

Your first budget will be the most difficult to develop—

but it will be worth the effort. The budget will help you analyze the results of your advertising. By your next business year you'll have a more factual basis for budgeting than you did before. Your plans will become more effective with each budget you develop.

Appendix B
A Table of
Yellow Pages
Usage and
Purchases

Since 1979, Simmons Market Research Bureau, Inc., has included phone directories in its annual "Study of Media & Markets." The following table gives its estimates of the number of people who referred to the Yellow Pages for different products and services in a given year and its estimates for the total number of people who purchased that product or service that year (whether or not they used Yellow Pages).

However, if 1,977,000 people referred to the Yellow Pages when considering automatic dishwashers and 2,503,000 bought dishwashers, that hardly means that 79 percent of those who bought dishwashers went to the Yellow Pages first. Obviously, not everyone who looks in a directory ends up buying—not by any means. In some categories—usually expensive luxury products—the number of people who look the product up even exceeds the total number of buyers. We all like to dream.

Still, in general, half of those who refer to the Yellow Pages buy within 48 hours. And more than three quarters of the rest say they're likely or somewhat likely to buy in the near future. (How many of these people are just dreaming is hard to say.) So a strong correlation between Yellow Pages usage and purchases does mean *something*.

Product/Service	Referred to Yellow Pages When Considering (figures in thousands)	Total Number Who Purchased (figures in thousands)
Adding a room (except a greenhouse)	1,945	2,504
Additions to home (greenhouse)	1.896	696
Air Conditioners, Central	1,327	931
Air Conditioners, Room (separate)	2,882	2,559
Airlines, Domestic Scheduled	15,594	28,133
Automobiles, New	6,590	10,892
Automobile Radio (separate from car)	1,581	10,862
Automobile Rentals	6,294	14,242
Automobile Rust Proofing	1,517	6,842
Automobile Telephones	724	988
Automobile or Truck Parts (except tires)	15,704	90,999
Automobile Tune-Up Service	850	65,209
Automobile Wax & Polish	9,398	54,132
Batteries, Automobile	5,376	25,287
Bicycles	3,644	7,048
Boats with Inboard/Outboard Motors	1,044	395
Boats with Outboard Motors	955	817
Burglar Alarm/Lock Systems, Home	967	403
Calculators	1,156	6,498
Cameras	4,276	25,543
Carpeting, Wall-to-Wall or Room Sized Rug	3,837	15,178
Chain Saws, Gas/Electric	1,725	2,440
Clothes Dryers (separate) Gas or Electric	2,997	5,020
Copying Service/Quick Printing	5,399	n/a
Department Store Chains	22,240	122,569
Discount Store Chains	11,478	93,363
Dishwasher, Automatic	1,977	2,503
Electric Blankets	679	5,394
Electric Shavers	1,007	8,130
Floor Tile/Vinyl Flooring	4,072	11,219
Freezers, Home (separate)	970	1,282
Furnaces, Home	4,342	4,336

Product/Service	Referred to Yellow Pages When Considering (figures in thousands)	Total Number Who Purchased (figures in thousands)
Furniture, Dining or Living Room	3.566	18,089
Games & Toys	6,680	80,359
Garage Door Openers Automatic	2,137	3,377
Garbage Disposers	1,078	921
Gasoline & Diesel Fuel	3,093	129,309
Golf Equipment	1,274	2,686
Grilles, Charcoal, Gas/Electric	1,000	4,819
Hardware Store Chains	10,955	n/a
Health Care Facilities	7,668	n/a
Hospital Equipment, Rental/Purchase	1,893	n/a
Hotels/Motels (business use)	3,599	24,602
Hotels/Motels (personal use)	12,174	63,166
Insulation for Ceiling, Floors & Walls	3,074	9,257
Insurance, Life	3,097	11,028
Jogging/Running Shoes	1,508	13,491
Loans/Real Estate Loans	3,766	20,332
Material Handling Equipment	1,613	n/a
Mattresses	4,270	8,669
Microwave Ovens (separate)	2,179	12,367
Motor Homes/Campers	2,671	7,058
Motor Oil	2,227	2,291
Motorcycles	1,900	109,448
Muffler Purchase/Repair	5,938	28,513
Outboard Motors for Boats	876	1,388
Paints, Interior	3,362	10,029
Paints & Stains, Exterior	3,531	26,166
Power Garden & Workshop Equipment and Hand Tools	6,577	12,389
Power Mowers, Gas/Electric	2,423	7,290
Real Estate Agents/Brokers	4,444	4,323
Recliners	1,165	4,069
Refrigerators	3,937	6,972

Product/Service	Referred to Yellow Pages When Considering (figures in thousands)	Total Number Who Purchased (figures in thousands)
Restaurants, Cafeteria	12,197	12,270
Restaurants, Family	23,561	34,488
Restaurants, Fast Food/Drive-in	11,087	73,587
Restaurants, Other	16,594	n/a
Rodent & Pest Control Services	3,584	25,085
Roofing	3,139	25,085
Room Air Purifiers	484	4,323
Satellite Dishes, Home	1,304	5,124
Securities & Investments	2,453	2,180
Sewing Machines	2,156	1,195
Shoes, Men's	2,667	26,549
Shoes, Women's	1,958	53,837
Snow Blowers	914	1,178
Spark Plugs	2,070	64,647
Stove/Range, Electric or Gas	2,750	3,250
Telephone Equipment Service	5,896	n/a
Telephones, Fixed or Cordless	2,135	5,735
Televisions	8,077	20,740
Tennis Equipment	835	4,027
Tires, Car & Truck	7,695	43,891
Trailer/Van Rentals	2,049	3,003
Transmission Service	2,738	19,982
Trash Compactors, Electric	179	99
Truck Rentals	2,458	5,472
Vacuum Cleaners	4,039	8,607
Washing Machines, Automatic	3,030	6,932
Water Heaters	2,956	8,399
Water Purifiers or Filters	1,334	1,122

APPENDIX C

Appendix C
The Influence of
Other
Advertising

The study of actual purchasers conducted by Statistical Research, Inc. for the Yellow Pages Publishers Association also examined the influence of other media in the purchase decision. For the following table, newspapers, radio or TV "influence" is defined as "swaying purchasers' decisions by affecting awareness and/or demand."

The "Effective Reach of Best Single Yellow Pages Combination" column gives the percentage of purchasers reached by the Yellow Pages and/or the other medium, discounting for purchasers who use both.

Product/Service	Percent of Purchasers Who Use Yellow Pages	Frequency of Newspaper Influence on Purchase Decisions	Frequency of Television Influence on Purchase Decisions	Frequency of Radio Influence on Purchase Decisions	Best Single Yellow Pages Combination	Effective Research of Best Single Yellow Pages Combination
Air Travel (contacted airline directly)	47.5%	22.0%	13.8%	8.6%	Yellow Pages & TV	56.9%
Attorneys	32.1%	1.6%	4.9%	3.3%	Yellow Pages & Radio	34.4%
Auto parts	29.5%	28.4%	11.2%	4.1%	Yellow Pages & Newspapers	47.8%
Auto repair	31.8%	12.6%	5.4%	5.2%	Yellow Pages & Newspapers	38.3%
Auto/truck rental or lease	51.6%	14.8%	14.2%	7.4%	Yellow Pages & TV	58.4%
Bank services	24.2%	17.7%	10.5%	9.2%	Yellow Pages & Newspapers	35.3%
Beauty salons	24.4%	11.6%	2.6%	3.2%	Yellow Pages & Newspapers	31.3%
Carry-out food (except pizza)	30.6%	16.1%	17.4%	3.3%	Yellow Pages & TV	41.7%
Electronic products: includes TV's, VCR's, stereos, home computers, similar products	21.0%	57.4%	26.3%	14.9%	Yellow Pages & Newspapers	64.8%
Floor coverings	24.0%	43.1%	19.1%	8.6%	Yellow Pages & Newspapers	54.9%
Florists	31.0%	9.1%	3.0%	4.5%	Yellow Pages & Newspapers	35.7%
Furniture	19.3%	50.1%	19.2%	10.8%	Yellow Pages & Newspapers	58.0%

Home contractors: includes plumbers, painters, carpenters, electricians, exterminators, and similar contractors	42.2%	9.1%	5.6%	2.7%	Yellow Pages & Newspapers	45.6%
Insurance	31.3%	7.6%	9.7%	5.3%	Yellow Pages & Radio	36.7%
Lawn & garden supplies: includes power equipment, hand tools, seed, plants, fertilizers, insecticides, similar products	13.0%	47.2%	22.1%	4.8%	Yellow Pages & Newspapers	52.0%
Loans	22.5%	17.0%	8.4%	7.3%	Yellow Pages & Newspapers	32.8%
Major Appliances	25.1%	51.4%	21.7%	13.6%	Yellow Pages & Newspapers	62.8%
New, used cars & trucks	19.7%	29.2%	16.2%	10.2%	Yellow Pages & Newspapers	37.9%
Pizza carry-out	38.1%	21.2%	22.2%	15.2%	Yellow Pages & TV	50.4%
Real Estate	29.2%	42.2%	13.5%	3.3%	Yellow Pages & Newspapers	55.5%
Restaurants	9.5%	9.3%	6.8%	3.5%	Yellow Pages & Newspapers	16.3%
Sporting Goods	17.2%	35.9%	13.7%	7.9%	Yellow Pages & Newspapers	45.7%
Tires	31.7%	36.4%	10.7%	8.9%	Yellow Pages & Newspapers	55.0%
TV/radio repair	45.2%	12.3%	8.1%	3.9%	Yellow Pages & Newspapers	51.5%
Average for these 24 product & Service categories	24.0%	25.1%	12.1%	7.1%	Yellow Pages & Newspaper	45.4%

Source: Research study on the role of Yellow Pages in the purchase decision, copyrighted by the Yellow Pages Publishers Association; conducted by Statistical Research, Inc., Westfield, NJ.

Index

Other Books From Aegis Publishing Group:

Aegis Publishing specializes in telecommunications books for non-technical end-users. Inquire about wholesale quantity discounts: Aegis Publishing Group, 796 Aquidneck Ave., Newport, RI 02842 800-828-6961; aegis@aegisbooks.com; Web: www.aegisbooks.com

Telecom Business Opportunities:
The Entrepreneur's Guide to Making Money in the Telecommunications Revolution (December 1997), by Steven Rosenbush
Item TC10 $24.95 ISBN: 1-890154-04-0, paper, 336 pages
This first-of-its-kind guide by *USA Today* telecom reporter Steve Rosenbush shows where the money is to be made in the evolving, deregulated telecommunications industry. Consists of fascinating case studies of real-life entrepreneurs who are carving out their share of profits in this enormous $200 billion industry.

Telecom Made Easy:
Money-Saving, Profit-Building Solutions
for Home Businesses, Telecommuters and Small Organizations
3rd edition (August 1997), by June Langhoff
Item TC19 $19.95 ISBN: 0-9632790-7-6, paper, 400 pages
"... a basic but thorough guide to phone systems and services, cellular phones, answering devices, paging, on-line services, modems, faxes, and networked systems... geared toward home businesses, telecommuters, and small firms." —*Nation's Business*

Winning Communications Strategies:
How Small Businesses Master Cutting-Edge Technology to Stay Competitive, Provide Better Service and Make More Money (August 1997), by Jeffrey Kagan
Item TC3 $14.95   ISBN: 0-9632790-8-4, paper, 219 pages
Real-world profiles of small businesses that use the latest technology to compete and win. Illustrates how the most powerful tools in business are available to even the smallest organizations, and how businesses can use technology such as fax-on-demand, voice mail, interactive voice response, intranets, video conferencing and computer-telephony integration in solving today's competitive business challenges.

The Telecommuter's Advisor:
Working in the Fast Lane (July 1996), by June Langhoff
Item TC2 $14.95 ISBN: 0-9632790-5-X, paper, 240 pages
". . . practical, 1990s real-world advice. . . This book is for anyone who

wants to improve their remote working skills and covers a broad range of topics, including designing a home office, selecting equipment, coping with e-mail, using groupware and wireless communications, and connecting internationally. . ." —*Booklist*

900 KNOW-HOW:
How to Succeed With Your Own 900 Number Business
3rd edition (August 1996), by Robert Mastin
Item TC1B $19.95 ISBN: 0-9632790-3-3, paper, 350 pages
Become a toll collector on the info highway. "If you have decided that you are nothing but road kill on the information highway, take a look at *900 Know-How* . . . For those in the information-providing business, the 900 number could be an attractive source of revenue." —*Wall Street Journal*

The Business Traveler's Survival Guide:
How to Get Work Done While on the Road
(October 1997), by June Langhoff
Item TC9 $9.95 ISBN: 1-890154-03-2, paper, 112 pages
This handy guide will be appreciated by every business traveler, covering remote working, data security, what to pack in the road warrior's toolkit, and a listing of business hotels with the best communications setups. The ideal travel companion.

Money-Making 900 Numbers:
How Entrepreneurs Use the Telephone to Sell Information
(July 1995), by Carol Morse Ginsburg and Robert Mastin
Item TC18 $19.95
ISBN: 0-9632790-1-7, paper, 336 pages, 5-1/2" x 8-1/2"
"... a thorough job of illustrating the incredible variety of pay-per-call services that have been done... an excellent overall view of the industry, and anyone thinking of starting a 900 number should read the book." —*McHenry County Business Journal*

Phone Company Services:
Working Smarter with the Right Telecom Tools
(September 1997), by June Langhoff
Item TC7 $9.95
ISBN: 1-890154-01-6, paper, 96 pages, 5-1/2" x 8-1/2"
From Call Forwarding to Caller ID to 500 Service to ISDN to Centrex, this book describes phone company services in detail, and how to put them to their best use in real-life applications.